Reading Lessons from the Eighteenth Century

Mothers, children and texts

Reading Lessons from the Eighteenth Century

Mothers, children and texts

Evelyn Arizpe and Morag Styles
with Shirley Brice Heath

First published 2006 by:

Pied Piper Publishing Ltd.
80 Birmingham Road
Shenstone
Lichfield
Staffordshire
WS14 0JU

All illustrations courtesy of the Lilly Library, Indiana University, Bloomington, Indiana.

British Library Cataloguing in Publication
A catalogue record for this book is available from the British Library.

ISBN: 0 9546384 8 4 paperback
       0 9552106 1 5 hardback

Printed in Britain by 4EDGE LTD, 7a Eldon Way, Eldon Way Industrial Estate, Hockley, Essex SS5 4AD

To my parents, Gracy and Jorge Arizpe, who let me find my own way through books.

E.A.

Writing this book has involved thinking deeply about families and the past. I should like, therefore, to dedicate this book to the memory of my maternal grandparents, Mary and Alec McRobb. Unlike Jane Johnson, they were both ardent socialists, but like her they worked immensely hard, devoted their lives to their families, and tried to make the world a better place for other people.

M.S.

Contents

Foreword

To anyone familiar with her, Jane Johnson is a beacon shining in the murky uncertainties of eighteenth-century history. In the first chapter of this book, Evelyn Arizpe and Morag Styles speak of 'drawing Jane out of the shadows' so that we can see her more clearly - a felicitous phrase to indicate one of the authors' purposes, to explain and interpret this ordinary yet extraordinary woman and rescue her from obscurity.

I have noticed that, when people write about Jane Johnson, images of light and dark come naturally to their minds.

Undoubtedly, while so few people knew of her, Jane Johnson could truly be said to have been lost in the shadows of the forgotten past. But the work done by the three researchers who have written this book has shown how Jane was her own source of brightness within the life she led and the family she loved. No shadows for her! - except, of course, the Shadow of the Valley of Death, the meaning of which she never once lost sight of. She would probably have denied that her own light was of any significance, attributing everything to God. 'Oh Lord send out thy Light and Truth,' she writes; and she approvingly quotes Thomson's 'Father of Light & Life...', adding her own humble prayer to the chosen extract.

Such imagery is traditional, perhaps commonplace. But this book shows how, combined with energy, intelligence and purpose, the brightness of Jane's faith enlightened her family and illuminated the world they grew up in, not only because of the firmness of her moral convictions but also because of the love apparent in everything she did and wrote. Her words are full of urgency and joy - uncompromising and demanding, but never dull - and always loving. As this book testifies, her influence over her children lasted all through their lives. They became intellectually curious adults, interested in the world they lived in, affectionate to each other, and devoted in their religion. Years later, Jane's daughter Barbara wrote: 'How often have I seen Joy brighten every Eye and Irradiate every countenance.' She is talking, in fact, about the pleasure of reading newspapers, but her choice of words is characteristic, just the kind of phrasing she would have learned from her mother.

To me, the daily domestic life of eighteenth-century history remains elusive and shadowy. Only fiction can show it with clarity and immediacy. I confess, for example, that middle-class life at the end of the eighteenth century and during the Regency period would be for me an unknown tract of wilderness if it were not for Jane Austen. This book works in a similar way. Rural landed middle-class England for almost the whole century is brought to life and brilliantly lit through this exploration of one family and its intimate friends. A lot of the material is fragmentary - gossip, letters, brief entries in a journal or a commonplace book. They provide a story of wills, inheritance, family scandal (perhaps), marriages, the deaths of children and parents; and, later, towards the end of the century, the subsequent lives of Jane's grown-up children and their families.

At the centre of the narrative is Jane Johnson herself, firm in her convictions, rooted in the realities of her day, active in her concern for the well-being and wise thinking of her loved-ones. And, above all, strong and vigorous *in words*: '… we must not expect,' she writes in her commonplace book, 'to be carried [to Heaven] Lolling at our Ease in a four wheel'd Post Chaise hung upon springs, but provided we get there at last, it is very well, even tho' we are jolted through the Cart Ruts in a Dung-Cart.'

This is the language of Henry Fielding and - much more to Jane's taste - Samuel Richardson. More significantly, it is also the language of John Bunyan - earthy, urgent, uncompromising, with an evangelical commonsense he would have recognised and approved of.

Shortly before her husband died, Jane wrote in her commonplace book:

> I gave a strong proof of my Courage, made a Bold Stand against Vice, but my forces were weak, & the Enemy soon got the better & drove me out of the Field. May Virtue for the future have a more powerful, & more successful Advocate.

We can only speculate upon the distress that led to this admission. It is immediately followed by four lines of writing crossed out so thoroughly that it is impossible to decipher her words. We should not be surprised that a woman like her might have second thoughts, or even secret thoughts. But such a determined erasure is so rare in her papers that it comes as something of a shock to see it, for Jane Johnson was a woman of openness. She believed in the value of using words to expose and express, to formulate and analyse, to convey love and faith - always to let in the light of understanding.

Shadows and darkness, ambiguities and secrets, were inimical to her. She was a woman of clarity and definition. So welcome to Jane Johnson's written world.

Victor Watson.
September 2005

Prologue: A Story about a Story .....

'... *no Boy was ever better belov'd than you are ...*'
a letter from Jane Johnson to her son, George, dated April 20 1755[1]

As this is an informal tale of researchers researching, it seems
appropriate to use Christian names for much of this narrative, once
new characters have been introduced. As we feel so close to Jane
Johnson, we refer to her as Jane throughout the book.

Beginnings

Once upon a time in the spring of 1994 a famous American scholar,
Shirley Brice Heath, came from across the sea to stay with me in
Cambridge. She was here to give a lecture on her latest research to an
eager crowd of British academics and teachers who had read her
seminal book, *Ways with Words*. Shirley wondered if a seminar on an
eighteenth-century Englishwoman who created a fascinating nursery
library for her own children might be of interest? The answer was a
resounding 'yes' as the group of us then teaching children's literature
at Homerton College, Cambridge, were very keen on its history.

It transpired that Shirley's uncle, Reed Voran of Muncie, Indiana, knew
about a holding at the Lilly Library, Indiana University, that he thought
would interest her. Shirley's uncle had been the executor of the estate
of Elisabeth Ball, daughter of a prominent midwestern family of
industrialists, whose penchant for collecting had included children's
literature. In particular, Elisabeth's father, George Ball, had bought two
large collections of children's books in the 1930s which were shelved
in Oakhurst, the Ball mansion in Muncie.

Other materials were stashed in the tops of cupboards throughout the
house. Far back on a closet shelf on the third floor of the mansion
nestled an old hatbox containing the first nursery library in English
consisting of 438 pieces created by someone called Jane Johnson[2]
(1706 - 1759). At the death of Elisabeth Ball in 1982, Reed Voran
called in Justin Schiller, New York expert on antiquities of children's
literature. In his final check of the house, Schiller found the hatbox. 'It
was during a general hunt, room by room, that we opened the door of a
rather tall closet, one that was essentially bare. Some empty wire
hangers were still arranged on the crossbar, but nothing else was there

except a big hatbox on the top shelf with some loose newspapers underneath' (Schiller 1997:17). Schiller goes on to describe Jane's nursery library as 'the most precious children's book treasure I have ever known... we found bright gilt-coloured eighteenth-century paper used as backing for 361 mounted cards, each with hand-lettered texts, a box of ornamental words, two miniature books, all with découpage and carefully hand-lettered manuscript text, prepared by a mother for her son[3] - a real nursery library from 250 years ago, the very time John Newbery was beginning to produce his first books for young children' (Schiller, 1997:19-22).

Intrigued by her uncle's story of Jane's nursery library, Shirley went to the Lilly Library to examine the collection. She knew it would shed new light on domestic literacy and the history of children's reading. Librarians[4] at the Lilly, including Elizabeth Johnson, Head of Technical Services, had determined the identity of the creator of the library and the means of classifying the unique set of artefacts.

In 1994, Shirley gave an illustrated talk on Jane Johnson's nursery library in Cambridge to an invited group of children's authors, teachers and lecturers in a range of disciplines. You could have heard a pin drop in the room as Shirley showed slide after slide of exquisite little reading cards which Jane had made for her children so long ago. The audience seemed to be aware that they had been given access to something quite exceptional. As I gazed at Jane's work, aware, on the one hand, of the sheer hard slog involved in her project and, on the other, of her multimodal originality so ahead of her time, I felt the first pangs of falling in love with a subject that was going to fill my spare time, off and on, for upwards of the next ten years. Who was Jane? Was she a typical mother of her period or someone very special? I had to know more.

To Witham we shall go

I was not alone in my desire to research Jane's life more thoroughly; my colleague, Victor Watson, a distinguished scholar of children's literature, was equally hooked and so was Shirley herself, the instigator of it all. She and I made a quick trip to London to read some family wills, then we set off with Victor and his wife, Judy (a primary teacher and school librarian) on 12 April 1994 for Witham-on-the-Hill[5] (which hereafter we will simply call Witham). At this point, all we knew was that Jane Johnson had lived in the manor house in Witham, now a school. Her husband, Reverend Woolsey Johnson (1696 - 1756), had built the home for his family at the same time as enclosing the park in 1752. Witham itself is quite a small village, attractive but not picture-postcard pretty, tucked away in a part of Lincolnshire that visitors are unlikely to encounter unless they have some business there. We arrived at lunchtime and had a sandwich at the pub; some regulars eyed us rather suspiciously as we enthusiastically discussed a certain Jane Johnson who used to live there.

I don't know why I expected Jane's old home to be a village school; of course, it was much too grand for that and had in fact become a private prep school. It turned out to be a handsome Georgian building with a vista of fields and woods in front and a delightful garden behind. It was the school holidays, so when we rang the doorbell, no one answered, although the front door was slightly ajar. We called out and tentatively took a peek inside. Immediately, a woman we had noticed at the pub appeared, and Victor went into her office to explain our purpose, while a student asked us what we were researching. When I mentioned the name Johnson, she said, 'Oh, we've got a book by her in the library'. Shirley and I followed her into what would have been Jane's parlour and looked with delight at the nicely laid out grass, paths and flower-beds beyond the French windows, while admiring the elegant yet homely proportions of a most attractive room.

The next coincidence of the day was about to unfold. The student - a girl aged about twelve - brought us a large handsome book entitled, *A Lady of Fashion*[6] which actually related to someone else in the Johnson family - Jane's daughter, Barbara, whose album of fashion and fabrics the Victoria and Albert Museum (which hereafter we will call the V&A) had acquired and which was presented here in facsimile form. The editor of this volume knew that Barbara's mother was a Jane Johnson, but she clearly knew nothing about Jane's particular claim to fame - the pride of the Lilly Library collection of early children's books. Shirley and I were on the floor (it's a large book), desperately jotting down sources and references, when a woman introducing herself as the Headmaster's wife asked us to leave forthwith. We apologised and tried to explain, but being Cambridge scholars cut no ice at all and we were bundled out with haste.

Before leaving Witham, we stopped at St Andrews Church in the heart of the village where Woolsey and his youngest son, Charles, had preached. There we found the family tomb, a marble pyramidal tablet set against the north wall of the chancel. Jane, Woolsey and their eldest son, George, are buried there. Nearby lies Robert Johnson, the second son of Jane and Woolsey, and Robert's son, Lieutenant General William Augustus Johnson, and grandson, Captain Robert William Johnson. Clearly, the Johnson family had a long connection with Witham.

The plot thickens

On the journey back to Cambridge we made plans. Shirley was leaving for America early the next morning, so it was up to Victor and me to pursue this new piece of evidence. I was in Cambridge University Library when it opened the next morning, poring over *A Lady of Fashion*. The book was edited by Natalie Rothstein; later I wrote to her at the V&A about our research, asking if she would be willing to send on a letter to Bill Blois Johnson, a descendent of Jane's we had not previously known about, who had provided much of the family information for the book. Meanwhile a busy summer term and holidays came and went before I managed to write to Bill on 13 October, 1994, asking if there were any circumstances in which he would allow me to examine some of the family documents.

In collaboration with William Cagle, then Director of the Lilly Library, Shirley set about raising money for a symposium in Cambridge to be centred around Jane's nursery library, while I approached the Fitzwilliam Museum, Cambridge, about the possibility of a small exhibition based round the Lilly Library collection. All of us were successful: the Fitzwilliam promised us use of their Octagon Room for an exhibition to coincide with our symposium, and William and Shirley obtained a handsome grant from the Ball Foundation[7] to enable the symposium to go ahead[8].

Then two wonderful things happened almost simultaneously in late October. I received a phone call from someone called Maggie Wilkins, a fabric historian, who had made an enquiry of the V&A about Barbara Johnson's book and was told there was a scholar at Cambridge who was also researching the Johnson family. 'I have, as we speak, my hand on an eighteenth century notebook written by a Jane Johnson' said Maggie, full of portent. 'It contains poems and a story written for her children, dated 1744.' I put down the phone trembling with excitement as 1744 is the key date for scholars of children's literature - the year that children's book publishing as we know it began in earnest. After arranging a trip to Maggie's Norfolk home, I bent down to open a letter on my desk with unfamiliar handwriting. It was from Bill Blois Johnson inviting me to visit him and his wife in Dorset to examine their family archive[9].

A Very Pretty Story

Victor and I set off for Norfolk where Maggie lived and found her in an artistic house full of beautiful artefacts and antique furniture. In her living room the ceiling was deep blue, decorated with stars and moons that you could almost imagine twinkling in the night sky. Maggie was a natural collector, and had spent her life picking up interesting objects from jumble sales and antique fairs. She had acquired Jane's notebook some years earlier, became aware of the value of her find and, understandably, was wary of strangers. Once she felt confident that our interest was scholarly and genuine, she brought out Jane's precious notebook containing *A Very Pretty Story*[10] and some poetry. We quickly realised that we had before us a most remarkable document. Here was a lengthy moral tale with considerable enchantments, featuring Jane's two eldest children as central characters. Maggie did not want to let something so valuable out of her hands, but she kindly agreed to write out the story by hand and send us a copy. In return, we shared our knowledge to date with her and invited her to the forthcoming symposium. By the end of that crisp autumn afternoon in Norfolk, there was another person who had fallen under Jane's spell. Soon after, Maggie decided to work on the research with us for a while and proved to be a talented archivist, providing us with family trees and other information. Indeed, it was Maggie who first spotted that the portrait the Blois Johnsons believed to be of Jane (a copy of which has adorned my study ever since) was probably of her mother, as the clothing she wore was of a style fashionable a generation before Jane's time.

Soon after, on 4th November 1994, I travelled down to Dorset to meet Bill and Cresson Blois Johnson. They turned out to be a charming elderly couple living in an old house that was full of character. After a delicious supper of roast pheasant with lashings of wine, I asked if I could see the archive. Bill took me upstairs to a room with a bureau and chest out of which tumbled dozens of letters, packages, notebooks, lists and jottings of all kinds, many of them by Jane. I noted with relief that her handwriting was easy to read and, in most cases, the ink had hardly faded. One look was enough to realise that I had stumbled on an amazing find and I couldn't wait to start work on it the next day.

The Johnsons could not have been kinder, giving me free access to the materials over the weekend. The first item I picked up was a tiny pristine white paper package (about 3 x 2 and a half inches) which easily fitted in the palm of my hand; on it Jane had written, 'for my son George William Johnson when I am dead. Jane Johnson'[11]. It looked as if it had not been touched since she signed it, so I opened it with the greatest care. Inside were exquisite, intricately designed paper cuttings in the shape of a heart, a sun, lovebirds and flowers. They had been made with a mother's tender care to delight her babies and Jane had wished to preserve them.

Next I picked up a poem in praise of Jane's first born, Barbara, who was clearly missed by her mother on a trip to London:

Then come Miss Johnson come away,
No longer in dull London stay.
But let the country be your choice.
We'll welcome you with heart and voice.[12]
(from 'Invitation to Miss Barbara to come into the country, 1 May 1747')

The next was a letter from Jane to George (who would have been fifteen) dated 20 April 1755, only one year before his father's death. It concluded with the words, 'Adieu my dear George and believe that no boy was ever better beloved than you are by Jane Johnson.'[13] Most moving of all was a letter Jane had written a few months later to Robert, her second son, on 30 July 1755 when he was only ten. It was full of motherly love and tenderness, but Robert was also firmly advised to get on with his lessons and to think of God in everything he did. It ended with four religious lines for him to memorise before he got home. Then as a sort of after-thought near the bottom of the page, Jane has added, 'Oh! Robert Live for Ever.'[14] Whether that was simply a religious way of signing off a letter or a mother's heartfelt longing, we shall never know.

By now I was now completely under Jane's spell. I began to look at all the material systematically, putting the things that seemed most important in one pile and those of secondary or little importance in others. I began to copy by hand - letters, extracts from Jane's commonplace book, poems, lists of words, drawings, notes to keep certain items for posterity and a beautifully fashioned interlocking chain with her children's names within (see Figure 1).

A Register of the Rev.ᵈ Woolsey Johnson's Children of Olney, Bucks.

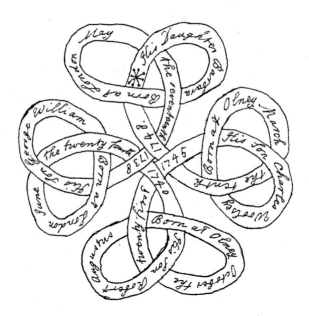

Figure 1.

I realised this archive would be of great interest to a wide range of scholars and gently suggested to the Blois Johnsons that they might consider lending the material to a university or public record office for safe-keeping. They generously loaned me Jane's commonplace book to work on. Not being a historian, I was unaware how valuable the piece was or I might have been more nervous of taking it away. As I travelled back to Cambridge on the train from Dorset, my head was brimming with Jane and full of anticipation for what Victor would make of the booty carefully carried in my briefcase. I now understood something of the appeal of detective work and the deep satisfaction of beginning to fit pieces of a jigsaw together.

Scrapbooks and Chapbooks 1995

While all these exciting developments were going ahead, plans for the symposium at Homerton College were taking shape. Paul Woudhuysen, then Keeper of Manuscripts & Printed Books at the Fitzwilliam Museum, was liaising with the Lilly Library about transporting Jane's nursery library from Indiana to Cambridge. A colleague, Mary Hilton, became involved and encouraged us to invite social historians such as Norma Clarke, Margaret Spufford and David Vincent as speakers. Topics for the symposium were extremely varied: women teaching reading to poor children in the seventeenth century; Samuel Richardson's Aesop; a defence of rationalist women writers of the eighteenth century; John Newbery and Tom Telescope and many more.

The wide range of academic disciplines represented at the symposium proved to be stimulating, while the attendance of the Blois Johnsons and Maggie Wilkins added to the rich mix. The conference also attracted the attention of early book collectors who were knowledgeable about the complex publishing history and precise dating of obscure publications. The heart of the symposium was our own Private View of Handmade Readings at the Fitzwilliam Museum where most of the participants, including myself, were able to view Jane's nursery library for the first time. The Blois Johnsons kindly lent us some of the family artefacts which were put on display at Homerton College[15]. The contributors were invited to submit written versions of their papers/lectures and *Opening the Nursery Door: Reading, Writing and Childhood 1600-1900*[16] finally appeared in 1997, a lasting tribute to a memorable event and an aid to scholars interested in the history of reading. At the heart of the book is Jane, our guiding spirit.

Figure 2. Front cover of Fitzwilliam Museum Catalogue for Handmade Readings.

The Journalist's story

Over the years I have told the story of Jane and how we came to know about her to many people. So keen is my enthusiasm for this project that, like the Ancient Mariner, I may fix my victims with a 'glittering eye' and spend rather too long on my tale! One person who listened with great interest was Geraldine Brennan, literary editor of the Times Educational Supplement (thereafter called the TES). She invited me to her office in East Smithfield near the Tower of London where she introduced me to fellow journalist, Victoria Neumark. At first, I wasn't sure whether Victoria would be gripped by what could appear a rather mundane story, but as soon as I began my tale, she was listening intently. When I came to Robert's letter, quoted earlier, Victoria actually wept in response. It turned out she was the devoted mother of three boys, one of whom was called Robert.

Victoria was commissioned to write an article about Victor and me as literary detectives for the TES in 1998. It was time to return to Witham and, as luck would have it, a new headmaster was installed who was more than willing for us to visit the school that had been Jane's home. This time our trip was most enjoyable and productive. The Headmaster could not have been more helpful, the atmosphere in the school was welcoming and informal, and we had time to stop and notice Jane's curse on a plaque still standing in the hall, a reminder that she was a spirited woman of her time.

> To the Intent that it may never be forgot
> This plate in inscribed to the memory of Reverend Woolsey Johnson [...] He was a man who from his infancy to the hour of his death was exempt from every vice, and adorned with many and great virtues [...] Cursed be the He or She that defaces or removes or causes to be defaced or removed this Inscription. Blessed be He or She that endeavours to preserve and keep it clean.
> June 5th 1756

We met some pupils who quizzed us on our research, while we in turn found out about their daily lives at school. We were taken up to the top of the house which must have contained the nursery and duly imagined Barbara Johnson there, joined by her brothers in the school holidays, for the children were growing up by the time they moved to Witham.

We were very lucky in our journalist and the rest of the team at TES[17]; Victoria wrote an excellent, liberally illustrated, article which brought our work to a wide readership for the first time.

I had previously met Jim Meacham who ran Witham's lively historical society. An American, settled in Britain, Jim had something of the pioneering spirit of early American settlers in his determination to investigate the social history of his adopted neighbourhood. He and his colleagues have since published a book on Witham called *A Piece of the Puzzle*.[18] More than once I enjoyed the generous hospitality of Jim and his wife. On one occasion (25 April 2001) I gave a talk about Jane in Witham Church Hall to a large, knowledgeable audience which included the church cleaner and the Head of Witham School.

Olney hymns

Once we discovered that several of Jane's children were born in Olney, Buckinghamshire, it was obvious that most of Jane's married life had taken place in that pleasant market town. Her husband, Woolsey, a third son who had been born in Olney, inherited the living from his father, William, in 1735 after the deaths of his older brothers. He married Jane the same year; he was 39 and she was 30. One sunny January morning in 1996, Victor, Judy and I set out to investigate further. The night before, I attended the annual T S Eliot Award reception at the British Library for the best new collection of poetry that year. Spying my friend, Margaret Meek, a well-known scholar of children's literature (who had attended Shirley's lecture in Cambridge and the Scrapbooks symposium), I rushed across the room to say hello. She had been talking to a man who had just left the Board of the Poetry Book Society of which Margaret and I were current members. She duly introduced us and he listened as Margaret and I launched into a discussion of mutual friends and gossip. Finally, I told Margaret that I was going to Olney the next day to investigate Jane's life further and propelled myself into a busy account of all that we had found out about her since last we spoke. When I had finished, the man whose name turned out to be Tony Seward told me that he was one of the trustees of the Cowper and Newton Museum in Olney. He offered to show me round the museum and to introduce me to a knowledgeable local historian, Elizabeth Knight. Another coincidence or Jane's benign ghost pushing things along?

We knew from parish records that the Great House Jane and Woolsey had lived in was no longer standing, but we hoped the church would provide some information. Olney, of course, is famous as the place where the inspirational preacher, John Newton, was the vicar some years after the Johnsons had departed. Here the poet, William Cowper, recovered his depressive spirits and collaborated with Newton on the Olney hymns which include the ever popular 'Amazing Grace', now famous worldwide. The Church of St Peter & St Paul sits in a pretty setting by some water meadows on the edge of the town. After examining all the records available and appreciating the architecture, we noted memorabilia for sale relating to Cowper and Newton. I turned to Victor and told him it was my ambition to see material related to Jane Johnson for sale in that church before I died.

Across the green from the church stands a handsome, substantial, Georgian house, surrounded by a wall. It was likely that this was where the curates used to live, but we speculated about whether Jane might have stayed there at any point. On the spur of the moment, and somewhat to Victor's discomfort, I knocked at the door and asked the startled owners if we could have a look round the house, briefly explaining our mission. The owners turned out to be a friendly retired couple who showed us round their most attractive home and garden. The upstairs bedrooms were perfect for a nursery, so we fancifully imagined Jane's children there, as well as Newton and Cowper scribbling their hymns by candlelight some years later. One intriguing feature of the house was that a lot of the decoration and furniture was eighteenth century in style and design. It wasn't really a surprise to discover that Mrs Wallace, like Jane, was gifted with her hands and particularly keen on Georgian furniture, material and wallpaper.

Evelyn joins the search

At the time when Jane came into my life I was in the middle of a major book which had to be completed, so with reluctance I put my research on Jane aside as I got to grips with three hundred years of poetry for children. I never forgot Jane (I even found a way of putting her in that book), but my priority shifted back to poetry. After that, I began a big project on visual literacy that took up every waking hour for several years. The unfinished business of Jane was always at the back of my mind, but my professional life was taken over with new interests.

One of the best things about the visual literacy project was that I had started working with Evelyn Arizpe who had recently completed her PhD in Cambridge on teenage fiction and Mexican readers. It was a most harmonious collaboration, and I was sorry when research grants ran out and there seemed no prospect of working together any more. Could I think up a small research project which would enable us to continue working together? Would Evelyn be willing to shift from working with children and artists on contemporary picture books to parachute herself into the middle of the eighteenth century to follow the trail of an obscure woman? For the nth time, I started my tale of Jane and her doings, quite sceptical about its suitability for Evelyn as a joint research project. By the time I had finished, with hardly a pause for thought, Evelyn had committed herself, and Jane became the primary interest in my life again. Evelyn showed herself to be an able, determined and resourceful researcher, and much of the new information that has come to light is down to her good offices. As ever, the 'year or so' has proved to be somewhat longer. We started work in 2002 and this book will not be published until 2006.

Evelyn now needed to visit the two main sites of pilgrimage, so one Saturday in 2002 we set off for Olney with her husband, Nigel, her two children, Isabel and Flora, and Victor and Judy. This time we had contacted the Wallaces ahead, and they welcomed us into their house again and did not mind the little girls racing round the garden. As we walked by the church and water meadows which Jane would have looked at every day of her life, I noted Evelyn's growing attachment to her story. On another occasion we went back to Witham School, where we happened on a lesson run by curators from a local museum on eighteenth century toys. We are quite blasé about coincidences now!

In April 2003 we travelled to Indiana on Helm Fellowships in order to inspect thoroughly Jane's nursery library and consult the Lilly Library's collection of early children's books. We were met by a smiling Breon Mitchell, Director of the Lilly Library who drove us to Bloomington. His friendliness was matched by that of other members of the library staff, particularly Elizabeth Johnson who looked after us in both a personal and professional capacity. The campus at Bloomington was beautiful in early spring with trees, blossom, woodland, as well as fine buildings to admire. By day, we worked hard in the library, examining every item, noting every detail and discussing it at every opportunity. From breakfast and lunch at the student refectory, through dinner in a different Bloomington eatery every evening, Jane and her children kept us company, morning, noon and night. Working on the Johnson materials will be an easier task for future scholars as the Lilly Library has recently completed an excellent website on Jane's nursery library.

Entangled on the web

The internet has become an indispensable tool for archival research, as websites link up together and more and more documents are made available on-line. It is relatively easy now to search catalogues of record offices and libraries as well as sites for genealogical history. However, on-line cataloguing is not by any means comprehensive and on-line searching does not prevent 'wild goose chases' although at least these can be done from the comfort of one's home. Although many hours were wasted in front of the computer screen trying to follow leads that went nowhere, Evelyn managed to locate a surprising amount of information on 'our' Johnson family.

It was incredibly exciting when some of the documents that were thrown up answered questions we had been asking for some time. Even so, several mysteries remain unsolved. For example, a marriage document confirmed that Lucy Russell (Jane's mother) and Lucy Ingoldesby, who died in Olney in 1752, were the same person. It revealed that she remarried in 1728 and although a second marriage is not surprising, the fact that Jane's mother was 48 when she married her 28 year old second husband was rather unexpected, especially as her first husband (Jane's father) was 27 years older than she was.

Thanks to the *DocumentsOnline* facility on the National Archives website, where one goes around adding wills to a shopping basket, some fascinating material relating to the Rainsford side of Jane's maternal family was discovered. We now have the wills of Jane's great-grandparents, grandparents and father, all of which confirm that the family had been a wealthy one, with houses in Lincoln's Inn Fields and St. James Westminster, Dallington, Northants and Whitton, Middlesex. Her grandmother owned 'a Cabinet from Naples' and a picture of Lady Falkland 'set round with diamonds' and she bequeathed a gold watch to young Jane.

One of the most exciting moments was when the will of Richard Russell (Jane's father) began to emerge from Evelyn's printer. We had hoped it would reveal something about his supposedly humble origins (history books describe him as a 'menial servant' to Sir Thomas Spencer at Claverdon), but it did not. However, it confirmed the existence of a daughter from a first marriage, a Mrs Plummerden, who was therefore Jane's half sister. It also threw up the bewildering fact that Richard Russell disinherited Jane's mother, his wife of sixteen years. Had she left him for her young lover who would have been nineteen at the time? If so, why did she wait eight years to marry him? Was she escaping from a drunk, violent man, so many years her senior? What did fourteen year old Jane make of all this when her father died in 1720? Unfortunately, at this point, we have not been able to find the answers to these and other questions, but we will never stop trying to solve this puzzle.

Record offices and libraries

As well as so many Johnson family documents having survived, it is surprising where some have ended up. Most of the papers are in

Buckinghamshire and Lincolnshire where the family lived, but we also found papers in record offices far from there. In Uppingham School and in St John's College, Cambridge, there were boxes of papers on earlier generations of Johnsons, as far back as the early sixteenth century, in particular relating to the Archdeacon Robert Johnson who founded Uppingham and Oakham schools.

Visits to record offices included The Centre for Buckinghamshire Studies in Aylesbury which contains documents from the seventeenth century, mainly letters to Woolsey's father from his parents, Anne and Thomas Johnson, some of them clearly organised by Jane herself when she went through her husband's papers after his death. (These papers have some marginal comments in Jane's handwriting.) The Lincolnshire archives, originally explored by Shirley in 1994, provided a wealth of documents thanks to the meticulous collecting of Lucy Johnson, the wife of General William Augustus Johnson, eldest son of Robert (who inherited the Witham estate). As a widow, around 1870 Lucy seems to have made a scrapbook for each of her children containing handmade copies of family trees, history, crests and letters, such as the letter from Jane to the Uppingham School headmaster complaining about the cost of educating and boarding her sons and extracts from Robert Augustus' diary, as well as sketches of the Great House in Olney and Witham Hall. One of these albums, bound in a lovely red cotton print with green and brown acorns, says that it was copied for a little girl and that Jane was her great great grandmother. Sadly, they also contain the obituary for Lucy's husband. It is another coincidence that someone not directly descended from Jane also had such an interest in collecting and preserving family documents and in particular, presenting them so beautifully.

After our symposium in 1995, Maggie had sold Jane's story to the Bodleian Library and it appeared in an attractive facsimile edition in 2001. Around the same time, the Bodleian also acquired the Johnson materials owned by Bill Blois Johnson, so the British archive is in good hands, carefully curated originally by Mary Clapinson. Evelyn and I came to know these materials well in the Johnson Room (no relation) with its helpful librarians.

Other library visits were necessary for obtaining more information about particular members of the Johnson family. The earliest known printed army list (1740), for example, which Evelyn finally located thanks to an enthusiastic librarian in the Manuscript and Rare Books Room in Cambridge University Library, turned out to have a mention of Jane's mother's second husband. This library (together with the electronic database, *Literature Online*) also provided books that helped track down some of Jane's sources for her commonplace book. The Map Room was also useful, and an A-Z of Georgian London[19] helped situate the various family houses in London.

Trips to London to the Society of Genealogists (see the invaluable *Boyd's Inhabitants of London*) and the Guildhall included a visit to St Andrew's Holborn and the nearby Warwick Court, where Jane and Woolsey probably had a house. A knock on the door of the only remaining house with an eighteenth century facade resulted in an impromptu chat with a lawyer with a great knowledge of history, and a visit to Gray's Inn Library where a kind deputy librarian provided information about this address. It did not confirm that Jane had lived there, but we did discover that a dark little ghostly figure can often be seen on the premises - an interview with the ghost might have yielded further information! It would have been tempting to continue following leads and clues to find out more about Jane's family, but eventually we realised that if we did so, this book would never get written.

Jane's legacy

So why all this fuss about family papers and a woman providing her own handmade reading lessons and a story for her children? Well, first of all, what shines out of these materials is love, Jane's love for her children (elsewhere we also find evidence of her devotion to her husband) which is the universal appeal of Jane's legacy. Secondly, Jane was a very special woman, described on her death by a young friend in these words, 'never could a woman more resemble an angel than she did in every action'; but she was an 'angel' with spirit and she was not slow to show her disapproval or stand up for her family when the need arose, as we will show. Thirdly, Jane's careful housekeeping (her instructions to keep documents for posterity are handwritten on many notes and letters) ensured the survival of a remarkable set of family papers spanning several generations. Finally, there is the quality and originality of her reading materials and what they suggest about mothers and children in the eighteenth century. As Gillian Avery put it: 'Her relationship with her children would have stood out as an unusually happy one at any period, but it is remarkable for its informality...'[20]. I hope that readers will find Jane and her family as fascinating a subject as we have done.

Morag Styles - Cambridge September 2005

Jane Johnson's Manuscript Nursery Library (Johnson, J. mss.) is held by the Lilly Library, Indiana University, Bloomington, Indiana. A finding aid for the collection with links to digital images of the materials can be found at the following web address:

http://www.dlib.indiana.edu/collections/janejohnson

We would like to thank the many individuals whose names are mentioned in this preface.

In particular, we are extremely grateful to the Lilly Library, Indiana University, for allowing us access to the Johnson nursery library and for giving us permission to reproduce material. Special thanks are due to Breon Mitchell for supporting and facilitating our research in various ways, and to Elizabeth Johnson, who is now a friend as well as colleague, for many kindnesses too numerous to mention. The lavish use of illustrations in the book comes through their good offices. In addition Michael L Taylor and Saundra B Taylor have been most helpful to us.

We would not have been able to do this research without the financial support of the British Academy who provided several grants enabling Evelyn Arizpe to work on this research. We are grateful to them and to the Research and Development Fund at the Faculty of Education, University of Cambridge which gave us enough money to complete our work. We are also grateful to the Lilly Library, Indiana University, for awarding Helm Fellowships which enabled both of us to travel to Bloomington and spend time there studying the collection.

We would like to thank Bill and Cresson Blois Johnson for their generosity in sharing the Johnson materials with us.
We took great liberties with Evelyn's husband, Nigel Leask's knowledge of eighteenth century literature and culture for which we are most grateful.

We would also like to thank Evelyn's brother, Andres Arizpe, for producing the Johnson family tree, Lawrence Klein for his helpful comments on Chapter 5, Justin Schiller for a useful tip and Martin Ingram for advice as well as hospitality on visits to Oxford. Several archivists, too numerous to mention by name, also helped us in our quest.

Victor Watson has been an enthusiastic collaborator and generous colleague and friend throughout the project. He and I researched the Johnson archive together ten years ago and it was his pioneering literary work which uncovered some of the sources of Jane's Pretty Story. He has stayed closely in touch since then and took the trouble of reading the entire manuscript before writing an insightful foreword for which we are deeply grateful.

We are indebted to Shirley Brice Heath for drawing the archive to our attention in the first place, for setting us off on the research trail, and for her dazzling chapter which ends the book. We could not envisage a better critical friend than she has been throughout the course of the project.

Notes

1. Oxford, Bodleian Library, MS.Don.c.190, fols. 2-4.

2. The Johnson materials were purchased from the British collector, Charles Todd Owen, in 1933 and were detailed in the typescript as item #1756.

3. The Nursery Library was prepared for Jane's daughter, Barbara, as well as her son, George, as close examination of the material makes clear.

4. Virginia Mauck was the librarian at the Lilly Library who carried out the initial cataloguing of the Johnson materials and who did all the genealogical work that went with it.

5. Sometimes called Wytham-on-the-Hill.

6. Rothstein, Natalie (ed) (1987) *A Lady of Fashion: Barbara Johnson's Album of Styles and Fabrics*, London: Thames & Hudson.

7. The Ball Foundation awarded the money to the Lilly Library, Indiana University.

8. Elizabeth Johnson curated the Handmade Readings exhibition, Fitzwilliam Museum (1994) with Shirley Brice Heath and Paul Woudhuysen, then Keeper of Manuscripts and Printed Books.

9. The dating and sequence of events is true to my best recollection.

10. *A Very Pretty Story* is discussed in Chapter 4.

11. Oxford, Bodleian Library, Ms.Don.c.190, fols. 5-6.

12. Oxford, Bodleian Library, Ms.Don.c.190, fol. 1.

13. Oxford, Bodleian Library, Ms.Don.c.190, fol. 4

14. Oxford, Bodleian Library, Ms.Don.c.190, fols. 9 -10.

15.   Victor and Judy Watson made a second journey to the Blois Johnsons in Dorset to collect material to put on display at Chapbooks and Scrapbooks Conference (1994).

16.   Hilton, M., Styles, M. & Watson, V. (eds.) (1997) *Opening the Nursery Door: Reading, Writing and Childhood 1600-1900*, London: Routledge

17.   'A different kind of love story' by Victoria Neumark, *Times Educational Supplement*, May 22, 1998.

18.   Witham-on-the-Hill Historical Society (2000) *A Piece of the Puzzle: the Journey of a Village through History*, Stamford: BJs Print Design Ltd.

19.   See J Roque's *The A to Z of Georgian London.*

20.   Avery, Gillian (2001) Introduction, *A Very Pretty Story by Jane Johnson,* Oxford: Bodleian Library, p. 7.

Introduction

Maternal Pedagogy and Histories of Reading

> Reading is for the improvement of the understanding. The improvement of the understanding is for two ends: first, for our own increase of knowledge; secondly, it enables us to deliver and make out that knowledge to others.
> John Locke (1750: 397)

We decided to write this book for a number of reasons. First of all we fell in love with our subject, Jane Johnson, and felt the need to tell her story to a wider audience. Her case study, together with that of her children, highlights the relationship between the history of domestic pedagogy and the history of reading. Our research into informal domestic literacy also sheds new light on the role of women as educators in England in the mid-eighteenth century.

We provide evidence that educated women played an active role in the education of their children, turning their talents to the creation of material for them and not just relying on, or borrowing from, published primers or other educational texts. These mothers valued this ephemera which could include a wide range of genres and both took account of children's experiences and drew on the material of their everyday lives. They had also the advantage of an intimate knowledge of each child's particular talents and weaknesses. We also show that mothers taught not only the first letters and basic principles of reading but prepared children for their future roles as adults in society, through writing letters and providing examples of other literate practices including drama. The reading and writing of Jane's children as adults prove that those homely methods could be successful.

Throughout this book it becomes evident that women's and girls' literate practices were intrinsically related to their multiple roles (present or future), as wives, mothers, teachers, household managers and social beings. These practices were actively engaged with and women readers conducted private conversations with male-authored texts and transformed them for their own purposes through their own writing and/or parallel readings.

1

Jane's nursery library and her original story, *A Very Pretty Story* (1744), offer fresh insights into the multiple and intersecting histories of books and readers, juvenile literature, and reading pedagogy. For example, *A Very Pretty Story* also confirms the fallacy of the division between fairy tale and didactic/moral tale, usually sustained under the false dichotomy of literature for children being either 'instructive' or 'delightful'.

Finally, from the wealth of family papers carefully preserved for posterity by Jane and later members of the family, we have a unique opportunity to try to make sense of the culture of a middle-income family in the eighteenth century, to find out more about their reading practices, as well as pursue informed hunches as to what reading meant to children and adults during this period.

In order to understand Jane as a woman, mother and teacher, it is necessary to place the Johnson family in context and to go back into her own childhood. We have, therefore, tried to gather together as much information as possible relevant to women (as mothers and teachers), children (their education and rearing) and reading (the practices and the texts) during this period. There are many studies that focus on one or two of these aspects, but there are few that bring together all three of them.

Domestic histories

Recently there has been a great deal of scholarly and popular interest in the histories of English families from the past. Like biographies and diaries, these historical reconstructions allow the reader glimpses into the everyday lives of men and women who lived in previous centuries. They are all the more tantalising because they can never be complete; we are forced to use our imaginations to fill in the gaps. In the more fortunate cases, there is extensive biographical information and perhaps even manuscripts or paintings. For the most part, these cases relate to genteel or aristocratic families and, of course, there are far more documents by and about men than women due to their privileged access to formal education and involvement in public life.

Recent research, however, has revealed previously neglected documents by women who were never famous but whose letters, diaries and manuscripts provide glimpses into their everyday lives (see, for example, the women discussed by Amanda Vickery in *The Gentleman's Daughter,* 1998). Some of these documents have shown that women played a far more influential role in the public as well as in the private spheres than was previously thought, and that in many respects the division between the two spheres is illusory (see also Leonore Davidoff and Catherine Hall, 1987). The documents discussed in Vickery's book show many women to be well-educated, well informed and unafraid to voice their opinions despite the patriarchal society in which they lived.

In his review of recent publications on gender studies in the late Medieval and Early Modern period, Martin Ingram considers the rise of 'new social history' and the women's movement. He points out that 'the weight of interest has focused on women and their relations with men' so that other aspects of women's lives within a patriarchal society have been largely ignored. One of these aspects is the relationship between parents and children and although Ingram acknowledges that 'there has been some distinguished work on children, adolescents, servants and apprentices, the total output is not as large as might have been expected, especially in relation to the very young' (Ingram, 2005: 734).

Classic histories of childhood in England, such as those by Rosamund Bayne-Powell (1939), Ivy Pinchbeck and Margaret Hewitt (1969) and Lawrence Stone (1977) have been revised using new perspectives on childhood. In their book, Neil McKendrick, John Brewer and J. H. Plumb (1983), for example, place childhood in the context of the consumer culture of the eighteenth century[1], while Linda Pollock (1983) uses primary sources such as diaries to focus on parent-child relations, and Keith Thomas (1989) looks at children's 'subculture', including lore and play, to stress the difference between child and adult values in early modern England. In a more recent book, Andrew O'Malley (2003) explores how childhood has been constructed in the late eighteenth century by focusing on the 'consolidation' of what he calls the middle class in England with their strong emphasis on education and reading. In *The Making of the Modern Child,* O'Malley also discusses reading pedagogy, the oral tradition and children's literature of the period, linking them to industrial, scientific and medical advances. Some of the essays in *Opening the Nursery Door* (Hilton et al, 1997) which look at the implications of women writing for children (including Jane Johnson), have also added to our understanding of the history of childhood. While this book is not meant to be a study of the history of childhood, we do attempt to bring together the research of previous historians and to explore some of the links between childhood, schooling and children's texts in this period through the Johnson family history.

Figure 3. [Set 11, leaf 37]. Final image in the miniature book made by Jane Johnson for George William. Courtesy of Lilly Library, Indiana University, Bloomington, IN.

Mothers as teachers: home education before school

We know that Jane was not the only mother who was closely involved in her children's early education. The diaries and letters from the seventeenth and eighteenth centuries analysed by Spufford (1981) and by Pollock (1983) reveal parental concern about their children's learning and show many parents taking some part in the education of

their children.[2] Interest in the education of the young appears to have increased at the beginning of the 1800s among middle-income families, probably due to the influence of John Locke's seminal treatise on education from 1693: *Some Thoughts Concerning Education.* Locke's idea that children's minds are like pieces of wax to be moulded and shaped, was the backbone of any educational activity in the eighteenth-century informed household. One way of moulding and shaping is evidently through carefully supervised reading, but in order to be able to select texts wisely and to impart knowledge more generally, it is also necessary for the 'teacher' to be well read. Jane and Woolsey, as well as many other English men and women who were having families around the middle of the eighteenth century, would have assumed that 'honour due to parents was based not on the role of parents in begetting their children, but their role in nourishing and educating them: an implicit contract' (Amussen, 1988: 65).

There were no clear guidelines as to who did the actual teaching. Wealthier families tended to engage governesses or tutors to ensure their children's learning before sending them to public schools. In middle-income families like the Johnsons, some parents taught the basics of literacy, numeracy and religious knowledge themselves, but their children could also be sent, together with those of lower-income families, to 'Dame' or 'Petty' schools. These small private schools were usually run by elderly women (some were little more than child-minders) who charged about 3d. per week. Their teaching included religious knowledge and reading and then perhaps practical skills leading to boys becoming apprentices and girls learning to be good wives and mothers (see, for example, Spufford, 1981). Later in the century Charity schools took over most of the education for poorer children.

One consequence of the pedagogical role of parents was scrutiny of their own behaviour, as it was considered crucial to set a good example to the children. In 1755 Jane writes in her commonplace book that:

> If a man [sic] would have Good & Virtuous Children, he must be Good & Virtuous himself, for it is not reasonable to expect that a Bad Tree should bring forth good Fruit.[3]

This had particular implications for women. In the second volume of Samuel Richardson's *Pamela* (circa 1740), the eponymous heroine (having finally got herself 'properly' married), concentrates on providing a virtuous example to the children in her care. Many novels from the later eighteenth century written by women, such as *Evelina* by Fanny Burnett (1778), *Millenium Hall* by Sarah Scott (1762) and *A Simple Story* by Elizabeth Inchbald (1782) stress the importance of a 'proper education' for women and blame either absent or unsuitable mothers for their daughter's failings. Along with conduct books, these novels assumed some of the responsibility for educating their young female readers.

Jane was encouraged by the popular literature on child-rearing to take her role as educator seriously. As well as Locke, Jane read the writings of influential educational philosophers and famous educationalists such as Fénelon (François de Salignac de la Mothe, Archbishop of Cambrai) and the French scholar, Charles Rollin. She also almost certainly would have read the second volume of Samuel Richardson's *Pamela*, with its long, digressive criticisms of some of Locke's recommendations. Jane was also familiar with popular primers such as those published by John Newbery and Mary Cooper. As some studies on women and education suggest (see for example Spufford, 1981 and Brewer, 1996), familiarity with such material seems to have been true of most genteel mothers of Jane's time. Although she followed their advice, she also drew on her own ingenuity and moral purpose.

Yet very little is known about how education in the home would have taken place in early to mid-eighteenth century, and who would have provided particular lessons. The diaries studied by Pollock (1983) show that several fathers were directly involved in teaching reading and writing as well as religious education. Other fathers seemed to act more as general overseers. Most appeared to have had clear ideas about what they wanted their children to learn. Even so, early education was mainly the mothers' concern.

We know that even before the eighteenth century mothers had instructed their children in religion, through the recitation of short prayers and psalms, and that throughout the Middle Ages there are indications that mothers were 'mediators' of book-learning (Clanchy, 1984).[4] Literate mothers would have based their teaching on the Bible

and taught the alphabet and reading as far as they themselves were able. In her articles on the history of literacy, Spufford (1981 and 1997) shows that in the early eighteenth century even mothers from lower-income households, such as a Mrs. Fretwell of Yorkshire, were successful in their attempts at teaching their children.[5] But how often did mothers create any materials of their own and, if they did, how did they link these to their children's interests and experiences? How did eighteenth-century mothers follow the methods usually found in the published primers? How did they make use of images? How did they take up references to popular culture of the time?

Recent historical and feminist research into women's roles in the domestic sphere in the eighteenth century helps us understand the context for domestic pedagogical activities and reveals interesting debates about the mother's power in the nursery.[6] As Terry Lovell writes: 'the figure of woman in early eighteenth-century England has begun to be recast in a much more active role: participant in, even producer of, aspects of that culture, *and a key agent in its transmission across generations*' (Lovell, 1995: 37 [*our emphasis*]). In the first place, the interest in rational thought during the eighteenth century was quickly followed by the realisation that if the mother was to inculcate the 'right' values and morals, as well as the 'proper' knowledge (as opposed to superstition and false notions), she had to be educated herself. Given Locke's highly influential view of the child's mind as a 'tabula rasa'[7] it was the mother who, for the first eight to ten impressionable years of children's lives, would 'form' the character and role of her offspring. Many of the 'conduct' books for women like *The Ladies Library* (published by Richard Steele in 1714) stressed this important task: 'The Principle Care of the *Mother* being to Educate her Children well ...' (Steele, 1714: 134).[8]

Steele, co-founder with Joseph Addison of *The Spectator*, and others actively encouraged mothers to participate in their children's educational development. When she becomes a mother, Pamela takes this to heart[9]:

> What delights have those mammas [...] who can make their babies, and their first educations, their entertainment and diversion! To watch the dawning of reason in them, to direct their little passions [...] and to prepare the sweet virgin soil of their minds to receive the seeds of virtue and goodness ... (Richardson, 1984: 405)

However, Richardson's Pamela also raises at least one very pertinent question:

> who I pray, as our sex is generally educated, shall teach the *mothers*? How, in a word, shall they come by their knowledge? [...] I would indeed have a girl brought up to her needle, but I would not have *all* her time employed in [...] those unnecessary things, which she will never, probably, be called upon to practise. (Richardson, 1984: 413)

As education became too important a task to leave to strangers, mothers were expected to teach more academic subjects such as Latin grammar, accounts and geography. In order to be able to do this, women's education needed to be improved. Reading was the main channel for self-education, helped by the increase in publications aimed specifically at women, as well as participation in the general literate culture through letter-writing, newspapers and circulating libraries.

One of the most popular books (despite his Catholicism in mainly Protestant England) was by Fénelon; in his *Instructions for the Education of a Daughter* (1687), he argued that children's brains harden as they grow and that they learn at different paces according to their age and ability. He advised educators to make learning enjoyable so that children would not take an aversion to study: 'Everything that rejoices or enlivens the Imagination, facilitates study' (Fénelon, 1713: 51). For the education of girls he recommended play and 'a pretty *instructive Reading*, a *Labour* which is by herself freely undertaken [and] a *Walk* or *innocent Conversation* which relaxes the mind after hard labour' (Fénelon 1713: 59). Another popular book which echoed the recommendations of Locke and Fénelon was Rollin's monumental *Methods for Teaching and Studying the Belles Lettres* (1726-1728). He advocated a highly structured method of instruction, but he also advised studying the character of the child and endeavouring to make study agreeable. In a final chapter on girl's education, he recommended that education should be the same for girls and boys up to the ages of 6 or 7.

After the ages of 6 or 7 it became a practice in England to send middle-class boys off to school rather than have them privately tutored at home, particularly after the 1720s. Woolsey and Jane sent all three boys to Rugby: George and Robert at the age of 10 and Charles at the

age of 8. Secondary and higher education was still mainly for boys of the gentry and bourgeoisie and the best schools were Eton and Westminster, with Rugby considered a 'lesser' public school on a par with Winchester or Harrow. The schools taught Latin, literature, rhetoric, vernacular grammar and arithmetic but little or no religious education. Boys would then go on to careers in the church, state, military or commerce. These public schools however, had a bad reputation among some parents and were considered to pose threats to both morals and health (Trumbach, 1978). As well as considering the cost, Jane might have thought her boys were better off at a smaller private school like Uppingham where she could have more of a say in their welfare.[10]

So what about the education of a girl like Barbara Johnson? Pollock (1983) shows that many diarists from the seventeenth and eighteenth centuries were interested in the education of their daughters as much as their sons, although differences still applied. According to Patricia Clancy (1982), on her arrival in England, Mme de Beaumont[11] was appalled at girls' education, as even those girls whose families could pay for it, gained very little from their schooling. Girls of well-to-do families were not usually sent to school, but they were taught to read, write and cast accounts by their mothers or governesses. They were also instructed in housekeeping tasks such as cooking, distilling medicaments, spinning or needlework ('the science of women' as Rollin puts it) and dancing, languages and music. While their brothers were at school, university or on the 'Grand Tour', girls would learn about fashion and polite society, making visits and attending social events until they married.

From around the mid-eighteenth century, this pattern changed, and girls started to learn Latin, arithmetic, history, French and Italian among other subjects.[12] Barbara would have probably been taught some of these subjects by her mother and although there are no direct mentions in Jane's writing about her expectations for her daughter's education, there are indications that she believed a woman ought to be capable of thinking for herself. She would have agreed with Mme de Beaumont who

> ... believed that the critical part of education was achieved through the incorporation of a mixture of moral lessons and practical knowledge into instructive conversation [...] She believed it was critical to teach children taste and judgement, giving them the tools to make rational decisions throughout their lives in favor of virtue over vice. (Shefrin, 2003: 84).

As the domestic sphere was accorded the important function of educating future generations, it also became the site of a power struggle between men and women. Even in the seventeenth century, women like Hannah Woolley and Mary Astell had recognised that although women should be educated as much as men, they must also be skilled at concealing their learning. This view continued well into the eighteenth century so that education for women involved a delicate balance between obtaining enough knowledge to instruct their children, for their own spiritual well-being and to become a better companion to their husbands, and not becoming overly intellectual and thereby risk social alienation.

In any case, by mid-eighteenth century, most genteel mothers like Jane would have considered their role as educator as a primary one. Thirty years later a woman like Anna Larpent 'consciously saw herself as a teacher' and 'devised a rigorous programme of reading for her growing young sons' (Vickery, 1988: 114). Hester Thrale, a contemporary of Barbara's, was also devoted to her children's learning, although she pushed her children to such extremes that 'she alienated the affections of all her daughters' (Pollock, 1983: 247). Writing in 1762, Rousseau endorses the pedagogical duty of mothers in his influential *Émile* where he stresses the importance of early education. Unfortunately Rousseau also promoted a more conservative view of women in which 'sensitive' girls should be not so much educated as restrained and moulded into the 'perfect' wife. However, by the end of the century, women like Anna Barbauld and Maria Edgeworth, were publishing didactic literature which, as Myers writes, 'signals a shifting female cultural ideal, a bourgeois reinvention of woman in the stylish new mode of enlightened domesticity' (Myers, 1986: 34).[13]

We can presume that many of these involved mothers also created materials of their own to teach their children to read and write and probably did it well, too. The very fact that Jane's materials survived may be an indication of the extent to which such creative contributions, fed by pedagogical and religious treatises, not only were part of daily life but were also cherished as part of family histories.

Histories of reading

In the Johnson archives we are fortunate to have access to unique and quite detailed information on what the members of this particular family read, especially Jane and her son Robert. By looking at how this information relates to the socio-historical conditions of the period, we can learn more not only about this particular family's reading practices, but also about literacy in eighteenth-century England in general. However, in order to make the most of this wealth of data, it is necessary to place it within the framework of other studies of the history of reading.

According to the French historian Robert Darnton, the 'first steps toward a history of reading' would include investigating 'the ideals and assumptions underlying reading in the past' (Darnton, 1990: 171). To this foundation, Darnton adds the history of education, records individuals have left about their reading habits (e.g. autobiographies), literary theories (such as reader-response criticism), and consideration of the physical appearance of the books themselves (design, binding, layout etc.). It is important to remember, however, that, as James Machor says, 'even the most complete historical record never discloses a pure presence but depends on our own mediating activities as interpreters and readers of the past' (Machor, 1993: xxii). Until the early eighteenth century we know most about reading aloud because it was public performance. Once reading becomes a more private activity it is harder to access. Our interpretation of domestic reading is analysed through the prism of the private documents meant for family members, current and future.[14]

Historians of reading all recognise the difficulties of interpreting domestic or private materials preserved primarily through accidents of history. A variety of interpretative approaches contribute to building an increasingly complex picture of reading in earlier periods. One approach analyses the audience that seems to be targeted by the materials written and/or published. An 'implied' reader, to use Wolfgang Iser's terminology, is conjured up. This approach however, can become a closed circuit because the only readers distinguished are text-based. Therefore, we may end up with only the author's view of who his or her intended reader is. Another approach examines the history of publication and distribution of books and other reading matter. The analysis of materials, such as wills, publishing company records, and library records (see, for example, William St Clair on the printed-book industry in the Romantic period) tell us what was available, but not what was actually read. Owning or borrowing a book is not equivalent to reading it.

At the opposite end of the spectrum from author and printer/bookseller are individual readers responding to particular texts. We have already mentioned some of the problems with these records, and it is ironic that on their own, these fragments may present little evidence of *how* people read, partly because they are fragments, partly because they are few and far between, and mainly because, as St Clair says, they were 'produced by their authors, within generic conventions of specific historical time, with implied readers and intended rhetorical effects in mind' (St Clair, 2004: 5-6). For example, even in her commonplace book, a 'private' text, Jane may have been choosing to transcribe particular moral passages from contemporary books with the expectation that her children would later read and learn from them.

Recent work on particular individuals, which follows in the general direction signalled in the work of the French historian, Roger Chartier (see, for example, *The Cultural Uses of Print in Early Modern France*, 1987), considers reading as a socially constructed activity and proposes using social history, textual criticism and primary sources to try to describe not only 'what' readers read in the past, but also 'when' and 'how' they read it. In order to do this, Machor argues in his introduction to *Readers in History* that reader-response criticism needs to explore 'the dynamics of reading and the textual construction of audience as products of historically specific fields, where social conditions, ideologies, rhetorical practices, interpretive strategies, and cultural factors of race, class, and gender intersect' (Machor, 1993: xi).

As we try to understand how the Johnson family read, we need to consider as many of these strands as possible. We attempt to do so· particularly for Jane through the commonplace book which gives us invaluable clues to her reading. We also go back a generation or so in the Johnson family history to help situate the family in terms of 'literacy' backgrounds and build a picture of what both Jane and Woolsey may have brought to their own family.

Mapping this book

Our book follows Darnton's steps, using a range of historical sources, reading theories, educational ideas and information on literacy in the eighteenth century, as well as the primary evidence found in the various Johnson archives. We shall also be touching on the history of publishing and its relationship to education and children's literature. In order to help chart readers' way through this book, we now set out a guide to the content.

In this Introduction we have attempted a brief general review of the histories of women, children and reading which contextualise our particular study of one woman and her family's reading practices over two generations. In so doing, we have touched on relevant historical and cultural studies literature with our focus firmly on what it meant to read and to be a reader in the eighteenth century.

In Chapter 1, we introduce the Johnson family by locating them within the context of 'polite' society, as well as in relation to the social, cultural, geographical, religious and economic worlds of their time. In addition, we touch on the earlier family histories of both the Johnsons (Woolsey's family of origin) and the Rainsford/Russells (Jane's family of origin). Finally, we try to bring Jane and her family alive for the reader by focusing on her multiple roles as wife, mother, domestic manager, writer and educator. Indeed, we make a modest attempt to travel 'in Jane's footsteps' by reconstructing her life story through examination of her literate practices and her domestic writing. These include a recipe book she wrote as a child; letters to friends, family and her children; private notes and poetry.

Chapter 2 concentrates on the changing world of reading and children's books in the eighteenth century. We document the rise of literacy in this period and examine who read what, where and when. We provide an overview of the publishing world in this period, particularly the rise of juvenile publishing and the growing commercial market in children's books. We probe what can be learned from reconstructing the reading practices of other early modern readers. We also consider the nature of the readings by which the Johnson family lived. These include the Bible and other devotional texts, the writings of Locke and Newbery's publications for children, as well as popular fiction of their day.

Chapter 3 is devoted to Jane's maternal pedagogy in the form of the reading materials and lessons she prepared for her children in the

English nursery of the 1740s. We show how her reading lessons contained traditional elements, alongside products of the new 'enlightened' thinking of her day. We also delineate the unique aspects of her highly visual, child-centred and varied approach to the learning and teaching of reading.

Jane's wonderful tale written especially for her own children, *A Very Pretty Story*, is examined in detail in Chapter 4 along with what were then changing tastes in children's literature - in particular, fairy tales and moral tales - both of which strongly influenced Jane's story. We then look at the religious and didactic strain in Jane's writing and consider the ways in which her children might have taken meaning from word and image through her texts.

In Chapter 5, we move on to Jane's commonplace book and, within the context of women as readers, we plot her own reading history and personal reading habits. Using critical discussion to guide our thinking, we review the influences on Jane - from Plato to *Pamela* - locating her reading within the intersection of gender and literacy, culture and religion of the first half of the eighteenth century.

The literate and cultural practices of the second half of the eighteenth century are examined in Chapter 6, our penultimate chapter, by looking at the Johnson siblings as adult readers. We scrutinise their diaries and letters and consider the wide-ranging choice of texts they used to communicate with one another; sustain, entertain and educate themselves; and, in Robert's case, reflect on his roles as a parent. Overall, we try to investigate what reading meant to Jane's family as they grew up and how their childhood and education might have influenced the literate adults they were to become.

In the final chapter, Shirley Brice Heath takes an anthropological perspective on the ephemera of literacy that handmade materials represent. She sets their transitory and temporary nature down within the contexts of leisure time, technological advances, and family routines necessary to support their creation. She brings us from what the Johnson family has taught us about literate practices in the eighteenth century, to a comparative frame on families' technological and aesthetic practices in the twenty-first century.

Notes

1. Part of Plumb's chapter in this book is from his article, 'The New World of Children', published in 1975.

2. Historians of childhood in England such as Pinchbeck and Hewitt (1969), Trumbach (1978) and Stone (1979) provided evidence that the nature of family relationships among the aristocracy and landed classes was transformed during the late seventeenth and early eighteenth century, as the rejection of the concept of original sin allowed parents to be less disciplinarian and to show more affection to their offspring.

3. Oxford, Bodleian Library, MS. Don.c.190, fols. 72-102.

4. Clanchy makes this argument based on the many images of the Virgin reading with the Child Jesus and on Chaucer's *Prioress's Tale* (Clanchy, 1984).

5. Mothers may have also been forced to take on the role of teachers if there was no school nearby. In Mrs Fretwell's case, she taught her children because she did not feel the 'old school-dame' was doing the job properly (Spufford, 1981: 128).

6. See for example Bowers, 1996; Lovell, 1995; McDermid, 1989; and Rafferty, 1997.

7. Locke was not the first to promote the belief that character was formed not by innate forces but by cultivation. As Ezell writes: 'The blank slate/white paper image stems from the seventeenth century, but it is not until the eighteenth that it acquires its expanded meaning and becomes a stock metaphor to describe children' (Ezell, 1983: 150).

8. Steele pretends that it was 'written by a lady', but he borrows from Locke and particularly from Mary Astell's *A Serious Proposal to the Ladies* (1694).

9. They also suggested 'methods' of teaching, such as when Pamela points to their ears and tongues when she says 'knowledge is obtained by *hearing*, and not by *speaking*' and Miss Goodwin says 'You have so many pretty ways to learn one, Madam, that it is impossible we should not regard what you say to us!' (Richardson, 1984: 427)

10. Also, by this stage Woolsey had died.

11. In Mme. de Beaumont's two works (*Education Complète ou Abrégé de l'Histoire Universelle, Melée de Geographie, de Chronologie*, 1753 and *Nouveau Magasin Français*, 1750-55) aimed at adolescent girls of upper and middle class families like Barbara Johnson, she incorporates many of Fénelon's recommendations as well as Rollin's method of presenting history.

12. On the curriculum for girls in the eighteenth century, see for example, Cohen 2005.

13. See also McCarthy 1999, Myers 1986, 1991 and 1999.

14. As Whyman reminds us in her insightful history of the Verney family and their correspondence in late-Stuart England, 'Let no one who reads a memoir, diary, or letter naively conclude that there is a simple correlation between content and "reality" [...] every author formulates a "pose" and erects a screen in order to present "the self" positively' (Whyman, 1999: 11-12).

Chapter 1

Family Fictions: In the Footsteps of the Johnsons

> I had rather be a favourite of Angels than of men, but I believe those
> that Behave as they should do, will commonly be a favourite of both.
> Jane Johnson, Commonplace book[1]

> To make a whippt syllabub[2]
> take a pint of cream 6 spoonfuls of sack the whites of 2 eggs 3 ounces
> of fine shuger and a burch twig bate it till it froth well skim it and put
> it into your syllabub glasses[3]

Jane's recipe for a delicious sounding syllabub dessert, written when
she was a little girl, introduces the reader to the Johnson family. In the
Preface, readers have already met Jane, a devoted mother of four
children, happily married to the well-to-do Reverend Woolsey
Johnson. Our aim here is to situate Jane, Woolsey and their children
historically and geographically, to give an impression of their social
and economic status and to provide a snapshot of their interactions
with friends, acquaintances and family. We go back in time to provide
a brief history of the Johnson and Rainsford (sometimes spelled
Raynsford[4]) families, and then look forward to the generations
following Jane and Woolsey. We do so, not just to tease out the strands
that run through their particular family, but also to consider them as
part of English social fabric from the beginning of the seventeenth to
the late eighteenth century. In a small way, by looking closely at a
family of some wealth and influence, noting the small but significant
choices they made in areas ranging from education, reading and
religion, to justice, colonisation and land management, we can arrive at
a better understanding of some aspects of the making of the English
middle classes during this period. Most importantly for our purposes,
we draw Jane out of the shadows and analyse the character of this
remarkable woman to find out, among other things, what drove her to
create such a special nursery library.

Johnson family fortunes before the eighteenth century[5]

The Johnson family documents that have survived range from the
sixteenth to the nineteenth centuries. As mentioned in the Preface, they
are not all collected together in one place although the two archives of
most interest to educators and historians are in the Lilly Library,

Bloomington, Indiana and in the Bodleian Library, Oxford. Other papers, which are scattered in various archives in the UK, although less directly relevant to Jane herself, are still linked to her, given that she meticulously collected papers from previous generations of Johnsons and passed on to her children not only the family history, but also her concern to preserve it for future generations. As she said in a letter to Mrs Brompton (Jane's aunt) in 1749, 'I think it a vast deal of pity that anything you write shou'd be lost …'[6] Several documents and letters have comments written in the margins in Jane's hand, probably for the purpose of clarifying some historical facts for her children. She seems to have read and organised her husband's documents after his death (1755), as most remarks end with 'Jane Johnson 1756'. Although several times she also wrote a comment to the effect that 'these papers are of no sort of use', she was careful to safeguard them.

Certain paths and interests of many English families have been followed across the generations. In the Johnson case, a strong religious vein emerges in the clerical profession, along with a concern for education, manifest in the founding of schools and Jane's nursery library. A love of reading and writing, an artistic bent and a passion for collecting and preserving, whether it be letters, books, moral maxims or fashionable textiles, was also evident across the generations and, indeed, sometimes in the spouses they chose. Those who had the opportunity also liked to travel (even Archdeacon Johnson living in the sixteenth century spent three years abroad in France), but in general the Johnsons remained attached to their lands in Lincolnshire and what was then Rutland in Buckinghamshire.

It is possible to trace the Johnson family tree as far back as 1540.[7] Bryan Matthews, historian of Uppingham School, provides an interesting account of these early Johnsons, particularly of Robert Johnson, Archdeacon of Leicester, a wealthy philanthropist and educator. Born in Stamford in 1540, he bought most of the estate of Witham[8]-on-the-Hill in 1625 from William Harrington to whom he had earlier lent £4000 to support Charles I before he came to the throne. His money came partly from his pluralities[9] of which there were many and partly from the property acquired from his first two marriages[10]. He founded two schools, Oakham and Uppingham, still thriving today. Both were for local boys with underprivileged parents who were to pay according to their abilities. He also founded two hospitals for the poor known as the Hospitals of Christ. In addition, he established sixteen exhibitions - the equivalent of student grants - for four students for each of the Cambridge colleges of St. John's, Emmanuel, Clare and Sidney Sussex, each worth around £6 per year. These 'Exhibitioners' as they were known, were elected by the Master and senior fellows of each college every fourth year, with preference to those who had attended the grammar schools of either Oakham or Uppingham for at least two years.

A devout Puritan[11], Archdeacon Johnson had friends in high places, including the Queen's most senior advisors, such as William Cecil and Nicholas Bacon, who helped his advancing career. Queen Elizabeth 1 herself provided some of the money for his projects. Just before his death in 1625, Archdeacon Johnson issued a series of 'statutes and ordinances' for his schools that declared that the schoolmaster should be 'an honest and discreet Man, Master of Arts, and diligent in his Place, painful in the educating of Children in good Learning and Religion such as can make a Greek and Latin Verse.'[12] His only son, Abraham, was handsomely educated; he had been taught Latin, Greek, French, Italian and Spanish as well as rhetoric, logic, music and singing. For all his learning, Abraham disappointed his father. According to Matthews, he called himself '"a philosophical engineer", which meant an inventor of ingenious devices, for the building of which he was often begging money from his father' (Matthews, 1984: 14). The relationship between father and son was so bad that at one point Robert Johnson wanted to leave only £100 in his will to Abraham and the rest to his favourite grandson, Isaac. (At the time of his death, the Archdeacon's estate was valued at £30,000, more than half a million pounds in today's currency.)

The said Isaac, and his half-brothers Samuel and Ezekiel, were all educated at Emmanuel College, Cambridge and were known as 'the Johnsons of Northants, Clipsham and Rutland'. Once he had inherited his grandfather's money, Isaac became a founding member of the Massachusetts Bay Company and emigrated to New England in 1630 on a ship named after his wife, 'Arabella', daughter of the Earl of Lincoln. This endeavour ended tragically as both Isaac and his wife died after a few months in Salem, she of 'sickness' because of the severe winter, and he, of grief.[13] Samuel died in 1658 and Ezekiel became Master of Uppingham School, as well as Lord of the Manor of Clipsham and Rector of Cranford. He had no male heirs, so his daughter Anne (born circa 1640) inherited the family estate. Unfortunately for Anne, she also inherited the annuity to be paid to the Cambridge colleges which had built up arrears over time. That her children were also 'Johnsons' was due to the coincidence of her marrying a Thomas Johnson of Olney (1633-1696), one of the Buckinghamshire Johnsons. He turned out to be an extravagant spendthrift who went to prison several times for debt (some of his letters from prison to his son have survived). On a document relating to the sale of Clipsham, Jane Johnson wrote touchingly about the horrors of debt, a theme she would return to again and again:

> This paper is of no manner of use, I only keep it to show posterity that the Reverend Ezekiel Johnson sold his Estate at Clipsam in Rutland, to one Mr Snow, for ten thousand pounds [...] a vast deal of money at that time of day, but it was thought Ezekiel Johnson sold Clipsom a great deal too Cheap. It was to defray the Extravagances of Thomas Johnson Esqr. William Johnson's father that he sold it [...] Thomas Johnson was once in Newgate for Debt, & several times in other Prisons. All he had at Olney was once seized on & his Wife, (Ezekiel Johnson's Daughter) & Family turn'd out of Doors [...] Oh to what Distress & inconveniences does Extravagances bring people. Let Thomas Johnson Esqr of Olney be a Warning to all his posterity never to run out their income.
> (Jane Johnson, 1756)[14]

The Johnson family of Buckinghamshire were connected with Olney from at least 1633 when they purchased the rectory and advowson of the parish. The family also owned property in Rutland, but they lived in the Great House in Olney which stood near the parish church (it was pulled down in mid-nineteenth century). They also owned property in Lincolnshire and in Milton Bryant, Bedfordshire. In 1692, the Cambridge colleges brought action in the Court of Chancery for the recovery of the annuity and arrears, representing Archdeacon Johnson's Benefaction, against Thomas and his eldest son, William (1665-1736). They agreed in 1694 to pay £2,100 instead of the annuity and eventually land was purchased by the four colleges to support the exhibitions in 1709. The family fortunes picked up when William, father of Jane's husband, inherited the Witham Estate and in 1689 married Ann (?-1737), daughter and heiress of Thomas Woolsey, Archdeacon of Northampton and Rector of Thornhaugh. William

Johnson was vicar of Olney; Jane was clearly fond of her father-in-law and made him an attractive keepsake of all his children's names and their dates of birth.

Woolsey Johnson and Jane Russell

Ann and William had ten children, but it is their fourth son, Woolsey Johnson, born in 1696, who eventually inherited both the living of Olney and the Estate at Witham after the early deaths of his brothers. After leaving Uppingham School aged eighteen in 1713, Woolsey was admitted to Clare College, Cambridge in 1714 with one of Archdeacon Johnson's Exhibitions. Several letters from his parents while he was at Clare survive, among them a letter from his father which reveals his Whig politics and strongly Protestant religion as he celebrates the defeat of the Jacobites:

> Nov 20 1715,
> To Mr Woolsey Johnson at Clare Hall in Cambridge
> I cannot but congratulate you on glorious news… defeat of Lancaster Rebells in Scotland […] to have a popish imposter [James II's son, 'the Old Pretender'] educated in the schools of Tyranny accustomed to behold the persecution of the Hugenots with pleasure is inconsistent with the welfare of a protestant nation.
> (W Johnson)[15]

In 1720 Woolsey was ordained deacon at the Peterborough diocese. He was sometime curate at St. Andrews, Holborn, then Rector of Wilby, Northants, as well as being Vicar of Olney from 1735, the same year he married Jane Russell. Jane and Woolsey lived in the Great House in Olney until 1756 when he died aged 60, after some years where he spent much time and money overseeing the building of a Manor House and enclosing the Park at Witham. Jane and the children moved to Witham without him; he was the first of his family to be buried there.

It is not clear how much money Jane Russell brought to her marriage. She is described as 'coheiress' of her father's estate, and this entailed half the money from the sale of Packwood Manor, Warwickshire, which Jane and her sister inherited, then sold to Horace Mann in 1727. Her father, Richard Russell (1654-1720), had bought Packwood Manor in 1715, from the Earl of Spencer but according to the histories of Warwickshire, he was originally a 'menial servant' in the Earl of

Spencer's other house at Claverdon.[16] Some family documents claim he was descended from Judge Richard Ward, but this claim may have been an attempt to hide his humbler origins.[17] Despite much searching, we were unable to find out where he obtained enough money to buy Packwood Manor. Perhaps he made his fortune in London, working with his future father-in-law, Francis Rainsford, a well-off merchant with a shop in Bow Lane and a house in St. James Westminster? Alternatively were his future wife's family reluctant about the match? At any rate, only one day before Lucy Rainsford married Richard Russell on 7 July 1704, Francis Rainsford gave over substantial lands to his daughter.[18] Their first child, Lucy Russell, Jane's sister, was born exactly one year later.

The Rainsfords were a well-respected, London based family. Francis's father was Judge Richard Rainsford, Lord Chief Justice of the King's Bench in 1676. At the time of his death, he and his wife Katheryn were living in Portugal Row, Lincoln's Inn Fields and they also had a house in Dallington, Northamptonshire, where they are both buried. According to Spence's *London in the 1690s: A Social Atlas*, St. James Westminster was a 'spacious, aristocratic neighbourhood' where household rents averaged £48, about the same price as those living in Lincoln's Inn Fields. Various Rainsford wills also reveal the family was wealthy and well connected; for example, Francis' wife, Elizabeth, was the daughter of Edward Atkins, Baron of the Exchequer from 1630-1698. It is therefore unlikely that Francis and Elizabeth would have let their daughter, marry a man who did not possess some kind of fortune.

Richard Russell was a widower of 50 when he married Lucy Rainsford, then only 23, in 1704. We do not know what happened in this marriage, but fifteen years later, when Richard Russell made his will in 1719, he left his wife only 'one shilling' which effectively meant that he disinherited her. He left everything else (apart from a small sum for his daughter from his first marriage, Elizabeth Plummerden) to his two daughters, Lucy and Jane. This meant that the sisters become the 'ladies' of Packwood Manor in Warwickshire. Although Jane was christened in St. Mary's, Warwick, we found no evidence of her ever having lived there.

It seems more likely that the family lived in London and, after their father died, the girls either stayed with their mother, or went to live with their grandparents. Mysteriously, Jane's mother is never mentioned in any of the family correspondence, despite the fact that her four grandchildren were living nearby when she died in Olney in 1752. The fact that no letters survive from, to, or about her could be simply a matter of bad luck. However, if she had behaved in such a way as to provoke her husband's disinheritance by flirting, or worse, with handsome young soldiers such as Captain Ingoldsby[19], it might be that her daughters also disapproved of her. We know certainly that Jane's mother married again, one Francis Ingoldsby, First Lieutenant in Colonel Wolfe's Regiment of Marines [20] 'of the parish of St Martin in the Fields in the county of Middlesex Gent aged twenty eight years and a Batchelor'[21] - on 10 December 1728, when she was 49, a year after her daughters sold Packwood Manor. The disparity of ages suggests she was either a great beauty or an engaging personality or simply had a large fortune. Could Jane's extreme devoutness, uprightness and anxiety about debt stem from having had a racy, spendthrift mother? It might simply be the case that letters between the women were unnecessary, because Jane saw her mother regularly once she moved to Olney. Lucy's soldier husband died ten years later and his widow outlived him by 12 years. 'Mrs Lucy Relict of Captain Francis Ingoldsby' died aged seventy, at a much older age than both her daughters.[22]

Woolsey and Jane knew each other for several years before their marriage in 1735. He witnessed the will of Jane's sister Lucy before her untimely death in 1731. When they married, Jane was 30 and Woolsey was ten years older which suggests it was a marriage born of friendship, and based on mutual regard and agreement, rather than an impetuous romance or something arranged by their parents. By this time, Jane had had her share of her father's inheritance, as well as £50 left to her by her sister and another £50 and a gold watch from her maternal grandmother. They seem to have lived a comfortable though not extravagant life, devoted to their religion and their four children. Barbara (1738-1825), their only daughter, was followed by George William (1740-1814), Robert Augustus (1745-1799) and Charles Woolsey (1748-1828). Another child, Frederick Augustus, died soon after birth in 1743. We believe Woolsey and Jane alternated living in

Olney and in Warwick Court, London at first, as George William was born and baptised in Holborn.

'I would not have a Husband without faults for the World, for that would prevent his excusing mine' wrote Jane with characteristic wit and honesty in her Commonplace Book of 1756. From her fond account of Woolsey, he seems to have been a good husband and father, though not perhaps the saintly person she depicts after his death. In the 'curse' she hung in the hall at Witham, she inscribes that 'He was indefatigable for the Good and Welfare of his Family', and in her commonplace book she composes a short epitaph: 'Here Lyes the body of W.J. a Man Exempt from all Humane Vices, & seem'd Virtue itself in Humane Shape. He never did anything Virtuous for the sake of seeming Virtuous.'[23] There follow indications of money troubles for the widowed Jane, presumably because most of the family's wealth was tied up in their land, as well as much of it being spent on rebuilding the Witham manor house. Jane's concerns over money matters are revealed in many of her letters. Writing to Robert in 1755, a year before Woolsey's death, she worries: 'I fear your Father's House costs so much Building he will hardly find money enough to send you to Rugby, but I hope he will, for you are so wise and good that it would be a pity you should loose [sic] any opportunity of improvement'.[24] Later, in 1758, Jane moved her two youngest sons from Rugby to Uppingham because of the cost of school fees. Whether the family really was in financial trouble, or it was just Jane's anxiety about having to manage it all on her own, is not certain.

The Johnson children grow up

The Johnson children seem to have been successful in managing the land and family money. When their mother died, George inherited the estate and the Reverend Edmund Smyth of Linford (Woolsey's nephew and the son of his sister, Barbara Smyth), rector of Filgrave, Buckinghamshire (near Newport Pagnall) was appointed guardian to the children in 1760.

Surprisingly, given his wealth and social status, George never married (there is no clue in the archives as to why he remained a bachelor). He lived comfortably at Witham, a liberal and enlightened landowner, letting most of the estate to tenant farmers, but also farming land himself. George seems to have had a very pleasant disposition if his sister's opinion is anything to go by. Here is an extract from a heartfelt letter after George's death.

> My dear Brother George William Johnson. Through life belov'd in death lamented for his many amiable Virtues which endear'd him to his numerous friends and acquaintance he had so much respect for the feelings of others that he never utter'd a harsh expression that could give pain to any one and was always hurt when anybody else did. He was himself remarkably temperate, but never so well pleas'd as when he entertain'd his friends with elegant and chearful hospitality. In him I seem'd to have another existence and if at any time ill or depress'd myself I thought it of little consequence if he was well and happy. Now Spring returns without my feeling it's chearful influence, all Nature seems a Blank![25]

George travelled frequently both in Great Britain and Europe, and his most regular purchases seem to have been books for he was a great reader and bibliophile. Although he lived a retired life in terms of social entertainment, he was very much a public figure. In 1784 he became High Sheriff of Lincolnshire and was also governor of the poor hospitals set up by Archdeacon Johnson.[26] Barbara was clearly concerned about his reclusive tendencies and writes:

> Nothing has given me more pleasure a long time than to hear of your intention of going out again, and the reason you give for it are very just, for Retirement is not calculated for your time of life, and by entering into the chearful [sic] Scenes, and Social Circles of the World you may lay up an agreable Fund for Recollection when Repose becomes more suitable [...] so I hope you will soon be prevail'd to quit your Hermitage.[27]

Robert often urged him to visit his family in Kenilworth or Bath, to little avail. Despite the closeness of the brothers (Robert regularly visited George in the family home and the letters between them are affectionate and cordial), Robert's children saw precious little of their uncle George.

Barbara Johnson, the oldest sibling, was a single lady, comfortably if modestly provided for and someone who enjoyed the regard and respect of friends and family alike. She lived off her inheritance[28], only occasionally asking George for money, more frequently turning down offers of financial help, but judging from her social life and her clothes, she lacked for little. Barbara often stayed with friends, but she also seems to have had a place of her own in Mercer's Row, Northampton, and later in Queen Square, Bath, where she died. Barbara regularly visited her brothers at Witham and Kenilworth. Although on excellent terms with her bachelor brother, George, she did not choose to live with him at Witham.

We can follow in Barbara's footsteps through her letter writing, and also through her album of fabric samples collected throughout her adult life, particularly those marking social events (ball gowns) or deaths (mourning dresses). This singular document which tells so much about fashion for the genteel lady in the second half of the eighteenth century is described by Roy Strong, erstwhile Director of the Victoria & Albert Museum, as unique in scope, offering '... a microcosm of the factors which determined fashion over a very long period' (Rothstein, 1987). She was passionate about books, music and theatre. We believe that the reason Barbara never married may have been because she was looking after her younger brothers in the years after their mother's death, when she would otherwise have been finding a husband. References in Barbara's letters show that at least in her youth she often attended balls, assemblies and dinners, mingling with other members of the gentry and occasionally the aristocracy. Later in life she seemed more content to receive fashion news and society gossip from Robert's letters and, eventually, his grown up daughters. She was a devoted aunt to Robert's children as this extract from a letter to George shows:

> I rejoice in Robert's happiness as much as you can do, he is in a situation quite suited to him, he seems vastly fond of his two little Girls, they are both beautiful indeed and now at an Age very engaging.[29]

Robert was the second son who became an affluent clergyman and ended up as the only family man of the four siblings. He was a good humoured, lively, generous-hearted, artistic man who adored his wife and children (the 'little folk'). We cannot find evidence of where Robert went to university, if indeed he did so, but it seems that he did not follow his brothers to Cambridge.[30] Robert spent a spell in the army, from 1765 to 1770, first as Ensign and then as Lieutenant in the 13th Regiment of Foot.[31] A close friend of the family, Ralph Abercrombie (whom we encountered in letters as a child when he came to visit Olney during Rugby school holidays) was also in the army at the same time.[32]

In 1773 Robert mounted a rung on the social ladder by marrying Anna Rebecca Craven (1745-1816) the sister of the sixth Lord Craven (1738-1791); she was the widow of a clergyman, the Reverend Ludford Taylor, but had no children before her second marriage. Robert and 'Nan', as she is known, seem to have had a happy and loving relationship; they had eight children including twins, one of whom died shortly after birth. Robert and Nan settled in Kenilworth, but they also had addresses in London and Bath. In addition, they regularly visited Coombe, Nan's brother's stately home.

We believe that in 1771 Robert reverted to the family tradition and entered Holy Orders[33] after leaving the army. His journals indicate few signs of active worship, though he sometimes writes of spiritual matters. In 1791 he was appointed rector of both Wistanstow in Shropshire and Hamstall Ridware in Staffordshire, although he does not seem to have spent much time in these parishes.[34] Occasionally, he asked George for money and sometimes invested money for him while looking after affairs at Witham when George was on his travels.[35]

We have less information on Charles, the youngest of the Johnson siblings, who gained his BA and MA at Clare College, Cambridge. He continued to be closely involved with his college where he became a lifelong Fellow. He showed more signs of a genuinely religious vocation, as well as being a university scholar. After being ordained, he followed in his father's footsteps by becoming Deacon of Peterborough in 1772 and Vicar of Witham 1772 - 1828. He settled down in Datchford, Hertfordshire where he was rector, though he simultaneously held a living at Whitnash, Warwickshire. Before his marriage, aged 40, in Stamford to Elizabeth Linton in 1780, he sometimes travelled abroad with George and often stayed with him at Witham or Stamford. He died childless at the age of 80, outliving all his siblings.

Robert's three sons, William Augustus, Robert Henry and Charles Thomas carried on the Johnson family name.[36] All three, and later some of their children, were educated at Rugby. William Augustus, born in 1777, inherited Witham from his uncle George on his death in

1814. He followed his father into the army, fought in the Peninsula War campaigns and served as Member of Parliament for Boston and later for Oldham as a radical Tory. He was also Patron of Uppingham and Oakham schools, High Sheriff of Lincolnshire, holding various other public posts. Like his father, he seems to have been devoted to his nine children and to his young wife Lucy Foster of Dowsby whom he married late in life at the age of 58.[37] According to the historian, Michael Lloyd, William Augustus 'detested the new Poor Law of 1834 which exiled paupers from their native villages to the new Union workhouses' (Lloyd, 1983: 30). His obituary reveals him to be well-respected, a deserving successor to his ancestors:

> The attention which General Johnson has devoted to the public service during that long period (32 years), the perseverance and ability which he has displayed, the independence of his personal character, his love of truth and desire to administer substantial justice, tempered at all times with consideration for the helpless and unfortunate …[38]

Both Jane and Archdeacon Johnson would have approved.

Who was Jane Johnson?

> Virtue like hers could fear not sudden Fate
> They only Dye too soon, who Live too late. [39]

Since the abundance of materials reveal Jane as a capable wife and mother in the prime of life, it is endearing to find some written evidence of her as a little girl. The earliest of Jane's writing to have survived, minus its cover, is a little recipe book about six inches square, which she must have kept when she was quite young. Given the contents, the girlish hand, the spelling errors, we suspect Jane was about seven years old when she started keeping her recipes, mostly for food, but for medicinal purposes as well. Jane made little decorations at the bottom of pages, the sort of thing children still do when learning to write. She practises her name over and over and tells us that 'Jane Russel [sic] was born 1706'. Sometimes she repeats the same recipe several times in improved handwriting, another indication of immaturity.

The majority of the recipes are for the sort of sweet dishes children might enjoy: cheesecake, gingerbread, custard, possets, sugar cakes, icing, rice pudding, damson tarts, carrit pudding, black cherry marmalett, whippt syllabub. However, it may be that Jane was also being taught how to cook herself, or oversee the cooking, of both elaborate and economical meals: cafe (calf) head hash, hare pye, eele pye, mince pies of neats Tongues, venison pasty, strond (strained) broth, frigasie (fricassee), force meatballs, as well as pickel Melons or grat Conceomber (grated cucumbers). Her recipe for gravy would not shame a celebrity chef today!

> Take a piece of lean beef cut it into large slices beat them with the back of a knife then season it with and a little saltpeter and nutmeg then fry it very brown with fresh butter but flower it well put in a pint of strong broth & a pint of claret a shalot or two, let it stew till it be a nough then strean it through a culinder and keep it for your use.[40]

The next time we encounter Jane in print, she is a young woman of at least twenty-five, as she writes sadly on the opening page that 'My Dear sister died on 25th June 1731.' This little commonplace book begins with three sentences in code which play with numbers, letters and dates of birth and death. For example:

> '79 P5663282's B29th d1y 3s th2 5 4f S2pt27b29' substitutes for
> 'Mr Pulliene's Berth day is the 5 of September'[41].

The same Thomas Pulleine was married to her sister, Lucy. We don't understand why Jane chose to write in code, as what she had to say was easy to decipher and innocuous. The rest of this pocketbook contains texts of a religious nature, both transcriptions and what appear to be original compositions, exhibiting ardent religious belief in the form of prayers and severe self-analysis, not untypical in the young:

> Tis **Virtue** only makes our Bliss below;
> ` And all our Knowledge is, **Ourselves** to know. [42]

Maxims, like this, were tucked into any spare bit of space she could find (a timely reminder that paper was expensive in those days) between extracts from religious and literary writers, published letters, epitaphs, verse, conversations with God and self examination: 'Act sincerely to all Men, & never affect to appear what you are not.' 'Remember that Virtue alone can make you happy.' 'Never speak well of they self, nor ill of others.'[43] We can see the fruits of these maxims in Jane's moral lessons written for her children.

What can we learn from these two, small, tattered booklets? (We devote most of Chapter 5 to a detailed discussion of Jane's much fuller commonplace book of 1756.) First of all, Jane's recipe book shows her going through the same stages that most literate little girls go through: being preoccupied by writing her own name; practising her writing by copying out the same piece several times over; taking pleasure in the decorative aspects of writing. On a wider canvas, the evidence suggests that Jane was being prepared to run a household where she would be knowledgeable about raw ingredients and cooking implements, recipes for everyday meals, as well as catering for special occasions.

The spelling errors in the recipe book are frequent and significantly non-standard, including confusion over homonyms ('flower' for flour). They parallel those a six year old of today might produce. Indeed, Jane's writing style throughout her life was somewhat amateur, informal and repetitive, but what she lacked in conventional skill, she made up for by the sheer honesty, wit and vitality of her compositions. She continued to make the odd spelling error once she matured, as her pocketbook shows, but there she is in good company with the poet, John Keats.

As Jane grew up, several features of her character come to the forefront - her piety, her loving nature (particularly with regard to her family) and her artistic inclinations.

> Oh! God give me knowledge sufficient to lead me to Eternal Life, give me Health & necessarys in this World, & I will wait for Pleasures till I get to Heaven.[44]

Virtually everything Jane wrote shows evidence of her deep Christian faith and scrupulous moral sensitivity. She is much more interested in living well according to Christian virtues than in following the social proprieties of her day. Indeed, Jane was more than willing to heap ridicule on those in any station who did not behave according to her principles. Not surprisingly, Jane was very fond of proverbs, aphorisms and analogies; these pepper her reading cards, letters and commonplace books:

> There is nothing in the World so Beautiful as Virtue! It is the greatest Ornament any body can put on! It is more Becoming than Rich Silks, Trimmings, Lace Embroidery, & Brilliants…

> Nothing but Good Works can make you happy in this World, & Live when this world shall be no more.

> Some people's wit takes away their senses, those are Silly Wits. But when Wit & Wisdom go together all is Right & agreeable, Wit is to Wisdom like Salt to our meat, Meat would be insipid without it, & salt without meat would be worse than nothing, And so is Wit without Wisdom.[45]

She tried to instil worthy values in her children, all of whom grew up to be decent citizens who made loving relationships with those close to them. However, although two of her children took religious orders, none of them matched Jane in religious intensity, though all of them appear to have lived morally upright lives at a time of some sexual and social licence.

'Piety alone can give true Happiness'

Jane's letters tell of her religious faith as almost obsessional at times. Writing to her cousin, Rebecca Garth (nee Brompton), when Jane was thirty-six, she begins by saying, 'Ever since I was a Girl, reading the scriptures has always been my favourite study…'[46] After that, Jane launches into a passionate, somewhat rambling, but very sincere disquisition about God as a loving father, in order, perhaps, to allay fears or doubts that her cousin had expressed about the retributive side of the Old Testament. As well as demonstrating Jane's strong religious convictions, the extract from this letter below also illustrates her liberal views on parenting:

> That he is our Father merciful, loving and kind, that he is our Father full of compassion and tender mercies, that he does not afflict willingly or punish the children of Men, any more than the earthly parent would afflict or punish his own children [...] For what good father upon Earth would be angry with, or punish, his own Child for little trifling faults or not forgive him Great ones upon his amendment [...] Can a woman forget her sucking child, that she should not have

> compassion on the son of her womb? [...] a Dutiful child will know
> how to avoid the displeasure of a reasonable and affectionate parent
> [...] it is only against wilful wickedness that he [God] is ever severe.
> (Jane Johnson, 8 July 1742) [47]

Jane evidently took the role of wise guardian to Rebecca. In this letter
and the one preceding it, Jane seems to be attempting to reassure the
probably newly married Mrs Garth that she could put her husband first,
obey him, and still please God. (Rebecca Brompton had married John
Garth, MP for Devizes). Here, Jane reflects unswerving docility
regarding patriarchal obedience, but she also exhibits a sense of fun:

> I always liked Mr Garth very well [...] and I hope you won't be jealous
> when I tell you I am quite in love with him. Was not my situation in
> this world already so happy […] I should almost be tempted to envy
> you [..] it is her (a wife's) principal duty to do as her husband
> commands her [...] if they command us to do a wicked action, for in
> that, we ought rather to obey God, than man, but of that there's no
> danger from Mr Garth …[48]

Writing at length to her aunt, Mrs Brompton, Rebecca's mother, in
1749, Jane probably reveals more about herself than in any other letter,
particularly as she describes a time of crisis in her own life. Jane half
pretends that she is writing about a lady whom, 'because I take
pleasure in the name shall be call'd Clarissa',[49] but she is clearly
writing about herself. We have already established that Jane was
artistically gifted, and this letter begins with Jane describing the
pleasure she took in making pretty things with her hands:

> … and being prais'd for her ingenuity, to obtain this intoxicating
> pleasure she spent all the time she cou'd spare from visits & other
> such like business in making Prizes, Flowers, Stomachers, needle
> books, cutting watch ˈpapers, & many other pretty things, some of
> which she was continually making presents off to her acquaintance
> [...] In a few years after the above nam'd age, she was married to a
> gentleman of great merit, & an easy fortune, to whom she made a very
> good wife, & in five years time made him a happy Father of a fine
> Boy and Girl, whose Education she took all proper care off, as she did
> of all other family affairs …[50]

Jane (or Clarissa) goes on to experience 'a fit of sickness' which was
life-threatening, so that 'Death and judgement appear to her with all
their terrors', until she realised the error of her ways and decided to use

what free time she had for practising religion ever more ardently and devoting herself to good works. Reading between the lines, Jane seems to have suffered from depression as she uses the language of 'despair', 'anguish of her soul', 'hope kept at a distance'. Here is an extract:

> ...she burst out in the following most earnest petition [...] that all the remainder of her days shou'd be spent to his Glory, in studying the Doctrine of the Gospel, & in practising every Duty taught from the mouth, & example of the Son of God himself [...] since that time the employments of her leisure hours are entirely chang'd. & instead of performing such works for which she gain'ed praise from human beings only, she now imploys herself in such a manner as to merit the Esteem & favour of God, of Angels, & all good people ...[51]

The tone is almost hysterical, as she castigates herself for an innocent pleasure that only the most extreme Christian fundamentalist would judge a fault. In so doing, she is almost brutalising her own artistic nature. Jane recounts how Clarissa works to help the poor; as well as using her skill to make clothes out of wool and hemp for those in need. Then the letter changes mood as Jane employs what could almost be described as a leaning towards early socialist views, or at least a conception of a welfare state, to alleviate the unfairness of a society which allows people to live in such poverty:

> To relate all the deplorable circumstances she meets with among the Honest industrious poor, wou'd fill a Book more properly than a letter. Sometimes she finds a man and his wife & five or six small children in a house little better than a Hogsty, with a small room above & a couple of beds in it, four of which family lye in each of them, eat up with vermin for want of change of Linnen, which with all their industry they can't get money to purchase [...] On seeing the miserys of others, she often laments that there shou'd be any such objects in such a nation as this, & says there must certainly be some great fault somewhere either in the Laws, or in the actions of Individuals to occasion it [...] the fault is not in Providence, but in Men, the Instruments of Providence; who ought to find out ways of making a proper Distribution of these things amongst one another [...] these things taken into consideration by all who have Power, or Riches, Great things might be done & the welfare of the nation vastly increas'd by proper methods of helping every distressed Individual ...[52]

Jane's mood darkened even further in 1756. It may be that Woolsey who died a few months later had a terminal illness or, at any rate, that Jane realised he was not long for this world. Whatever the circumstances that led up to it, on 28 February that year, Jane wrote an extraordinary letter to her Aunt Brompton in which she dreams that:

> ... (Arachne-like) I was metamorphosed into a spider as big as the full moon, & sat upon a Throne in the Center of a Web of my own spinning as large as Lincolns-inn-Fields. As soon as I awaked, I wonder'd what this extraordinary Dream could portend, & not having any Magician, Astrologer, or children to report to, explain'd it myself, to signifie, that I must this day spin out of my own Brains a Long Letter to Dear Mrs Brompton...[53]

Jane regularly denigrates herself in letters to others, but here she goes further, describing herself as someone with many 'faults and imperfections', 'good for nothing' and 'unworthy'. Though 'full' of 'the Dismals', Jane attempts in the letter to rouse herself from depressing thoughts and focus on the positive. Clearly this takes some effort and at first she conjures up ice, frost, cold and hardness, imagery that Christina Rossetti would harvest so memorably more than a hundred years later in her hymn, 'In the Bleak Midwinter'. Yet the act of writing about her blessings has the desired effect and in lyrical prose Jane goes on to glory in the natural world in winter.

> What can be more beautiful that a Hoar-frost! That shews every fibre & string in a Spider's Web. What makes the Ice so hard? The snow so soft, & white & Light as Air [...] The Snow-Drop, bowing down its Drooping Head as if it mourn'd [...] the crocus, Iris, primrose, & Violet, begin to display their Lovely sweets and contours & and are all delightful to my fancy, & charm my Dazzled sight, but nothing pleases me so much as the moon, & all the Gems of Heaven glittering round her! this is to me a far more delightful sight, than Mrs Spencer encircled with jewels when she was presented to his Majesty [...][54]

Jane then goes on to wish that she could have attended the above-mentioned glittering occasion and to praise Lord Spencer for his kindness and charity to the poor. She admires him for marrying for love rather than money and the rest of the letter is devoted to the benefits of married life. As she is about to lose her own husband

(Woolsey dies two months later), Jane writes:

> For promoting matrimony is promoting everything that is Good [...] it
> is obeying the will, & the command of God whose First injunction,
> over & above what he had wisely ingrafted in our nature, I say his first
> command in Word as well as in nature, was, increase & multiply, but
> this command we cannot obey without being married [...] no Man
> should have more than one Wife, nor no woman more than one
> Husband for this is the law of nature.[55]

A Mysterious urge to express oneself in verse

Jane is responsive to poetry: she transcribes it in her commonplace
books, composes rhymes for her children and tries her hand at writing
it herself. Although we would not make any claims for her as a fine
poet, Jane does display some of the qualities of eighteenth century
women poets identified by Roger Lonsdale (1990) in his book of that
title.

> There is a strong line of interesting and engaging verse running
> through the century [...] There were in fact dozens of women at all
> social levels who, with variable ambition and competence,
> experienced the mysterious urge to express themselves in verse and,
> by one means or another, found their way into print. [...] such literary
> activity [...] took place in the shadow of an oppressive patriarchy. [...]
> The positive aspects of such verse, for some readers at least, will be
> the unaffected conversational ease with which it can describe
> experiences unmuffled by stylistic and generic inhibitions and
> obligations. (Lonsdale, 1990: xxi)

Jane's verse was commonplace, modest in scope, obviously the work
of an amateur and occasionally touching. She struggles a bit with
metre and rhyme, but she has the virtue of never trying too hard to be
pretentious or 'poetic' which Wordsworth described as the prevailing
vice of eighteenth century poets. We provide a few examples below,
written at different times in Jane's life.

'On Wisdom' (1733) is a poem written two years before Jane's
marriage when she was nearing thirty. Technically, it is a perfectly
respectable sonnet and the attitudes express the typical devotional
yearnings of a young woman living in the age of reason. It shows Jane
so earnest in her religious aspirations that it sometimes works to the
detriment of her poetry.

Wisdom's my Guide 'tis Wisdom's Rules I Read.[56]
And by those Rules my future Life I'll Lead.
'Tis Wisdom shows how frail is Humane Bliss,
That Piety alone can give true Happiness;
I'll frett no more let things go as they will
I'll be content be Fortune Good or ill.
To my Creator's Will still mine shall bend
He knows What's best, & that to me He'll send.
In Praising Him my Greatest joy shall be
I'll Praise my God to all Eternity.
O! God, my God hear this my Earnest Prayer,
Pour down Thy Grace, grant I may persevere;
Let Wisdom still my every action sway,
And then I shall all Thy Commands obey.[57]

Fourteen years later, a busy mother of four, Jane wrote one of her most ambitious poems, 'Stella and her Guardian Angel'. Although the jaunty anapaestic metre of this long poem might suggest light-heartedness (a critical flaw in a poem with a serious subject), it is as devout as the one which precedes it. But there is a change. There is no light relief in 'On Wisdom', whereas 'Stella and her Guardian Angel' is full of rich sensual language: Gabriel appears on 'a beautiful night', a 'star light night'; fair Stella with 'dazzling orbs' looks with delight on 'glories admird' and 'yon Blue Sky' [...] until she anticipates the joys of Heaven with its 'millions of angels' hiding in the clouds. The poem makes constant reference to pleasure, visual delights and love. This is far more the language of *A Very Pretty Story* (see Chapter 4). Perhaps it was the intimacy of marriage and having children that opened up Jane's softer, more creative side which she clearly enjoyed expressing in poetry. As for influences, Milton is probably foremost as, not only do we know that Jane was familiar with his work, but most well educated women of her time would have known Paradise Lost backwards! Indeed, in Milton's poem the Angel Gabriel appears to Eve. Other poems which make reference to Stella (which means star, of course) and which Jane might have read include Sir Philip Sidney's sonnet sequence, 'Astrophel and Stella' and Swift's 'Journal to Stella':

In a Beautiful night when the Stars shone most clear,
And God's Wisdom in them did Refulgent appear,
Fair Stella walked out, at the age of nineteen,
In Innocence Dress'd, with a Mind all serene.

The Dazzling Orbs that surrounded her sight
Fill'd her Soul with Devotion, her Eyes with Delight,
Whilst Gazing with pleasure, with Virtue Inspir'd
To her Maker she Bow'd, & these Glories admird.
How Happy says she shall I be when I Die!
By Angels Conducted! to Tread yon Blue Sky!
To Visit each Star! & see all that's done there!
What pleasures on Earth, with these can compare?
....
As Thus she was musing, & walking alone,
The Angel Raphael, Her Guardian came down,

....
Angel. Oh! Stella thy Wisdom, thy Choice I commend,
I am Raphael they Guardian, Raphael thy Friend.
Whole Millions of Angels unseen by Mankind,
Observe when to Good, or to ill they're inclin'd.
For once in your Sight I'm allowed to appear,
Oh! Stella be stedfast, till Death Persevere,
Then with pleasure your Guardian will on you attend,
And Shield you from Dangers, till Life it shall end,
Then Waft you to Heaven, to the Angels above
Who now all behold you, with pleasure & Love.
Thus saying, all Radiant, He ascended the Skys.
And left his Fair Charge fill'd with pleasing surprize
Who till hid in the Clouds, She pursu'd with her Eyes.
... ...
'This was composed by Jane Johnson in the year 1747'[58]

In the same year when her daughter was visiting London, Jane wrote
'An Invitation to Miss Barbara Johnson to come into the Country'.
Although this is slight in terms of the quality of the verse, it has a sort
of simple, good-natured charm which is calculated to appeal to
children.

How Fine and Sweet it is to see
The Flowers grow on every Tree,
To hear the pretty Cuckoo sing,
And welcome in the joyous Spring...
... ...
The Butterflys with painted wings,
Are prettier than such tawdry things.
All Nature smiles, and all looks gay,
The Men and Maids are making Hay.
How sweet it is to walk the Fields,
What joy! what Bliss the country yields![59]

Jane was the most sympathetic of friends and neighbours. Here she puts into verse a focus on the joys of heaven in a tender response to a young woman's early death in child-birth. While it is full of conventional sentiments for her time, the poem is sincere and reads well:

> Mark well this monument ye Blooming Fair,
> How short this Life! How little worth your care
> Are Beauty, Riches, Titles, Pomp or Birth,
> Or any Good ye can possess on Earth!
> Since Trans'ent[60] all-in haste they post away,
> And Virtue only suffers no decay:
> Then Tune your souls to meet the Bless'd above,
> Where all is Beauty, Harmony, & Love,
> Where ev'ry joy will last for evermore,
> Nor Friends with Tears the Loss of Friends deplore.

('On Reading the Inscription on Mrs Stonhouse's Monument who Died in Child Bed of her fourth Child in the 24th year of her age' 1750[61])

In 'A Psalm for an Afflicted Person' (March 1752), once again Jane is moved by the sufferings of others. Here she was, perhaps, influenced by Isaac Watts' musical hymns. By now we can see that this gifted woman could turn her hand to quite a variety of verse writing, but such poetic talent as Jane had was always subsumed to her religious convictions.

> On God alone I Trust,
> On Him alone rely,
> He sees the sorrows of my Heart,
> And Weepings of my Eye.
>   2
> In his Due time He'll send me help
> Down from his Holy place,
> In his Due time He'll send me help,
> Who sees my wretched case.
>   3
> To Hell for help I ne'er will go,
> But Trust in God alone;
> For Sin will only strengthen woe,
> And Double every Groan.
>   4
> Oh Lord send out thy Light and Truth,

And ['lead' crossed out] keep me in thy way,
And from the Paths of Innocence,
Oh! never let me stray.[62]

'the finest child ever ...'

The first we hear of Jane's children is in a letter she wrote to Rebecca Brompton about Barbara. Despite being a devoted Mamma, Jane demonstrates self-knowledge with a touch of irony:

> Your inquirys about my little girl are very obliging. I wish you would come and see how you like her; she is I thank God at present very well and as much like herself as ever you saw a little girl in your life, but as to who she is like besides there are various opinions. I think her the picture of Mr Johnson's mother whom you never saw, she is extremely fair, her cheeks look as though they were covered with rose leaves and her lips are like the coral she wears. Her Papa and Mama think her the finest child they ever saw with their eyes, but I do not believe there is one body living besides of that opinion.
> (Jane Johnson, 1739)[63]

Five years later, Jane praises admirable qualities in her daughter in a poem:

> All sweet, & soft of ever Charm possest!
> That can Adorn, or Grace the Human Breast.
> Her Soul Capacious, Large, Extensive, Wise!
> Without one thought that needs the least disguise,
> Such Worth on Earth will never more be found,
> When her Sweet Form is Buried under Ground.
> (from 'On Miss Barbara Johnson' March 16 1752[64])

Jane frequently reminded the children of their religious devotions in her letters, but she did so in an affectionate manner. In a letter to George when he was fifteen, she writes:

> ... since there is no way of being happy but by being good & making God our Friend, so I wish you may be the very best young man in England, & then you will be the happiest.
> (Jane Johnson Olney, April 20 1755)[65]

In a letter to Robert aged ten, in the middle of family news and greetings to friends, she writes:

... my dear Robert, Remember God Almighty in every thing you do & wherever you go, and pray continually to him to make you wise & Good, Remember this was King Solomon's prayer that his mother taught him when he was a little Boy as you are, & because he pray'd to God to make him wise, God was so well pleased with him, that he not only made him wiser than all the men on the earth, but likewise gave him more Riches than anybody ever had before or since.
(Jane Johnson, July 30th 1755)[66]

Several solicitous letters to George and Robert have survived. For Jane, loving her children meant attending closely to all aspects of their lives, including their education, of course. Sometimes, she could also be quite sharp, as in the following letter to Robert when he was eight years old. (In the original, words of more than one syllable are indicated with hyphens.) Two years later, in the second extract, Jane still isn't sure of Robert's reading ability and offers advice, but, once again, she softens it with a mother's heartfelt post-script:

Dear Robert

It gave me great pleasure to hear by Jacky Ansell that you are very well, but I am sorry you would not come home with him, for I want sadly to see you, besides am fearful you neglect your Book [...] Your brother Woolsey [who was then 5] has read every word of the other side of this letter very well. Everybody says they don't think you can read it half so well, but I hope they are mistaken for I think my Robert will never be such a Fool as to let a little Boy outdo him [...]
(Jane Johnson, 15th November 1753)[67]

Your sister gives her love to you, pray give my compliments to Mr & Mrs Ansel [sic], don't eat too much fruit, Read a chapter in the Bible every day, & be sure to Remember that

Whoever breaks the Holy Sabbath Day,
Unbless'd shall the other six away.
I Love you Dearly, & your Happiness is the constant wishes of

Jane Johnson
Olney July 19. 1755

P.S.

Oh! Robert Live for Ever
... ...

If you can't read all this Letter yourself pray let Miss Pruey tell you any of the Words that are so ill wrote that you can't make them out. Read it two or three times over.[68]

In a letter to George when he was at Rugby School aged 10, she makes arrangements for him and some friends to ride home for the holidays. As well as writing in a large, easy-to-read copperplate hand, Jane concluded the letter with a picture of the boys riding home on horseback.

Figure 4. Jane's letter to George from May 9 1750

Although she was a serious person, Jane had a caustic wit and did not suffer fools gladly. One can imagine, for example, the Head Master of Uppingham School quaking on receipt of Jane's letter on the subject of school fees in 1758, particularly as it was a Johnson family member who set up the school in the first place! There is a shrill tone that we rarely see in Jane's correspondence which might reflect an unhappy and anxious state of mind after her husband's death.

Sir I am very sorry you don't think proper to abate your terms, for notwithstanding all your Eloquence, I am still of opinion that they are too high, and that it would be pretty near as reasonable to Demand above Twenty pounds a Year for the Board of each of a Parcel of

> Hogs as a Parcell of School Boys, since the one would cost pretty near as much feeding and require almost as much waiting upon as the other generally meet with. But however it is my fancy and the Children's choice to come under your care and I design sending them about the middle of next week and with them two pairs of good new sheets, two silver spoons and one dozen of good new towels. I choose to send sheets etc instead of the entrance money into the House.[69]

According to Oliver Ratcliff, Jane 'had great disputes and squabbles with Moses Browne[70] (who succeeded Woolsey as Vicar of Olney), not withstanding he had obtained the benefice principally through her recommendation and patronage' (Ratcliff, 1900: 50). We never found evidence of these squabbles except for one letter about cutting down some trees, but we don't doubt that Jane still felt she had to keep an eye on the vicarage. Jane also had a long-running dispute with Thomas Trollope over who owned the Toft and Hound Inn in Witham.

Barbara had several traits in common with her mother: she inherited her interest in art, design, fashion and fabrics; she was like Jane in having a warm heart; and she was in tune with Jane in her desire to preserve family papers for future generations. Thanks to this latter instinct, we can include Barbara's fresh and personal account of a very pregnant Jane jumping into the River Ouse to save her son's life:

> It is worthy of remark that my dear Brother George William Johnson went coursing when he was only three years and three months old was on horseback seven hours leap'd over two ditches and brought home a hare. That day fortnight after riding out he came into the Garden to call my Mother to Tea, the River Ouse ran by the bottom of the garden at Olney in Bucks. My Brother had childishly thrown his waistcoat over his face and slip'd in the River. My Mother who was in an adjoining Summer-house immediately jump'd in after him, at the extreme hazard of her own life, she being very big with child, she was just in time enough to save my Brother who was fast floating down the River which would very soon have taken him to the Mill-Wheel. This happen'd Sept 24th 1743.
> Taken from an old Memorandum and I beg it may be preserv'd. Barbara Johnson[71]

Most moving of all is a letter from Henrietta Ingram, a friend of Barbara's, who was with her just after Jane's sudden demise. As well as telling us how Jane was valued by those around her, it also shows us how death was reacted to, or at least written about, between family members in that period.

from Henrietta Ingram, Witham to Nanny Feb 24 1759

... I am grieved that in return I cannot recite some of the delightful schemes [...] But will think it I dare say sufficient reason when I inform you that my Excellent friend Mrs Johnson was [..] taken very ill of an inflamation in her Bowels of which disorder she expired in less than a week. The excessive grief she left her family in, together with the sense I had of having lost a very Valuable friend, rendered me for a few days completely miserable, but I have now got the better of that tho' I must ever lament her, which I acknowledge to be wrong as I should rather rejoice that she is and I think I may say almost- the happiest of Angels; never could woman more resemble an angel than she did in every action, while upon Earth & She is now no doubt rejoicing with them in heaven, a place much more proper for such heavenly a woman than this, only her Eldest son and daughter were at home at the dreadful time, (the 2 youngest sons at School not old enough to be sensible of their great Loss) a very dreadful time to them indeed! We were here by ourselves for three days & then some of their relations came, but they all left us this week & Mr Johnson is gone to Cambridge again, so that Miss Johnson and I are quite alone at present. I can't leave her thus by her self, so intend staying till one of her relations come again which will not be these 3 weeks...[72]

What is so refreshing in the multitude of Johnson family papers is the picture we get of Jane as an admirable, gifted yet flawed human being - like the rest of us. We can trace her life story from the eager little girl acquiring the skills to run a household, to the devout adolescent trying to be the perfect Christian lady. We acknowledge her as the devoted, fulfilled wife and the warm, attentive mother who kept a keen eye on the children's educational and religious progress. We respect her as a scrupulous and devoted friend and relative and sympathise with her penny-pinching angst in the lonely years after Woolsey's death where Jane, in increasingly erratic handwriting, sets about ordering, explaining and protecting the fate of the family papers for posterity. But even in her distress, the quality of Jane's character, her keen eye for observation and her interest in people shines through, as she tidies up and annotates a parcel of her father-in-law's letters. Through Jane's good offices, they still survive.

This parcel of Letters are no sort of use. I only keep them because they were wrote by Thomas & Ann Johnson whose pictures are drawn with a Great Dog, his, & hers with a mournful look Leaning on her [his? sic] arm. These Letters were wrote by them to their son William Johnson Esq. whose Picture is drawn a little Boy with his hair over his forhead. The girl with the flowers in a Basket, & she with the Lamb his sisters. She with the flowers died at thirteen, she with the Lamb Died an old maid.[73]

Finally, on Jane's death, we have the 'angel' described by a close friend of the family. As readers, we can share in her domestic happiness which came relatively late in life, admire the tenacity and skill with which she set out to educate her children, wish her to be less soul searching and hard on herself as a Christian, and empathise with her loving nature, wit and kindness. Perhaps the greatest compliment we can pay our heroine is to conclude this chapter with the ending from George Eliot's Middlemarch (1872) which, it seems to us, suits Jane Johnson almost as well as it does Dorothea Ladislaw.

Her finely-touched spirit had still its fine issues, though they were not widely visible. Her full nature [..] spent itself in channels which had no great name on earth. But the effect of her being on those around her was incalculably diffuse: for the growing good of the world is partly dependent on unhistoric acts; and that things are not so ill with you and me as they might have been, is half owing to the number who lived faithfully a hidden life, and rest in unvisited tombs. (Eliot, 1965: 896).

Notes

1.   Oxford, Bodleian Library, MS.Don.c.190, fols.72-102.

2.   We have used Jane's original spellings in this chapter.

3.   Oxford, Bodleian Library, MS.Don.c.190, fol. 103 -118.

4.   As readers will be aware, not only did the spelling of names often change between the seventeenth and nineteenth centuries, but non-standard spelling was commonplace, even by educated people. There are several cases where the spelling of people's names in our research either changed over time or were spelled differently on different occasions by different people. Sometimes the name on the birth certificate is spelled in a different way on the marriage certificate or in a letter by a member of the family. In these cases, we have indicated both spellings and used the most standard form.

5.   The following information on the Johnsons has been taken from various sources, in particular, Lloyd 1983, Matthews 1994, Ratcliff 1900,

Rothstein 1987, The Lincoln Record Society 1936, Venn and Venn 1922, *Johnson of Wytham-on-the-Hill* (1875) and also from unpublished and often unreferenced documents and letters found in various archives. Where possible we have provided a reference.

6. Oxford, Bodleian Library, MS.Don.c.190, fols. 11-24.

7. *Pedigree of Johnson of Wytham-on-the-Hill, co. Lincoln* compiled by Everard Green and *Pedigree of Johnson*. Record Office for Leicestershire, Leicester and Rutland: Johnson Family collection, (DE5122/241)

8. Sometimes spelled Wytham

9. Robert Johnson was simultaneously Canon of Peterborough, Canon of Norwich, Prebend of Rochester, Chaplain at Gorhambury and Minister of St Albans before becoming Archdeacon of Leicester in 1591.

10. Archdeacon Johnson was twice a widower (Susannah Davers and Mary Herd) before marrying his third wife, Mary Wheeler.

11. In 1571 he was suspended from his religious duties for publicly expressing scruples about the Prayer Book of 1559. He eventually submitted and accepted the three Articles.

12. *The Statutes and Ordinances of me Robert Johnson Clerk, Archdeacon of Leicester, for and concerning the Ordering, Governings, and Maintaining of my Schools and Hospitals of Christ in the County of Rutland, whereof I am Founder and Patron.* (Stamford, 1753)

13. From a document which says the extract was taken from the *History of the British Dominions in North-America*, printed at London for W. Straham and J. Becket in the Strand 1773.

14. Uppingham School Archives.

15. Centre for Buckinghamshire Studies, Aylesbury: papers of Johnson of Olney D/X 827, AR 16/84.

16. Dugdale 1730; Burman 1934; Belton 1951.

17. The only link we found with Judge Ward was that his great great nephews were Richard Russell's executors.

18. Francis Rainsford ceded about 300 acres of land as well as cottages and a farm in Wotton, Islip and Northampton to his daughter Lucy the day before her wedding in 1704. Lucy Rainsford, in turn, passed those lands over to Jane and Woolsey in 1741. Source: Lease and Release, DE5122/154/1 and 2, Leicestershire, Leicester and Rutland Record Office.

19. Sometimes spelled 'Ingoldesby'.

20. Army List of 1740.

21. Vicar-General Marriage Licence Allegations.

22. Olney Parish Register.

23. Oxford, Bodleian Library, MS.Don.c.190, fols.72- 102.

24. Uppingham School Archives.

25. Oxford, Bodleian Library, MS.Don.c.191, fol. 87.

26. A letter to George in 1781 (Bodleian Library, MS.Don.c.194, fol. 42) reads:

    D:r S:r:

    Ever wishing to be a Friend to the Needy & Distressed, & persuaded your Feelings are Similar to my own, I beg Leave to become an Advocate on the Behalf of a poor Widow Woman for a Place in your Hospital at Oakham. She is far advanced in Life; of a Decent Carriage; & a proper object; otherwise I shd. not take upon me to recommend her to your Mention.

    Your Charitable Compliance of this request will rejoice the Heart of declining old Age, & greatly oblige
    Dr. Sr. your obedt. & affte: Hble. Servt.: R: Lambert

27. Oxford, Bodleian Library, MS.Don.c.193, fols. 15-16.

28. Her actual income was £60 per annum, though when George died in 1814, she invested the additional annuity of £50 in stocks.

29. Oxford, Bodleian Library, MS.Don.c.193, fols. 15-16.

30. Nor did Robert go to Oxford. There are a couple of years unaccounted for assuming he left Uppingham at age eighteen (like his brother Charles) before he went into the army aged 20.

31. Great Britain, War Office Army List (1765-1770).

32. Abercrombie (or Abercromby) went on to have a distinguished army career, becoming Commander of the British Army in Egypt and defeating the French at Aboukir in 1801. (Rouse, 1898: 114)

33. Despite considerable efforts, we have found no record of where Robert was ordained.

34. *Clergy of the Church of England Database* (www.theclergydatabase.org.uk) and Shropshire Registers (we are grateful to Stewart Minton Beddoes, Churchwarden for Wistanstow for this information). The appointments were made through his influential patrons, William Lord Craven and Lady Mary Leigh.

35. Although not wealthy himself, Robert seems to have had a lucky star in terms of money. For unknown reasons, in 1780 he and Nan are given £10,000 -a very substantial sum— by a Mrs Leigh, probably of Stoneleigh Abbey and lady of the manor of Hamstall Ridware who later had him

appointed as rector in this place. In his letters he refers several times to the Leighs, they would have been his neighbours in Kenilworth. (In 1806, Jane Austen stays at Stoneleigh; had Robert lived a few years longer, he might have met her there!). We have no evidence that the Leighs referred to in Notes 34 and 35 were the same person, but this does seem likely.

36.   Robert's four daughters were Harriet, Maria, Georgiana and Selina. Harriet married John Hamilton Dalrymple, eighth Earl of Stair (1771-1853). She lived for a time in Oxinford Castle in Scotland and also had an address in Upper Grosvenor St. London. She died childless in 1821.

37.   Around 1874 Lucy Johnson made albums of the Johnson family history for her children some of which have survived. One of her sons, George Woolsey Johnson kept a diary and a photograph album of his stay in South Africa in the 1860s, which has also survived.

38.   Lincolnshire Archives, Johnson I/2, p.12.

39.   This epigram is attributed by Jane to 'C.J.' but we have not been able to find out to whom it refers.

40.   Oxford, Bodleian Library, MS.Don.c.190, fols. 103-118.

41.   ibid

42.   ibid

43.   ibid

44.   Oxford, Bodleian Library, MS.Don.c.190, fols. 72-102.

45.   ibid

46.   Oxford, Bodleian Library, MS.Don.c.190, fols. 21-22.

47.   ibid

48.   ibid

49.   This signals the importance of Richardson's novel which had just been published (1747-48).

50.   Oxford, Bodleian Library, MS.Don.c.190, fols. 11-12.

51.   ibid

52.   ibid

53.   Oxford, Bodleian Library, MS. Don. c. 190, fols. 13-14.

54.   ibid

55.   ibid

56.   We are not certain that the two words at the end of the first line after 'Rules' are correct. It might be 'Rules of Need' or 'Rules I Need'.

57.   Oxford, Bodleian Library, MS.Don.d.198.

58.   From 'A Conversation between Stella & Her Guardian Angel, One Star Light Night, in the Garden at—' Oxford, Bodleian Library, MS.Don.c.190, fols. 26-8.

59.   Oxford, Bodleian Library, MS.Don.c.190, fol. 1.

60.   We think this is a shortening of 'transient'.

61.   Oxford, Bodleian Library, MS.Don.e.198, fol. 17.

62.   ibid

63.   Oxford, Bodleian Library, MS.Don.c.190, fols. 15-16.

64.   Oxford, Bodleian Library, MS.Don.d.198, fol. 17.

65.   Oxford, Bodleian Library, MS.Don.c.190, fols. 2-4.

66.   Oxford, Bodleian Library, MS.Don.c.190, fols. 9-10.

67.   Oxford, Bodleian Library, MS.Don.c.190, fols. 7-8.

68.   Uppingham School Archives.

69.   Lincolnshire Archive, Johnson I/2, pp. 69-71.

70.   Moses Brown was a most distinguished Evangelical preacher and was followed in that position by the better known, John Newton. We wonder whether the Evangelical tradition, evident in Olney by the late 1750s, had already begun, or indeed been fostered, during Woolsey's time a s vicar of Olney.

71.   Oxford, Bodleian Library, MS.Don.c.190, fol. 88.

72.   Oxford, Bodleian Library, MS.Don.c.191, fols. 62-3.

73.   Oxford, Bodleian Library, MS.Don.c.196, fols. 24-35.

Chapter 2

The Changing World of Books and Reading in the Eighteenth Century

> The Books that are to be Read by All that would be Eloquent, Polite, Genteel & agreeable; Wise in this World & Happy in the next; are the Bible, Homer, Milton, The Guardians, Spectators & Tatlers. These should be Read over & over again, & short Extracts Learn'd by Heart, out of them; these are the only Books necessary to be read for improvement, all others only for Diversion. Whoever following this rule will think justly, & write, & talk eloquently.
> Jane Johnson[1]

This authoritative comment by Jane appears in her commonplace book and neatly summarises not only the texts and the methods, but also the perceived consequences of reading of her time. During the eighteenth century the world of books and reading in England underwent great changes. In this chapter we attempt to provide a picture of these changes and place the information we have about Jane's family in the context of the histories of literacy and publishing. This in turn gives us clues for reconstructing Jane's literary background as well as her own and her children's reading experiences.

Who could read? Literacy facts and figures

According to historians, during the eighteenth century there was an unprecedented demographic growth which had consequences for all aspects of society, among them, education and literacy. The number of young people in England was rapidly increasing: in 1701 the population under the age of 24 was just under two million; by 1801, the number had risen to three and a half million (from Wrigley and Schofield cited in Hunter, 1990: 80). The causes for this growth have been ascribed to better nutrition and environmental conditions and also to a parallel economic growth. The expansion of industry and business meant an increase in available employment, especially for workers who could read, write and count, as well as keep abreast of news, including politics. There was also a demand for literacy because of the possibilities it offered in terms of prestige, social mobility, cultural expectations and intellectual development.

Although the exact figures for literacy within the population are debatable (for reasons which will be discussed below), historians are certain that literacy increased rapidly between 1600 and 1750. In 1600, approximately 25 percent of the adult male population was literate. Male literacy rose from an astonishing 45 percent in 1714 to 60 percent in 1750, which meant that about two million men in England and Wales could read (Hunter, 1990: 66). Female literacy, although based on less reliable evidence, rose in parallel from 25 percent in 1714 to 40 percent in 1750 (Brewer, 1997: 167). Spufford's research into seventeenth century autobiographies provides evidence that even boys from relatively poor households would have probably had a year or two of schooling up to the ages of six or seven by which time they may have learned to read. If they stayed on at school, by eight they may have also learned to write. (Spufford, 1981b: 148).

Although Houston concludes that by the end of the century, England could boast of 'mass literacy' in comparison to other European countries (Houston, 1988: 65), historians in general remain cautious about literacy indicators. In the first place, they are usually based on signatures in local records, which may not be an indication of a wider ability to read or write. In terms of female literacy, for example, women were not usually required to sign legal documents until after 1753. However, it was usually women - mothers, older sisters or 'school-dames' - who introduced children to their first letters and taught them to read, whether or not they could write themselves.

Another reason to be cautious about widespread literacy is that, as Hunter shows, readers were more likely to be urban than rural dwellers; especially people living in highly populated areas. London, for example, had the highest and most rapidly increasing level of female literacy from 22 percent in 1670 to 66 percent in 1720 (Brewer, 1997: 167). The number of urban readers grew every year as more of the population moved into towns and cities. In his study of the people living in the capital between 1650 and 1750, Earle affirms that '... all Londoners, men and women, London-born and immigrants, were... amongst the best educated and most literate people in the early modern world' (Earle, 1994: 37).

If we look at Jane and Woolsey's ancestors in this context, the Rainsfords and the Johnsons were almost certainly highly literate families. Books were owned by almost all professional literate people (Weatherill, 1996: 189) and in the sample of inventories in England between 1675 and 1725 which Weatherill collects and which corresponds to Jane and Woolsey's parents' generation, one can see that trades of high status such as the clergy owned even more books than the gentry (Weatherill, 1996: 168). With an income of at least £1000 a year, there would have been plenty to spend on books.[2] Weatherill calculates that 3-4% of the annual expense of a medium or higher income family would have been spent on books per year.

As a clergyman educated at Cambridge, Woolsey would have been building up his own library. Living in London until a few years after her marriage, Jane would also have come into contact with much of the printed matter of the day, including all sorts of 'novelties', especially as, according to Hunter (1990), young people in London were most 'modern' in their reading tastes and they were also the main readers of novels. Certainly, growing up in the early part of the eighteenth century meant that Jane and Woolsey would have had greater access to a much wider range of texts than any previous generation.[3]

The women in the Rainsford/Russell and Johnson families had probably been literate for at least three or four generations before Jane's. An interesting case is that of Richard Russell, Jane's father. If it is true that he was a 'menial servant' in the Spencer household in Warwick and then obtained enough money to buy Packwood Manor, he seems to fit the description of the ambitious young man as described by Hunter: '... those most likely to learn to read were those most likely to wish to change their circumstances, to be dissatisfied with their lots, to have ambition above the station they were born into' (Hunter, 1990: 76). Richard Russell clearly gained enough formal education to make money to enable him to marry Lucy Rainsford and to put 'gent' and 'esq.' after his name.

What was read? Changes in the world of publishing

In the eighteenth century culture became a commodity. The publication, promotion and distribution of books increased rapidly, adding new genres, functions, and outlets for the printed word. The spread of dramatic productions throughout the countryside, as well as urban areas, fed interest in reading (see chapter 7). As well as collecting prints, people with some means attended plays and concerts.

(We know from his diary, for example, that Samuel Pepys did all these things in the seventeenth century.) Books could be bought at the booksellers, through mail order or borrowed through 'circulating libraries'. Buying, borrowing and lending books, as well as recommending or commenting on them in letters, were common activities. According to Brewer's study on English culture,

> Books, prints and readers were everywhere. Not everyone was a reader, but even those who could not read lived to an unprecedented degree in a culture of print, for the impact of the publishing revolution extended beyond the literate [...] in homes, taverns, coffee houses, in fields and in the street, oral and literature cultures were married through the ministrations of the public reader. (Brewer, 1997: 187)

James Lackington, a bookseller, estimated in 1792 that 'more than four times the number of books are [sic] sold now than were sold twenty years since' (quoted in Porter, 1990: 236).[4] Yet for those with low incomes, new books were still expensive objects: a newly published novel cost at least 7s. 6d., while a work of history or 'belles lettres' cost a guinea or so (Porter, 1990: 235). However, second hand copies, collected editions and pirated editions could be had more cheaply as well as pamphlets, cartoons and ballads.

The economic well-being of the century contributed to, and was partly a result of, the circulation of print. Printing presses and bookshops opened all over the country and by 1800 every major town had a printer and bookshop. Circulating libraries made thousands of books available for a couple of guineas per year. Porter notes that by 1800 there were 122 circulating libraries in London and 268 in the provinces (Porter, 1990: 235). This would have meant that even though Jane and Woolsey were mainly living in rural Olney, they could still have access to new publications and may have shared them among their friends or family, as their grown up children certainly did twenty years later.

Freedom of the press meant that newspapers, magazines and periodicals flourished in this period and were considered important not only for the acquisition of knowledge but also for the development of critical opinions: 'Contemporaries believed that, of all the media, newspapers shaped opinion the most' (Porter, 1990: 234). In 1700, all newspapers were printed in London, but by 1760, 35 provincial papers were in business selling 200,000 copies a week, doubling sales by end of century (Porter, 1990: 234). By the time George, Robert and Barbara Johnson were adults living in the provinces, they would have depended on newspapers to keep up with national and international events, financial reports (they had investments in stocks) and the latest fashions.[5]

Better transport also meant better circulation of print. In 1785, Robert writes to his brother George who was travelling on the Continent that: 'Palmer's plan of the mail coaches is now established throughout the Kingdom, the expedition they travel with is astonishing, we have the evening papers here the morning after they are printed'.[6] There are several mentions of newspapers among the sibling's letters as adults; for example, an amusing, ironic letter from Barbara to the publisher, Baldwin, complains about a proposed additional tax on newspapers:[7]

> ... for what is Life without a Newspaper? [...] how often have I seen Joy brighten every Eye and Irradiate every countenance in a large Circle by the arrival of a Newspaper [...] I look upon it as one of the glories of the present Reign that as Lord North has calculated upwards of twelve Millions of News-Papers are annually printed and if it be still further consider'd how many Persons at an average read each paper the Number becomes immense, how is happiness and knowledge by this means generally diffus'd [...] I had rather live upon Water-gruel and go in Rags, still bless'd with the sight of your Paper, than without it to be cloathed in Purple and fine Linnen, and fare sumptuously every day.
> (Clara Quidnunc)[8]

Periodicals such as the *Spectator* and the *Tatler* (both often quoted from by Jane in her commonplace book), appearing daily or monthly, also increased their print runs during the eighteenth century. By 1900 there were around 250 periodicals, providing information and opinion on every aspect of culture and politics and specialising in subjects from religion to fashion (Porter, 1990: 235). Some, like *The Gentleman's Magazine*, reached a circulation of up to 10,000 per year. Periodicals specifically for women also began to appear around 1750, both responding to and defining an emerging women's culture.[9]

At a more familial level, what part did print and reading play in a literate household such as the Johnsons? Darnton reminds us that, 'To pass from the *what* to the *how* of reading is an extremely difficult step', yet in the next two sections we want to try to build up an idea of how books, periodicals and other printed material would have generally been a part of life in a family like the Johnsons using the work of scholars who have provided fascinating glimpses into readers from the past.

Reconstructing eighteenth-century readers

In this section, we will touch on Darnton's reconstruction of the reading practices of Jean Ranson, as well as considering some other readers from the early seventeenth to the late eighteenth century: Victoria E Burke for Anne Bowyer; Kevin Sharpe for William Drake; E Jennifer Monaghan for Cotton Mather and his children; Naomi Tadmor for the Turner and the Richardson households and John Brewer for Anna Larpent. Although these readers cover quite a wide span in terms of age, gender, culture and chronological and geographical location, we have selected them because of similarities to the Johnson family: Anne Bowyer and William Drake, like Jane, kept commonplace books; Cotton Mather and Anna Larpent were deeply involved in their children's learning and reading; the Turners and Richardsons were Jane and Woolsey's contemporaries, highly literate and keen readers; and Jean Ranson was starting a family at the same time as Robert. Another reason for looking at this diverse group of readers is that, as Sharpe argues in the case of his subject, even if Drake was not a 'typical' reader, his reading leads us to other texts of the time and to contemporary ideas on education and culture. In these ways, the examples which follow have something to teach us about the likely reading practices of the Johnson family members.

The first case is that of Anne Bowyer about whom few details are known except that she was a member of 'an upwardly mobile family of urban craftsmen with links to the gentry' (Burke, 2001: 26), who compiled a commonplace book in the early seventeenth century. Through careful analysis of this notebook and a few surviving documents, Burke shows how Bowyer had clearly had a good education herself and how she, in turn, oversaw at least the religious education of her only son who had this to say about his mother:

> She was competently read in divinity, History and Poetry, and was continually instilling into my Eares, such Religious & Morall Precepts, as my younger years were capable off. Nor did she ever faile

to correct my faults, alwaies adding sharpe reproofes & good Lectures
to boote. (quoted in Burke, 2001: 10)

Burke surmises that there was probably a large library in her family
home, containing, among others, works of Chaucer, Spenser, Drayton,
Warner and Ralegh and observes that 'the taste reflected in the choice
of many of these works is for a stern moral subject matter which
yielded short, extractable, memorable lines' but that there was also an
interest in works about 'England's development as a nation' (Burke,
2001: 26). What is interesting is that Bowyer transcribes passages from
these sources but often alters either the subject or language in order to
bring out a particular message (as Jane sometimes does in her
commonplace book) or make them particularly relevant to women.
This practice is telling, given that it means that a writer's words could
be taken and moulded according to the reader's purpose and even a
female reader would have been able to freely respond to and adapt the
words of these established male authors. In other words, it provides
evidence that readers brought their own experiences to the text.

Born exactly one century before Jane Johnson, William Drake (1606-
1669) was a 'promoter and patron of letters' as well as a wealthy
landowner and politician who kept the largest collection of
commonplace books known today (Sharpe, 2000: 71). Like Anne
Bowyer, Drake is an example of 'a reader who very much made his
own meaning' (Sharpe, 2000: 41). Drake transcribed proverbs, fables
and emblems and other time-honoured texts of advice; however, as he
carefully glossed and cross-referenced his entries, he was also creating
his own text, related to his own tastes and preferences, experiences and
thoughts.

A particularly interesting case in terms of reading and teaching is that
of Cotton Mather (1663-1728) who was a Puritan minister in Boston,
USA. As well as being the author of a great number of sermons and
other religious works, he meticulously kept a diary in which he
included observations of, and plans for, his children's literacy
education. Samuel, one of only two of sixteen children that survived
their father, was born in 1706, the same year as Jane Johnson.
Monaghan's study of this family's literacy through Mather's diaries
show his particular interest in writing and how he not only acted as a
teacher, but also as an interpreter of text and encouraged his children to

comprehend and reflect on their reading and other matters through their own writing. His involvement was mainly in his sons' education; texts were allocated on the basis of his children's gender and even the older daughters would be 'read to' by the younger sons.

Monaghan observes that reading aloud was part of the daily routine, from the reading of Scripture during morning and evening prayers to lessons and the reading of suitable books, such as those by James Janeway[10] before bedtime. At other times, Mather listened to his children reciting their catechism and commented on particular passages. The children were also encouraged to keep the equivalent of a commonplace book. In one of his diaries Mather equates 'improving in Reading' with 'improving in Goodness' (quoted Monaghan, 1991: 354) so that, like the other readers we discuss in this section, 'he constructed bridges between life, language, and literacy' (Monaghan, 1991: 364).

Tadmor carried out studies of reading in the eighteenth-century households of Thomas Turner and Samuel Richardson. Although Turner (1729-1793) was a relatively humble Sussex mercer and draper, his diary mentions over 70 items of literature. Richardson (1689-1761), the famous author and printer, lived in London with his wife and daughters. Tadmor argues that the practice of reading in both these households was not idle or frivolous, but that 'sociable reading, devout reading, intermittent reading and the combination of reading, discipline and work, formed part of the encounter of readers and texts' (Tadmor, 1996: 174). Another interesting practice is that reading was done intermittently, 'texts were read in combination with other texts and genres, and texts were also read in combination with - or while doing - other things' (Tadmor, 1996: 166). Therefore any children in the house would be listening to a variety of texts during the day and in the evening, from magazines and plays, to Milton, Locke and Richardson himself - but this reading might be frequently interrupted by social activities such as entertaining guests, playing music or card games.

In the Richardson household, reading was a sociable activity as well as part of a religious and moral discipline. Mrs Richardson would read aloud from the Psalms to her daughters in the morning; after breakfast, lessons for the day would be listened to. During the day and especially in the evenings, reading sessions made the burdens of housework lighter and were combined with other activities such as needlework or drawing. Conversation about some of the texts would have surely ensued, combining enjoyment with interpretation. All these practices would have contributed to the way in which the members of the households made sense of their reading, strengthening the connection between the moral and the literary, a theme Richardson interweaves throughout his novels which are themselves developed from conduct literature. Furthermore, Richardson also had an interest in pedagogy and children's reading (he composed his *Aesop's Fables* in 1740) and given his popularity with female readers in the eighteenth century (including Jane Johnson[11]), it is reasonable to suppose that his views on reading as a social and moral act had great influence, especially on mothers who assumed the role of educators.[12]

Even the case of a reader in a country other than England allows us insights into the role of published texts among the second generation of Johnsons. Darnton bases his reading reconstruction on a French merchant's book orders over eleven years, as well as his letters to a publisher. Interestingly, one third of the orders were either for pedagogy or books for children. Born in 1747, Jean Ranson became a fervent admirer of Rousseau and his reading practices were influenced by the ideas of this great thinker. Darnton tries to understand how Ranson 'look[ed] at a book when he took it in his hands' given that 'books as physical objects were very different in the eighteenth century from what they are today, and their readers perceived them differently' (Darnton, 1984: 216). Ranson was concerned with the quality of the paper and binding, formats and typography and comments upon them in his letters (we find Robert making similar sorts of remarks about books in letters to his brother). Ranson owned at least two copies of *Émile* but it is his correspondence with the publisher about the French philosopher which leads Darnton to conclude that he was Rousseau's ideal reader and shows just how much an individual could be influenced by his reading:

> He entered into parenthood through reading and relied on books in order to make his offspring into so many Emiles and Emilies. This behavior expressed a new attitude toward the printed word. Ranson did not read in order to enjoy literature but to cope with life and especially family life, exactly as Rousseau intended. (Darnton, 1984: 234)

Ranson's reading also provides an interesting link between old ways of child-rearing, according to traditional oral sources and the new ways, where parents consulted the printed word (Darnton, 1984: 230).

A final case is that of an Englishwoman born just a decade after Robert Johnson, Anna Larpent (1755-1824). Because her husband, John Larpent, was an 'Examiner of Plays', Larpent was in constant touch with the latest literary developments, but she still read religious rather than imaginative works. She also read many of the same authors as Jane - Pope, Swift, Milton, Young, Thomson, Richardson and Rollin - and like Jane, helped her children in their studies. Every day she read either the Bible or the Psalms or a pious text, and on Sundays sermons and scripture. Family reading and conversation also occurred during other times of the day and Brewer emphasises that the main objective of these activities was to strengthen their Christian faith. Like Mather, she read aloud to her children and listened to them reading and Brewer says 'she treated this form of instruction as a way of increasing her pupils' curiosity and of opening up new paths of inquiry' (Brewer, 1996: 241).

Books and reading in the Johnson household

Reading reconstructions such as those above reveal a complex picture of readers' interactions with text, yet all these cases provide us in some way with likely parallels for Jane Johnson's family and their particular reading practices. The best evidence we have of Jane's reading is her commonplace book from 1755-56 which mentions publications that had just appeared within the last five years of her entries such as Nathaniel Cotton's, *Visions in Verse* (1751) or Frank Coventry's, *The History of Pompey the Little* (1751). At least forty texts, ranging from conduct books and novels, to plays and periodicals, are recorded in the commonplace book; whether they were inherited, bought or borrowed is impossible to know. Later, in the last third of the century, judging from their letters, the Johnson children certainly regarded the purchase of books as a regular, indeed necessary, activity (see chapter 6).

According to Brewer, most books published in the eighteenth century fell into four categories: religion; social sciences; literature (including drama, classics and other foreign literature and poetry which was the most frequently published genre); and geography (including history and natural history). Probably all of these genres would have been found in the Johnson household. Alongside books, there would have been pamphlets, tracts and sermons, as well as ephemeral material such as newspapers, handbills, memorandums and almanacs. Some of latter may have even been used for lessons in numeracy, as they contained information about weather and agriculture, essential learning for those involved in overseeing the work on their lands such as George would need as the heir of the Witham estate.

During their childhood, the Johnson children may have had access to print and booksellers, including the Coopers in Paternoster Row and Newbery's in St. Paul's Churchyard. From their infancy the children would have watched and heard their parents reading all sorts of books; they must have been tantalised by the titles of *Letters writ by a Turkish Spy*, *The Arabian Nights* and the *Adventures of Telemachus* among others mentioned by Jane in her commonplace book. These books were probably read to the children as they grew older together with texts by Shakespeare, Spenser, Milton, Pope, Richardson, Swift as well as the ancient classics like Homer, Juvenal, Plato and Plutarch.

When and where did the Johnsons read? Looking at the description of the Richardson household above (admittedly a more literary one than average), reading seems to permeate daily activities and to take place at various times throughout the day and in different parts of the house. According to a table by Weatherill which shows estimates of time spent doing various household activities in the eighteenth century (in presumably privileged families), up to two hours daily were spent reading (Weatherill, 1996: 143). Lady Charlotte Finch, governess to George III and Queen Charlotte's children, describes the reading in a typical day in the royal family's life in 1759: Psalms together at 8 o'clock in the morning; reading, writing, French and other lessons after breakfast and then, after the day's other activities, reading aloud by candlelight until supper at 8 o'clock (Shefrin, 2003). Although this was certainly not a typical family, her account gives some idea of the amount of daily reading within elite households. We surmise that together with the examples mentioned above, that the Johnsons would have spent at least two hours a day in literacy-related activities.

In the eighteenth century, it seems likely that reading continued to be more of a public than a private activity, at least among women and children. Like other parents, Jane would have read to her children until they were old enough to begin reading themselves. Barbara and the boys would have read to Jane during 'lesson times' but perhaps also throughout the day, while she and Barbara did their sewing or other chores. Woolsey probably joined them in the evening, reading from some religious text, perhaps even from his own sermons. Reading as a collective enterprise would have also been helped by the rise of domesticity towards mid-eighteenth century (Trumbach, 1978), where a more intimate relationship, not only between husband and wife, but also parents with their children, would have encouraged general conversation around the shared books.

Scholars in the eighteenth century were concerned that reading should be an exercise in understanding, evaluation and judgement (Bartine, 1989) which meant that it was not just a matter of being able to sound out the words. As Isaac Watts says in his preface to *The Art of Reading and Writing in English* published in 1721, reading well means 'accenting' the meaning of words and sentences so that it makes sense to the hearers (Watts, 1972: xvi). In Richardson's novel, Pamela writes to Mr B that Miss Goodwin 'loves reading, and makes very pretty reflections upon all she reads, and asks very pertinent questions' (Richardson, 1984: 413). As we shall see in the next chapter, Jane's reading cards and other texts were geared towards encouraging questions, conversation and reflection, the same notions that she and Woolsey would have tried to apply to their own reading.

Although in her comment (quoted at the beginning of this chapter) on books which everyone should read, Jane dismisses most books as 'only for Diversion', in the Johnson household reading was not always about improvement. We are familiar with Locke's point that reading can also afford pleasurable entertainment for children, but he stresses the same for adults:

> There is another use of reading, which is for diversion and delight. Such are poetical writings, especially dramatick, if they be free from profaneness, obscenity, and what corrupts good manners: for such pitch should not be handled. Of all the books of fiction I know none that equals Servantes his *History of Don Quixot* in usefulness, pleasantry, and a constant decorum. (Locke, 1750: 403)

Jane's sense of humour, which shines out of her teaching materials and letters, may have led to purchasing or borrowing some 'pleasant' books to divert the whole family (maybe including *Don Quixote*). Perhaps Jane even permitted some of the more 'popular' literature traded by 'chapmen' - traditional stories, joke and riddle books and English legends - to enter the house, although one can imagine she kept a watchful eye on what was read by her children and probably the servants as well. In any case, more and more of these 'easy, pleasant books' became available for the Johnson children to read as the children's book trade began to develop. Before discussing texts for children, however, it is important to look into the increasingly important role of the visual in the development and practice of literacy in the eighteenth century.

Visual literacy

Figure 5. Set 21, item 1. Courtesy of the Lilly Library, Indiana University, Bloomington, Indiana.

Along with print culture, visual culture in the eighteenth century underwent a dramatic change through the invention of new technologies. Prints reproduced both cheap woodcuts and quality engravings; they were of all prices and most people could afford at least the cheapest ones. As Plumb writes:

> Art materials were to be found in every provincial town, and so were drawing masters, who taught in the home as well as in the school. Prints of old masters and modern artists were a commonplace of provincial as well as London life. (Plumb, 1983: 308)

The use of pictures became an important educational device, supported by Locke, Fénelon, Watts, Rollin and others. Rollin considers engraving 'the writing for the ignorant' (Rollin, 1742: 432) and Fénelon advised the use of prints and pictures as they 'may add to other Discourse, the better to enliven it, and print it deep on the Minds of Children and Young Persons' (Fénelon, 1713: 88). Publishers and print-sellers also took advantage of these notions and their catalogues contained more and more prints aimed specifically at children. At school, battledores brought pictures into the classroom, eventually replacing the more sober hornbooks. Images were also used for play and games; for example, in a catalogue issued in 1738, John Bowles advertised 'Lotteries, one hundred different sorts, many of them new designs, and very prettily graved: they are small prints of Men, Women, Fish, Flowers &c and are chiefly intended for children to play with...' (quoted in McKay, 2001: 131). Other sheets included familiar images such as toys and games, sports, street traders and other tradesmen. As O'Connell (1999) suggests in her book on popular print culture, these prints must have had great appeal and children would have swapped them and used them in their games, one of which involved sticking pins through the images.

Like other genteel families, the Johnsons would have collected the better quality prints to adorn their house and would have bought maps and charts for educating the children. Jane would certainly have taught her children to draw and paint, to make little books, card and other paper games (as well as combining these skills with needlework in the case of Barbara). Most importantly, she fostered an appreciation of colour and texture and an eye for detail, fashion and natural beauty. These qualities are evident in the fashion album that Barbara kept for more than 70 years (Rothstein, 1987), as well as in Robert's descriptions of people and landscape in his adult letters.[13] The generation that the Johnson children belonged to were lucky in this sense, as Plumb concludes about the eighteenth century, 'Visually it was a far more exciting age for children than ever before' (Plumb, 1983: 308).

Juvenile publishing, a growing commercial market

Looking back at the history of publishing in his in-depth study of books and reading during the Romantic period, William St Clair declares that, judging by print runs, 'one of the largest constituencies of readers during the whole print era has been young people, much of whose reading has been prescribed by adults' (St Clair, 2004: 21). This statement leads us to a consideration of three of the main features of children's book publishing during the eighteenth century: the definition of this 'constituency', the way in which childhood was regarded by adult buyers (which determined the demand for books) and the commercial and technological aspects of the book trade (which determined the supply). There is no space in this section (nor is it our purpose) to go into detail, but in what follows we shall briefly discuss these main features as a context for understanding Jane's writing and her children's reading.[14]

It was mainly through books that parents of the middling and upper ranks were given the arguments to support a more relaxed, loving and liberal attitude towards their children and it was also through books that parental interest and affection was made manifest. Parents were more willing to invest in texts that helped promote social mobility through teaching 'proper' habits and virtues that would enable their children to become 'gentlemen' and even 'gentlewomen'. The writing of stories and the publication of books especially for children both triggered and were a result of changing perceptions of childhood. As Myers says 'Because children's tales perform a variety of cultural functions, they are crammed with clues to changes in attitudes, values, and behavior. Above all, these key agents of socialisation diagram what cultures want of their young and expect of those who tend them' (Myers, 1986: 33).

Before the eighteenth century, the book industry did not consider books for children as separate from the general body of published works. With some exceptions, lesson books, moral treatises, courtesy books and chapbooks were not designed to appeal to a specific audience; they were read (or read out to) by people of all ages with an unambiguous instructional purpose. Locke had famously written that he did not know of any books, except for *Aesop's Fables* and *Reynard the Fox,* which were suitable for children. Enterprising publishers, John Newbery foremost among them, began to extend their business to include books which would appeal to this new market of readers. His motto of 'Trade and Plumb-cake for ever, Huzza!' is a precise description of intent behind his business.[15] As Plumb points out:

> ... the new children's literature was designed to attract adults, to project an image of those virtues which parents wished to inculcate in their off-spring, as well as beguile the child. Those alphabet and reading books, by their simplicity, also strengthened the confidence of parents in their ability to teach their children to read in the home. The new children's literature was aimed at the young, but only through the refraction of the parental eye. (Plumb, 1983: 82)

Newbery provided books which contained information on science and new inventions, such as *The Circle of the Sciences*, for a public eager to be in touch with new knowledge. Locke's influence also led Newbery and others to produce toys, games, maps and puzzles which would both educate and entertain, thus adding to the publisher's financial gains.

Because of the scope of Newbery's business and the playful tone he adopts when addressing his readers, he is usually considered to be the 'founder' of the 'new' children's literature, particularly with his *A Little Pretty Pocket- Book* (1744).[16] In writing about Newbery, Alderson notes that: 'There can be no doubt that the Pocket-Book occupies a "key" position, both for its original composition and as a portent of how books for children would develop, but it was only part of the revolution rather than the prime mover (Alderson, 1999: 186). Although we agree with Alderson that there were other novel publications for children, this particular book embodies not only the educational ideals of the time - to instruct and to entertain - but also the marketing ploys of plenty of illustrations, colourful binding and book-related toys. Like Newbery, other authors and publishers were producing purportedly 'pleasant' works for children. For example, the miniature books by Thomas Boreman, published between 1740 and 1743, give historical and descriptive accounts of buildings in London and included illustrations and humorous details, although he clearly believed that children should move on from the 'ill concerted artless lyes' of folktales like Tom Thumb and Jack the Giant-Killer (Boreman, 1741). Fortunately, these characters were kept alive by other publishers such as the Coopers and Newbery himself; in 1744 Mary Cooper published a little book for pure entertainment, *Tom Thumb's Pretty Song Book* which contained forty rhymes full of fun and humour while the preface of *A Little Pretty Pocket-Book* is supposed to be written by Jack the Giant-Killer.

During the last third of the century, even as the trend towards a more moralistic, rational view of education and reading became more widespread, writers and publishers continued to make their books appealing. Although old wood blocks were still sometimes used, original wood engravings and later copperplates were commissioned to provide a more handsome appearance. During this period publishers like John Marshall began to cater for different ages and capacities. Books for younger children, for example, were designed with larger print and more spacing. Marshall published 'improving' books but he also printed many popular tales. Also, the books themselves became objects of play: 'Popular stories - or portions of them - reappeared as dissected puzzles, writing sheets or table games, in abridged, pictorial, hieroglyphic or emblematic form [...]' (Shefrin, 1999: 251-2).

According to Jackson (1989), in the 1770s there was a sharp increase in publications for children given that the business was proving a lucrative investment. At the same time, the ideological balance was swaying towards the almost exclusive objectives of cultivating virtue and disseminating rational information. Conservatives regarded the ludic character of Newbery's texts as a waste of time, and stories about enterprising, upwardly mobile youths were seen as a threat to the establishment. Rousseau's influence on children's writers also began to be felt; they considered themselves to be the guardians of children's morals and censored from their writing that which might agitate their imagination. Fortunately, Rousseau's advice in *Émile* (1762, translated into English in 1763) that children should not be given books until they are twelve, with the exception of Defoe's *Robinson Crusoe*, was not heeded. However, his ideas struck a chord with some reformists who attempted to develop sensibility and feeling through direct experience in order that 'children learn to cope with the "real" world, a world rationally and scientifically describable' (Hunter, 1990: 147).

Towards the end of the century some of Rousseau's ideas on 'practical' pedagogy appeared in the books by a group of mainly female writers including Anna Letitia Barbauld, Maria Edgeworth, Sarah Trimmer, Mary Wollstonecraft and Ellenor Fenn. The result was a children's literature which has since been much maligned for its crassness, lack of humour and outlawing of the fanciful. It is true that Sarah Trimmer refused to allow her book *The Robins* to be illustrated as pictures could 'enflame childish imaginations' (quoted in Jackson, 1989: 143), yet she wrote the accompanying notes for a series of biblical and historical prints which were to be hung on nursery walls. Recent scholars have revised the one-dimensional view of "moralist" writers and revealed 'the rich imaginative and cultural uses of the "rational" tale for the woman writer in Georgian England (Myers, 1991: 102).[17]

The market for juvenile books continued to grow and push against the accepted boundaries (as it still does). At the end of the century when Jane's grandchildren were learning their letters, as well as moral and didactic stories, there was also plenty to amuse.[18] Despite shifting educational trends, chapbooks, for example, continued to be printed and in the second half of the eighteenth century began to be expressly targeted at a juvenile audience. These chapbooks included, among other texts, the abridged adventures of Robinson Crusoe and Lemmuel Gulliver, nursery rhymes, fairytales and oriental tales. They were cheap enough for poorer children to buy for a few pennies. Even at the turn of the century, during the poet John Clare's childhood, they were often the only literature (apart from religious books) that children and adults knew:

> I was fond of books before I began to write poetry these were such that chance came at 6py [penny] Pamphlets that are in the possession of every door calling hawker & found on every bookstall at fairs & markets whose titles are as familiar with everyone as his own name shall I repeat some of them 'Little Red Riding Hood' 'Valentine & Orson' 'Jack and the Giant' [...] such were the books that delighted me & I saved all the pence I got to buy them for they were the whole world of literature to me & I knew of no other. (Clare quoted in Deacon, 2002: 38)

It is telling that when leading Romantic writers, like William Wordsworth, Samuel Taylor Coleridge, Charles Lamb and John Clare, recall their childhood reading, it is chapbooks they cite (and defend) with great affection, rather than any of the 'new' children's literature of their period.

Whatever the truth is about actual literacy figures, about the amounts of books bought and how and when texts were read, there is definitely a sense that the importance of being able to read, as well as the possibility of reading as a pleasurable experience, was recognised during this period. A family like the Johnsons could only benefit from these developments.

Notes

1. Oxford, Bodleian Library, MS.Don.c.190, fols. 72-102.

2. A case recorded by Weatherill, for example, shows that one Sarah Fell of Swarthmore Hall spent 40 to 100 shillings a year on books out of an income of £350.

3. To give an example, the texts cited in her commonplace book (for just 1755-56) range from books first published in 1586 (Geffrey Whitney's, *A Choice of emblems and other Devises*) and 1677 (Owen Felltham's, *Resolves, divine, moral, political*) to poetry by Swift and Thomson published just before her marriage (Oxford, Bodleian Library, MS.Don.c.190, fols. 72-102).

4. The ubiquity of such publications and the ability to read to oneself however, was a cause of anxiety for many in positions of authority as it was believed that indiscriminate reading, especially among women, children and the lower classes, might cause serious damage to the moral and political health of the nation. In particular, the emergence of a new genre, the novel, was regarded with alarm by traditionalists and moralists.

5. The local newspapers would have been the *Northampton Mercury* (for Bucks. and Northants.) first published in 1720, and the *Lincoln, Rutland and Stamford Mercury* (for Lincolnshire) first published in 1714.

6. In this case he must refer to the London newspapers. Oxford, Bodleian Library, Ms. Don.c.193, fol. 110.

7. 'Quid Nunc', Barbara's pseudonym, was commonly used to describe young men in coffee houses or gossipmongers who continually asked 'What news?' or 'What now?' Unfortunately this letter is not dated and there were several generations of Baldwin's with connections newspaper publishing. It was probably addressed to Richard Baldwin I who was bookseller, publisher and newspaper proprietor between 1746 and 1810. Lord North was Prime Minister of Britain between 1770 and 1782.

8. Oxford, Bodleian Library, Ms. Don.c.192, fol. 93.

9. There is no mention of these in Jane's commonplace book.

10. James Janeway was a Puritan whose book, *A Token for Children* (1672), about the conversions and early deaths of young children was the most

widely read book in the seventeenth century after the Bible and John Bunyan's *Pilgrim's Progress*.

11. She mentions *Clarissa* and *Charles Grandison* in her letters and commonplace book; it is almost certain she would have read *Pamela*.

12. See, for example, Watson 1997 and Whitley 1997.

13. Later, Robert's daughters also do fashion sketches in their letters to Barbara (Oxford, Bodleian Library, MS.Don.c.195, fols. 86-9).

14. Information for this section has been put together from various sources: Hunt, 1995; Jackson, 1989; Kinnell, 1996; Pickering, 1981; Spufford, 1981a and b; Summerfield, 1984 and Thwaite, 1963.

15. For a detailed biography see Rowe Townsend (1994).

16. The first edition was advertised and probably published in 1744, but no copy of this first edition has ever come to light.

17. For more on women writers at the end of the eighteenth century, on their pedagogy and views on the imaginary, see Richardson, 1994; Clarke, 1997; McCarthy, 1999; Myers, 1986 and Tucker, 1997.

18. Jackson refers to the list of children's books published by Elizabeth Newbery (the widowed wife of John Newbery's nephew, Francis) in 1800 as evidence for this (Jackson, 1989: 196).

Chapter 3

Reading Lessons from an Eighteenth Century Nursery

> I am not ignorant of what it is to teach Children having taught all my
> own and several others to read without any assistance and always took
> a pleasure in it, and am so far from thinking it a trouble to have the
> care of Children, that I have often wished that Mr Johnson had been a
> schoolmaster. If I was to get my living any way it would be my choice
> to be a School Mistress ...
> Jane Johnson[1]

The above quote from Jane's feisty letter to the Headmaster of
Uppingham School (1758) confirms that she used the materials from
her nursery library to teach her own children 'and several others' to
read. In an earlier letter from 1747, where she tells the story of 'Miss
Clarissa' (see Chapter 1), she writes that this young lady was mother to
a boy and a girl 'whose Education she took all proper care off [sic]'.[2]
Like other genteel mothers, Jane evidently took her teaching role for
granted, and even took over teaching Latin to her son Robert after his
father had died.[3] However, it is clear that Jane embraced this role
whole-heartedly and made use, like 'Miss Clarissa', of her 'ingenuity
and dexterity'[4] in this task, not just because she loved children, but
also because, as her methods show, she took a keen interest in
childhood and in the intellectual development of the young.

Good fortune has allowed us more than a glimpse into how these
children learned to read in the eighteenth-century nursery. In this
chapter we scrutinise the nursery library created by Jane to teach her
children to read, looking in particular at the methodologies behind
Jane's teaching of reading. We also briefly describe some eighteenth-
century primers and their methods, as well as other educational
materials popular with parents and teachers at that time which were
likely to have influenced Jane's approach to teaching reading.

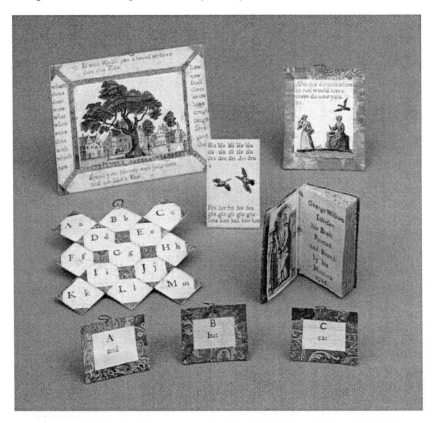

Figure 6. Jane Johnson's Nursery Library. Courtesy of the Lilly Library, Indiana University, Bloomington, Indiana.

A Hand-made nursery library

Here is a description of the nursery library, now housed at the Lilly Library, University of Indiana, Bloomington:

> The Jane Johnson papers comprise 438 pieces arranged into 24^5 sub-groups, all bordered or backed in Dutch floral paper, many illustrated by printed scraps (plain or hand-coloured) of people, birds, animals, and objects. Frequently these cards have small string loops so the items can be hung, probably on a nursery crib. Alphabet cards, lesson cards, and story cards can be used like modern flash cards with vowel sounds, syllables, short words. (Schiller, 1997: 20)

The beautiful hand-made reading materials are small enough to fit into the bottom of a hat-box, perhaps the very same one in which they were found by Justin Schiller in Oakhurst, the Ball mansion in Muncie, in

1982. In the middle of an embarrassment of riches, Schiller knew he had struck the 'leprechaun's pot of gold' and describes Jane's nursery library as 'the highlight of the entire collection...' (Schiller, 1997: 220). It was made to last and has remained more or less intact, surviving in surprisingly good condition for more than two hundred and fifty years. The individual items are beautifully constructed through intricate cutting and trimming, composing and transcribing text. Jane's writing is clear and consistent, usually in black, red (now faded) and perhaps brown ink which still reads well today. Evidence suggests that Jane created the collection between 1742 and 1747.[6] (Details of the different sets of cards within the nursery library are provided in this footnote.)[7]

Influences on Jane's reading materials

As noted earlier, Jane's pedagogical approaches would have been in large part both typical of her period and influenced by educational treatises, such as those of Locke. Certainly she believed, like Locke, that once children had mastered the alphabet, they should read for pleasure, though no doubt she also agreed with him that reading matter should not 'fill his [sic] head with perfectly useless trumpery' (Locke, 1693). F J Harvey Darton argues that in the eighteenth century writers for children, presumably including those, like Jane, who wrote without thought of publication, were either disciples of Locke or Rousseau.[8] Darton goes on to suggest that one of the reasons for Locke's success as a philosopher and educationalist was that he based his theories on knowledge of English domestic life: [Locke] '... was typically English, down to the smallest practical detail [...] and he knew [mothers'] long-established habits' in relation to their children (Darton, 1982: 111). Parents like Jane must have been relieved to follow Locke's edict that it was permissible, indeed advantageous, to make lessons amusing.[9]

For centuries, apart from religious works, schoolbooks were either abecedaria, primers, grammars or classical texts, with hornbooks being used for teaching the youngest children their letters and familiarising them with short prayers. The 'Criss-Cross-Row', as hornbooks were sometimes called, referred to 'the cross that headed the text or to an earlier arrangement of letters strung on wire in a cruciform' (Rowe, 2000: 147). One of the lesson cards made by Jane contains just such a rhyme[10]:

> A Schoolboy was once so dull in his way,
> He cou'd not be taught so much as great A
> His Schoolfellows jested upon his thick Skull
> Nay, hold, says the Youngster, I am not so dull;
> But if I learn A, which I cou'd soon do,
> They'll put me to B, C, & all the Cross Row: [...]
> (Set 14, item 28)[11]

In the eighteenth century battledores became common. As well as containing letters and texts, these folding books were illustrated with woodcuts.[12] By this time there was a flourishing trade in primers which also made use of visual aids for teaching. Although writing was usually taught much later or not at all (and was based on copying and obtaining a 'fair hand' rather than on the child's own composition), there were also books which helped children to practise this skill.[13] Jane's cards are written in clear handwriting, and some of her letters to her children are written in a neat copperplate, presumably meant for them to emulate.

Reading methods nearly always involved learning the alphabet by heart, recognising individual letters and then moving on to identify syllables, whole words and phrases. However, as Frank Davies shows, in some very early pedagogic works there is already an awareness of grading material for different ages and also of making it more interesting for children, either through the use of rhyme or illustration (Davies, 1973: 123). John Brinsley, for example, encouraged understanding rather than rote learning. In his *Ludos literarius* from 1612, he argued that learning should be a form of play and suggested using games, performing plays and telling stories, as well as using rhyme and music for teaching reading. In 1649 George Snell suggested in *The right teaching of useful knowledge* that 'the method of instruction ought to be closely related to the everyday experience of the pupil' (quoted in Neuburg, 1971: 66) and in 1660, Charles Hoole (who translated Jan Amos Comenius' *Orbis Pictus*) advocated various 'new' methods of teaching reading in his book *A New Discovery of the Old Art of Teaching Schoole* which rely less on memory and more on play and familiar experiences of childhood (Hoole, 1660).[14]

Locke discouraged the use of the *Bible* as a primer as it could confuse children and advocated instead the use of educational games and toys such as alphabet blocks (which existed from Tudor times), word cards and lotteries. Rollin went as far back as Quintilian for the idea of putting individual letters on cards or engraving them on wooden or ivory blocks which could be 'thrown' as part of the learning game (Rollin, 1742: 422). In *Jewell House of Art and Nature*, published by Hugh Platt in 1594, children are described as having 'good sport' with alphabet dice and cards where grammar rules have been printed (Platt, 1594: 45). He depicted various alphabetical artefacts including 'a little wheel' with holes where one letter at a time may be seen. Hoole also recommended 'pictures and letters printed [...] on the back side of a pack of cards, to entice children, that naturally love that sport, to the love of learning their books' (Hoole, 1660: 8). Playing cards was the most popular form of entertainment, especially during mid-century, so it is not surprising to find some of Jane's lesson cards with playing card symbols on them. She does not seem to have shared Pamela's worries about this kind of play leading to gambling.

Commercially produced reading materials would have found their way into the Johnson household. Any primer, instructional manual or spelling book of the late seventeenth / early eighteenth century contains examples of many of the same sorts of lessons as Jane prepared for her children.[15] Closest are those from the Coopers' and Newbery's primers. Thomas and Mary Cooper's *The Child's New Play-Thing: Being A Spelling-Book Intended to make Learning to Read, a Diversion instead of a Task*[16] which is 'adapted to the capacities of children', begins with the alphabet and a syllabary, and includes fables and lessons, moral and religious precepts, English proverbs, songs, riddles, moral dialogues, prayers, numbers and some stories with illustrated woodcuts. This primer also contained an 'Alphabet to be cut into single squares for children to play with' on which upper and lower case letters are set within decorated borders in a manner very similar to Jane's cards.[17] Jane takes the text of several of her lesson cards, almost word for word, from this primer. She copies lists of syllables and vowels, occasionally adding or missing out words or changing the order. She also transcribes 'Lessons of One Syllable' containing the names of 'Beasts', 'Birds', 'Fishes', 'Insects', 'Parts of the Human Body', 'Parts of the World' and 'Fruits, Flowers, Herbs, Trees'.

Newbery's *Pretty Book for Children* (issued circa 1743) is subtitled *An easy guide to the English tongue: perfectly well adapted to their tender capacities...* 'and is design'd as well for the more easy instruction of those that can but just read, as for the entertainment of others that are a little more advanced ...' It contains most of the above genres as well as alphabets in different characters, and the alphabet rhyme 'A was an angler' in little squares with flowered margins, again, similar to Jane's. Among the stories are Red Riding Hood, Cinderella, Fortunatus and Joseph and his brethren. Newbery's *Little Pretty Pocket-Book* (1744) was more suitable for fluent readers. Among other things, it contains four fables: three of them - The Wolf and the Kid', 'The Husbandman and the Stork' and 'The Shepherd's Boy' - are reproduced on Jane's cards (Set 14, items 3, 30 and 35), identical except for a few words.[18] In Newbery's *Pretty Book for children* we also find a mention of the game of 'Squares' which 'joins instruction with delight'. There is one surviving copy of the *Directions for playing with a set of squares upon the plan of Mr Locke* printed for Newbery and Collins circa. 1745.[19] Given the dates when Jane was producing her nursery library, it shows that she must have been quick off the mark to acquire these newly published texts.

Jane's view of reading

Margaret Meek, a distinguished British scholar of children's literature and reading, once said in a lecture that 'we teach what we think reading is'. Jane's nursery library shows us what one wife and mother thought reading could be for her children and family. First of all, we can be in no doubt that she enjoyed teaching her children to read from the evidence of the letter to the Headmaster at Uppingham quoted above which goes on to say:

> For sure nothing is so agreeable as to have a parcell of young brisk agreeable Children about me especially when one is so well paid for it! And as for the noise they make and the little mischiefs and unlucky tricks they do their sweet innocent looks and sprightly actions more than compensate for that trouble and the satisfaction of seeing their daily improvements is beyond all other pleasures.[20]

As a devout person, Jane would certainly have been familiar with Watts' *Divine Songs* (1715). The copious use of rhyme within her reading materials suggests that she shared his view of verse as a useful

'Furniture, for the Minds of Children' (Watts, 1971: 144). As babes in arms, Barbara and her brothers would probably have heard their mother sing lullabies such as this one she appears to have composed herself:

Rock on, rock on
my pretty Boy.
And you shall be
your Mother's joy.
(Set 17, item 33)

Although child-rearing books of the time strongly advised parents to discourage babbling, one can imagine Jane, so attuned to the rhythms of her children's language and a versifier herself, ignoring this advice and answering their early attempts with some form of what we now call 'motherese'.[21] In spite of a distrust of the folk tradition and the Puritan attempts to stamp it out, the children would have picked up on other rhymes, poems, ballads and songs through their parents as well as through servants or their own peers. Many of their games would have involved singing or reciting, and later, they would have been expected to commit catechism and other lessons to memory, an important skill and specifically linked to religion.

Jane encouraged the young readers in her care to make up their own narratives, including personal anecdotes, as well as to enjoy the words of others. Stories would have been central to Jane's pedagogy. Fénelon, for example, encouraged parents to recount stories (mainly Biblical) through 'lively representation' and then let the child retell it to someone else 'without reprehending her for her faults' (Fénelon, 1713: 77). Rollin also recommends children recounting fables 'in the natural, unaffected dress of his own words' (Rollin, 1742: 343). Fénelon went as far as to advocate having several children represent the characters in a story to help fix it in the memory, a dramatic practice which the Johnsons might have enjoyed. From Barbara's letters we know the Johnson children staged *The Earl of Essex* while at Witham, presumably one of many plays they acted.[22]

The lesson cards in set 18 of the nursery library would have been particularly good for story-making as they include large attractive pictures, some rhyming text and two sets of words which the children would have drawn on to make up their stories.

Figure 7. Set 18, item 5. Courtesy of the Lilly Library, Indiana University, Bloomington, Indiana.

Take item 5, for example, which would have hung in the nursery. Jane is still indicating words of more than one syllable with a hyphen, so the card is catering for a fairly early stage of reading. The image is dominated by a handsome townscape with a large blooming tree at the centre. There are small figures who could be engaged in buying, selling, socialising or even begging which would be in line with the wise caution about wasting money within the text. The list on the left includes mostly function words that relate to place and time. However, the list on the right is much more various: some words are put together which have similar spelling families - 'how' and 'vow', 'cough' and 'laugh', but Jane's propensity for loving lessons can't be ignored with the last three words reading 'give' 'them' 'love'. Similarly, her beautiful word card (set 10) again features function words, but there at the heart of it is 'love' again.

Figure 8. Word card. Courtesy of the Lilly Library, Indiana University, Bloomington, Indiana.

Then as now, there were arguments over how to teach reading and whether understanding and judgment should be taught together or separately. In schools for the lower classes, teaching of reading stressed the pronunciation of words rather than understanding the ideas in the text, while children of the middling and upper classes were expected to develop their powers of reasoning along with their letter learning. For Jane, both understanding and judgment went hand in hand: the gradual build-up of knowledge of letters is accomplished through clear directives as to what 'thinking justly', a quotation from her commonplace book, meant.[23]

Jane chose to use a mixture of teaching methods, realising that reading is not one skill, but a great many that have to be mastered if children are to become not merely functionally literate, but also enthusiastic, critical readers able to master a wide variety of texts. We know Jane succeeded in this endeavour since her children's letters and journals as adults document a lifelong, rich and varied fascination with all sorts of texts, as well as interest in the natural world, fashion, society, architecture and the arts. But let us return to the beginning: evidence suggests that Jane began to teach her children to read as soon as they could talk. This is corroborated by a letter where Jane says that at around four and a half, her son Charles could already read most of the words in that letter.[24]

Little books for little hands

Among the different artefacts for teaching that Jane created are two miniature books. The smallest measures 5.5 x 4.5cms and contains 32 numbered leaves. The first page contains the words 'A New Play Thing', a variation on a title common to printed books of the time, such as some of the primers mentioned here. Next is a page with the words 'good boy good girl' and after this, every opening contains a letter of the alphabet in upper and lower case, a word that begins with that letter and then a list of vowel and consonant sounds. By page 27 there are monosyllables composed of two, three and the four letters and finally, on the last page, the words 'The end of this Book'. Both books are carefully hand-printed and bound with cord ties in gilt Dutch paper, the same that Jane uses to bind the manuscript of her story and to frame some of the lesson cards.

The other book measures 8.5 x 5.3 cm and consists of 36 leaves. The title page reads 'George William Johnson his Book. Printed and Bound by his Mamma 1745' (he would have been five at the time). The facing page (as well as the front endpapers) shows two statues in emblematic poses: a woman holds a compass and a man carries a large volume in one hand and raises the other in a gesture of instruction or admonition. There is also a more homely coloured picture of a smaller woman and a sheep. It is likely that Jane's book for George was meant to inspire a sense of pride in its possession as well as to personalise its content. Although early miniature books[25] were produced for a variety of purposes, such as evidence of a printer's craftsmanship or as talismans, the fact that they could be easily carried and concealed, and in a sense 'possessed', made them especially attractive to children. Most miniature books from the fifteenth century onwards were produced for children's pockets. Boreman's *Curiosities in the Tower of London* (1741) is an example from the first half of the eighteenth century. Later, at the end of the century, Marshall became famous for his miniature libraries, sold in imitation bookcases or little decorated boxes.

In her analysis of 'the miniature' in literature, Susan Stewart notes the link between 'the aphoristic thinking of religious didacticism with the miniature book's materially compressed mode of presentation' as well as with 'the diminutive world of childhood' (Stewart, 1993: 43). She notes that 'The invention of printing coincided with the invention of childhood, and the two faces of children's literature, the fantastic and the didactic, developed at the same time in the miniature book' (Stewart, 1993: 43). The first, in the form of chapbooks, presented a 'realm of reverie', the second, in the form of lesson books, introduced 'nuggests of wisdom'. Thus Jane's small books fall within the latter type as she condenses her moral beliefs to fit a tiny page which she would presumably enlarge upon as the children grew older.

The book for George illustrates very clearly this almost inseparable link between instilling knowledge and religious and moral instruction, common in early primers. In this case, letter learning and moral education are literally back to back. George is instructed to read all the right-hand pages first (which contain simple rules to practise); the left-hand pages, written in a now-faded red ink, have pictures and more elaborate text for the more experienced reader he would become after he had mastered the exercises. The book is written in large letters, with plenty of spaces and margins, making it eminently suitable for a young reader.[26]

Alphabets

We cannot be sure of the order in which Jane used the reading materials, but we can certainly make an educated guess. She would have started with the alphabet mobiles with their little thread loops, probably hung about the nursery to familiarise the babies with their letters. Jane made her mobile alphabets appealing by decorating the little individual squares pasted together. To each, she affixed one, two or three triangles cut from Dutch floral paper in orange, green, red and blue. The squares tessellated to make an attractive pattern, as do the internal colourful triangle patterns within the whole. Afterwards, the children probably graduated to the alphabet cards which contained upper and lower case letters. In addition, Jane made a set of alphabetic word chips mostly related to food with playing card symbols on the back, presumably to make recognition of words into a game like the commercial materials mentioned earlier in the chapter.

Figure 9. Word chips and box. Courtesy of the Lilly Library, Indiana University, Bloomington, Indiana.

To reinforce alphabetic knowledge, Jane also produced two original alphabet rhymes ('A was an Alderman', 'A was an Ass'), although she could easily have copied several others that were in print at that time (including 'A was an Archer' from Cooper's primer which she must have owned). Jane's alphabets have her own unique flavour. For example, she was a good Anglican and couldn't abide what she calls Popery or Non-Conformism (which gets into her alphabet rhyme). There are also those caustic, ironic touches so typical of Jane - the lady whose beauty was frail, Aesop's ugliness, as well as references which she knew the children would enjoy, both exotic and homely - to animals, naughty boys, pirates and Xerxes fighting the Greeks. Each couplet is accompanied by a picture in the centre of the card serving a purely decorative function, as it is unconnected to the verse. Jane selected mainly one-syllable words for her alphabet rhymes and used hyphens to help inexperienced readers break up two syllable words.[27]

Figure 10. Set 5 item 11. Courtesy of the Lilly Library, Indiana University, Bloomington, Indiana.

> A Was an Al-der-man, in a fine Gown,
> B Was a Bar-ber, that shaved his Crown
> C Was a Cob-ler, and liv'd in a Stall.
> D Was a Draw-er, Pray Sir do you call?
> E Was an Em-press, en-rob-ed in black.
> F Was a Fox, with a Goose at his back.
> G Was a good man, that bought and sold hogs
> H Was a Hunt-er, quite fond of his Dogs.
> I Was an ink-horn, as black as a Crow.
> K Was a Keep-er, and shot at a Doe.
> L Was a La-dy, whose beau-ty Was frail,
> M Was a Mon-key, with-out a-ny Tail.
> N Was a nough-ty Boy in his dish,
> O Was an Ot-ter, that eat up the fish.
> P Was a Py-rate and Rob'd on the Seas.
> Q Was a qua-ker, as stiff as you please.
> R Was a Rab-bet, as brisk as a Bee.
> S Was a Squir-rel, and Tripp'd on a tree.
> T Was a tra-der, and ga-ther'd up pelf.
> U Was as ug-ly as Aesop him-self.
> W Was a Wa-ter-man, and ply'd in the Creeks
> X Was that Xerx-es that fought with the Greeks
> Y was a Yeo-man could Blust-er and strut
> Z was a Zea-lot, and liv'd in a Hutt.

Phonics and Flashcards

Next, the children were likely to be familiarised with sound and letter correspondence through cards which had mostly a phonic bias. We know that Jane began with initial consonants (because this set of materials is numbered) followed by the vowel sounds (ba, be, bi…) which get practised using two or three letter common words (in, of, to…). She moves on to phonic blends with single vowels (bla, ble, bli…). Next she introduced consonant digraphs (ch, sh) followed by three-letter words practising common letter strings. Jane's early lessons include familiar letter strings, suffixes, prefixes, syllables, diphthongs, tripthongs and other simple linguistic features related to the early mechanics of spelling and reading.

Figure 11. Set 1, item 13 Courtesy of the Lilly Library, Indiana University, Bloomington, Indiana.

From the start Jane seems to be keen to link her phonic lessons with real words, though there are occasional nonsense examples (jod, bur). Most of the words use the same letter strings (aze, ark, ick), but sometimes she tried homograph combinations where the 'rime'[28] part of words look the same, but sound different (kind, wind). The children would then encounter vowel digraphs (ee, ou, oo) in familiar words before Jane, introduced those tricky letter strings that can't easily be learned by phonics (augh, ough), as well as common usage words the children were bound to encounter. Finally, the children would move on to four letter words, including those with split digraphs (or magic 'e' as they are commonly known, where the final 'e' lengthens the preceding vowel). Some of those words could be worked out phonetically, others only by whole word recognition.

Most teachers of young children get them to recognise their own names (and Mummy, Daddy etc) before, or at the same time as, teaching phonemes. Many reading schemes today use whole-word recognition as a major strategy in the early stages of reading. Jane understood this principle and, like Cooper and others, introduced whole words to learn in her first set of cards, focusing on common items of food, animals, weather and body parts, starting with simple single-syllable words and gradually progressing to longer, more irregular words.[29] Jane produced attractive flashcards which could be played with, as well as card games, ditties, word lists artistically displayed on thread hangers and single words combined with pictures. Like the alphabet cards mentioned above, these cards may have been used in games such as the one recommended in the Preface to *The Child's New Play-Thing* where they are put into a box and read by the children as they are thrown or drawn out.

Rhyme and rime

Jane's phonic lessons probably helped the children with their writing and spelling as well as learning to read. Though her word lists are similar to those in print at the time, Jane made her lessons less tedious by using familiar words whenever possible and adding pictures for light relief.

Figure 12. Set 17, item 23. Courtesy of the Lilly Library, Indiana University, Bloomington, Indiana.

Jane's natural instinct is to use rhyme[30]: nine sets of cards are written in verse from rhyming couplets, to religious maxims. In his Introduction *to Divine Songs,* Watts talks about using verse to help children remember texts:

> What is learnt in verse is longer retained in memory, and sooner recollected [...] there is something amusing and entertaining in Rhymes and Metre, that will incline Children to make this part of their Business a Diversion ...
> (Watts, 1715: 146)

Jane seems to have seen the value of this advice; she combines a sense of humour and child-centred understanding with the capacity to write simple, appealing rhymes. Her moral verse so typical of this period is supplemented by much more vibrant ditties which call to mind Cooper's *Tommy Thumb's Pretty Song Book* (1744)[31] and anticipate *Mother Goose's Melody* (circa 1760):

> Then she set her
> Rump, upon a stump
> And took at pinch of
> Snuff.
> (Set 17, item 36)

Here are some examples which demonstrate the variety of Jane's use of verse. Jane could conjure up a brisk piece of nonsense:

> A young Bull fell in Love
> with a red and white Cow
> And each day when he met her
> he made her a Bow
> and said pray my Dear
> how do you now.
> (Set 18, item 7)

She drew on the oral and chapbook tradition:

> If all the world was paper
> and all the Seas were ink
> and all the Trees, were bread and cheese
> What would we have to drink?
> (Set 18, item 4)

She tells a good tale:

> A Fox caught a Goose,
> and eat her for dinner,
> A Man Shot the Fox
> while the Goose was within her.
> (Set 17, item 13)

She personalises a moral message (Jane could not abide alcohol):

> Dear Madam your Tea
> is exceedingly Fine,
> I had rather drink Tea,
> than the finest of Wine.
> (Set 17, item 8)

She could show her prejudices and have a bit of fun at the expense of the French:

> Such short Gowns as these, are much used in France;
> And the Men, and the Women cut capers and dance.
> The Ladys they Paint, and their backsides they show
> The Men hop, and skip, and each one is a Beau
> Would you see men like monkeys; to France you must go
> (Set 21, item 5)[32]

Even in light rhymes, Jane could show her independent spirit:

> Pray Madam come this way, one Gentleman crys,
> This Walk is more free from Sun-shine and Flys;
> No Sir says the Lady, it is this way **I** choose
> If that walk you like, pray your Liberty use.
> (Set 21, item 15)

Finally, Jane uses verse to impress on her audience moral and religious lessons as well as expanding their vocabulary with increasingly difficult words:

> Remember the Liar
> Has his part in Hell-Fire.
> Shun the Wicked and Rude,
> But converse with the Good.
> Transgress no good Rule,

At Home, or at School.
Vie still with the Best,
And excell all the rest.
(Set 24, item 5)

Word and image

Jane was most interested in the visual nature of texts; all her reading materials are attractively designed and most are multimodal. She clearly recognised that children would be more likely to want to learn to read if they were offered some visual diversion. The images she chose make reference to the Bible, the arts and natural history, as well as to fashion, society and popular culture. There are many pictures of plants, landscapes, cupids and mythical animals. There are also real animals, birds and insects, as well as people reading, painting and playing music. There are children playing games and pictures of swings, tops, hobby-horses and dolls. Finally, there are also pictures which refer to learning itself, such as children reading, going to school, and being punished by a schoolmaster.

Figure 13. Set 23, item 36. Courtesy of the Lilly Library, Indiana University, Bloomington, Indiana.

The multitude of images remind us once again of the value of Watts' advice: 'A thousand objects that strike their eyes, their ears, and all their senses, will furnish out new matter for their curiosity and your instructions' (Watts, 1859: 301). Jane would certainly have been familiar with *Orbis sensualium pictus* (1659), one of the earliest books using labelled pictures to make learning easier for children, conceived by the educational reformer Comenius. In fact, Comenius intended his books to be more than just appealing aids to reading; he believed in visual imagery 'as the cornerstone of a programme meant to revolutionise teaching by relating all learning, form infancy onwards, to its basis in sense experience' (Watson, 2001: 530). As we have mentioned, Fénelon also recommended using pictures which will 'strongly imprint what they see' on the minds of young children and predispose them for more learning' (Fénelon, 1713: 88).[33] Perhaps, most interestingly, the images Jane chose are often dramatic, drawing young readers in and lending themselves to sharing with an attentive adult.

Most of the pictures came from 'Lotteries' (the commercially produced sheets of images described in Chapter 2), which Jane would have cut out and used to her own particular devices.[34] There are several examples where Jane used pictures to complement the written text, such as some religious stories where all the main characters and the setting are depicted. In one, there is a picture of a soldier holding a baby by its leg, running a sword through its heart, while the mother looks on in despair. Jane's reaction is heart-felt as the accompanying text shows:

> More instances of wicked
> King Herod's cruelty
> in killing the young children. O!
> What a sad vile creature he was,
> who wou'd not rather be a Beggar?
> a Chimney Sweeper? nay or a
> Tom-Turd-man than such a king.
> (Set 14, item 22)

Figure 14. Set 14, item 22. Courtesy of the Lilly Library, Indiana University, Bloomington, Indiana.

In these instances, the text must have been constructed to accompany the picture. In other cases, a picture is used because it bears only slight relation to the text. There are also many examples where the picture is purely decorative and bears no link to the text. Occasionally, a serious religious message is softened by a light-hearted picture which accompanies it, almost like the technique found in ironical picture books today. Here are some examples where the image could be said to lighten the tone of the religious text:

> Image: Two ladies and two gentlemen are sitting down to tea while the maid boils a kettle.
>
> There is but one God,
> and he is Great, and
> High above all things...
> (Set 23, item1)
>
> Image: A fiddler plays while a young man and woman dance.
>
> Remember the Sabbath
> Day to keep it Holy: in
> it thou shalt do no manner of Work.
> (Set 23, item 21)
>
> Image: The monkey with a jaunty red hat who is smiling mischieviously is defecating into what appears to be a hat![35]
>
> Those that Love God, and keep / his Com-mands will all go to / Heaven, when they die, and / be a vast deal more happy / than they can be in this World. (Set 22, item 27)

Figure 15. Set 22, item 27. Courtesy of the Lilly Library, Indiana University, Bloomington, Indiana.

It is easy to see where Barbara developed her interest in fashion. However much Jane tried to suppress that side of herself (she confides this 'weakness' in a letter discussed in Chapter 1), so many pictures tell of her pleasure in introducing her daughter to well- dressed young ladies in elaborate costumes. We believe that Jane coloured most of the pictures herself with meticulous care (some of the rougher ones might have been done by the children), and her eye for colour, design and the gorgeous detail of dresses reveals her own interest in the subject. There are two cards, for example, which show the same lady, but in each case her dress is illuminated with different colours as well as patterns (Set 22, items 4 and 43).

Text-to-life

Like all good reading manuals, Jane started with simple text and gradually introduced more complex and challenging material. Sometimes she gave moral advice; other times she told little stories. Many of these 'tales' combine the domestic with interesting social detail. In the example below, young readers might savour the colourful variety of vegetables for dinner, as well as learning how to spell them, while discovering the names of the Duke of Northumberland's 'Page' and 'Gardiner'. This card is also a subtle lesson in social hierarchies and morés, particularly as black page boys were very fashionable and something of a curiosity at that time.

> Oronoko, a Black Boy, Page to
> his Grace the Duke of Northum-

> berland, telling Oliver Brom-
> field the Duke's Gardiner; that he
> must bring in some Cucumbers
> green Pease, Kidney-Beans, Horse-
> Radish, Asparagus Artichokes &
> Colly-Flowers, ready for Dinner.
> (Set 14, item 24)

The next offers lessons about the social world. through the characters (surely known to the children) and their doings, though Jane was keen to emphasise Edward Percival's diligence at reading, no doubt to encourage her own offspring.

> Rowland, & Rosamund Percival
> an honest country man & his wife
> walking to Sturbridge Fair to sell
> Eggs, Apples & Turneps, & to buy
> a new Hat, Stockings, Shoes, Lea-
> ther Breeches, and a Knife and
> Fork for their little son Edward
> who is a very good Boy & cou'd write
> & Read before he was eight years old.
> (Set 14, item 27)

At other times, Jane wanted to impart historical, political, religious or literary lessons.

> Plato, Socrates, and Seneca, three
> of the Ancient Wise Philosophers
> talking together about the immor-
> tality of the Soul, the Happiness of a
> future life & the shortness of this...
> (Set 14, item 26)

> Simon Lord Lovat; sitting in the
> Tower leaning upon a stone Pillar;
> and Edmund Newton his servant
> bringing him a large glass of French
> Brandy. On thursday April the
> ninth, one Thousand, seven-Hun-
> dred, & forty-seven his Head was
> Cut off, on Tower Hill for High Treason.
> (Set 14, item 29)

Jane was always aware of the importance of putting the child at the centre of things and she understood the power of the name. How proud George must have been of the special book dedicated to him. We presume Barbara was equally pleased to find herself in written and visual text. Beside a well-dressed lord and lady dancing, Jane writes:

> Lord Mountjoy, &
> Miss Barbara John-
> son, Dancing a
> Menuet together at
> a Ridotto in the
> Hay Market.
> (Set 19, item 3)

Figure 16. Set 19, item 3. Courtesy of the Lilly Library, Indiana University, Bloomington, Indiana.

You can almost hear Jane's arch voice in the last card we will mention which must have been designed for Barbara's pleasure. This playful ditty has the ring of a 'real' nursery rhyme.

> Indeed, little Madam
> you Ride very grand
> With a Crown on
> your Chair, and a Fan
> in your hand.
> (Set 17, item 24)

Although Jane's reading lessons are in many respects similar to published instructional materials for children, they also contain features original to her. All of it was produced without thought of profit or the public domain, yet it provides an exquisite illustration of domestic literacy, created out of love by a mother anxious to do the best by her children. What begins with delight at the sheer beauty of these tiny items, becomes respect for the painstaking tenacity of Jane's enterprise.

There are some continuities with the way reading is taught in the early twenty-first century. Jane did not experience the current controversies about which methodology for teaching reading is in fashion, but she appears to have understood that children find their own idiosyncratic ways into reading. She knew that learning to read requires frivolity, storytelling and diversion as well as diligence, rigour and repetition. Jane certainly grasped the importance of interactive learning where the text does the teaching and she knew how to employ the visual and dramatic. There is still much we can learn from her enlightened reading lessons today.[36]

Notes

1. Lincolnshire Archives, Johnson I/2, pp. 69-71.

2. Letter to Mrs Brompton, 1749. Oxford, Bodleian Library, Ms.Don.c.190, fols. 11-12.

3. Lincolnshire Archives, Johnson I/3, p.182.

4. ' Miss Clarissa' was not only very good with her needle but also at fine cutting, as she cut 'watch-papers' which were small circles of paper or fabric that protected watches from dust, often made as gifts. They were either cut in elaborate designs, handpainted or embroidered.

5. Schiller mentions 23 sub-groups, but the material was sorted into a further group at a later stage by Shirley Brice Heath and Elizabeth Johnson.

6. 'Factors for dating the material are derived from a figure on a card which bears a printed identity (set 1, item 36: Sir John Bernard, alderman and Lord Mayor of London, 1738); one of booklets (no. 11 - George William Johnson, his Book, Printed and Bound by his Mamma [Jane Johnson] 1745); and a card (no. 14 - Simon Lord Lovat) which notes that Lord Lovat was beheaded on April 9, 1747).' Scope and Content Note, Johnson, J. mss.
    http://www.dlib.indiana.edu/collections/janejohnson

7. The twenty-four sets that comprise the collection are grouped mainly according to their size, design, image or decoration. Some cards, for example, have the image and text on the same side, while others have the

text on one side and the image on the verso. Other sets all have gilt paper margins. Some are clearly numbered; one set (Set 22) shows roman numerals as well. Some cards and sets are discussed in detail in Chapters 3 & 7 but a brief overview helps give an idea of the whole.

Sets 1 to 4 were probably the first Jane created, as they are mainly for learning the alphabet and in Set 1 there is a reference to the year 1738 (the year Barbara was born - so although this may not necessarily indicate Jane began her pedagogic task that year, it must have been soon thereafter). Following the teaching of the letters, sets 5 and 6 contain two 'A was a ...' rhymes. Sets 7 to 10 teach mainly words, some linked to a common theme, but also show syllables. Sets 11 and 12 are two little handmade books. Sets 13 and 14 comprise cards with religious and secular topics, most of which are in verse. Set 15 is mainly religious verse. Set 16 is more miscellaneous, with different genres and formats. Forty-four cards with short verse make up Set 17 while in Set 18 most of the cards have longer verses as well as lists of words and have a distinct design and set of images. The cards in Set 19 all have texts on one side which are related to the image on the verso. Set 20 contains only one card, perhaps from an unfinished or lost group. As in Set 19, cards in Set 21 also have related texts and images. Sets 22 and 23 are made up of religious and moral sayings, some of which can be found in the little book in Set 11. Finally, Set 24 contains six cards with moral lessons in verse.

8.   *Émile* was not published until after Jane's death, but it is interesting to note that her children discussed his ideas with great enthusiasm as adults.

9.   In the seventeenth century most primers seemed more concerned with children's souls than with their minds. For example, as a child, Jane may have been given Benjamin Harris' *Protestant Tutor for Children,* originally published in 1690 which combines the teaching of letters, syllabaries and writing with accounts of martyrs of Popish tortures and massacres and is illustrated with woodcuts of some of these horrific sights. Fortunately, there were also a few more cheerful books such as *The Father's Blessing* by William Jole from 1674 which aims to 'allure' children to read through 'Godly and Delightful' verses, stories, riddles, fables, jests as well as proverbs and rules of behaviour. It is also adorned with cuts of animals and familiar objects.

10. A similar rhyme called 'The Naughty School-Boy' appears in Thomas Harris's *A New Playbook for Children* which appeared in 1749 (also bound in Dutch gilt paper).

11. Unless otherwise stated, all references to Jane's texts are from the Manuscript Nursery Library at the Lilly Library. These references include the set and item numbers (some of the cards were numbered by Jane). We have left Jane's original spelling in all the transcriptions.

12. Rowe also reminds us not to forget the sampler, with letters, texts and pictures (Rowe, 2000: 149).

13. See, for example John Bickham's *Fables, and other short poems: collected from the most celebrated English authors*. The whole curiously engrav'd, for the practice & amusement of young gentlemen & ladies, in the art of writing, from 1737. This book contains a sampler of alphabets in different hands as well as an introduction to drawing.

14. He suggests that the best time to begin to teach reading is between the ages of three and four, when 'a childe hath great propensity to peep into a book' (Hoole, 1660: 2).

15. Similar lessons can be found in an early primer, William Ronksley's *A Child's Weeks-Work* (1712) which is 'nicely suited to the Genius and Capacity of a Little Child' and aims to 'allure' the child into reading. Other primers include *A Guide for the Child and Youth* (1730) T.H., 'teacher of a private school', whose 'easy and pleasant' method included pages of small images next to rhyming couplets and *A New Play Book for Children or an Easy and Natural Introduction to the Art of Reading* by Thomas Harris (1749) also aimed at teaching through 'play'.

16. The first edition was printed for both husband and wife, the second edition from 1743 includes only Mary Cooper's name.

17. In his *Discourse on the education of children and youth*, Watts suggests 'may not some little tablets of pasteboard be made in imitation of cards [for teaching]' (Watts, 1859: 342)

18. The comparison was made with a Newbery edition of 1767 but it seems to confirm that there was indeed a first edition of *A Little Pretty Pocketbook* published in 1744.

19. Alderson (1999) dates the game even earlier, to the late 1730s.

20. Lincolnshire Archives, Johnson I/2, pp. 69-71.

21. Trumbach (1978) suggests other mothers and nurses probably did the same.

22. Vickery (1998) reports one mother in the 1770s reading a play to her children and then presiding over the staging of it.

23. Oxford, Bodleian Library, MS.Don.c.190, fols. 72-102.

24. Oxford, Bodleian Library, MS. Don.c.190, fols 7-8.

25. Miniature books technically means any book measuring less than 3 inches.

26. This is a practice in books for children that became popular later in the century with Anna Barbauld's lessons for children, also written with a particular child in mind. Had Jane been born a few decades later, she

might have felt more encouraged to publish and make her work available to a larger public.

27. In the original, Jane actually uses lower case letters to introduce the alphabet - 'a' was etc.

28. See Goswami & Bryant (1990)

29. Hoole called this method of making syllables into easy and familiar words 'the letter sport'. His examples are similar to Jane's: 'then, fable, bible, noble/ and, band, land, sand/ black, block, clack, clock' (Hoole, 1660: 15) Rollin also advises selecting familiar words like 'day', 'night' or 'sun' and 'when he is able to join words, short phrases containing some story or curious particular'. (Rollin, 1742: 426)

30. Jane may have had some intuition about what Usha Goswami (1990) and other psychologists have recently described as phonological awareness. Their evidence suggests that most children have to learn to recognise individual letters and phonemes (usually in the early months of schooling), whereas by about three years old most children instinctively notice rhyme at the end of words (what they term - *rime*), followed by becoming aware of the beginning of words (what they term - onset). At any rate, Jane certainly finds many different ways for her children to learn and practise syllables, onset, rime and phonics.

31. One of the rhymes in this book begins in the same way as one of Jane's cards, 'There was a little man, and he had a little gun' but the rest is completely different.

32. 'To dress like a monkey' was a term used for men who dressed extravagantly (Jones, Notes to *Evelina,* 2002: 422)

33. Rollin called pictures 'the writing for the ignorant' and, recalling Locke, wishes 'that we had a greater number of such prints, calculated purposely for children, which might instruct them in an entertaining way...' (Rollin, 1742: 426)

34. Découpage, or the art of using paper cut-out to make a design or tell a story, was a common craft for genteel women in the eighteenth century. Fine scissors were used for this intricate work.

35. This monkey creature (as well as the other monkey-men on some of the lesson cards) bears a strong resemblance to the monkeys dressed as men which appear in paintings by David Teniers the Younger, such as, for example, *Monkeys in the kitchen*, where monkeys wearing plumed hats drink and play cards. See also footnote 3 in chapter 7.

36. An earlier version of this chapter appeared in *Children's Literature in Education*, 35 (1), March 2004, pp53-68.

Chapter 4

A Mother's Story: Moral Texts and 'Pretty' Readers

A good Boy will be a good man. Love to Read your Book.
Jane Johnson[1]

… they all Learn'd to read their Books together, which they took so
much pleasure in, & Read so well that they were the admiration of all
the Gentlemen & Ladys [sic] that Lived near them in the Country.
Jane Johnson (*A Very Pretty Story*)[2]

In all of Jane Johnson's writing for children there is a tension between
the attempt to make reading an interesting and enjoyable task and her
deep concern for her children's spiritual growth; in other words,
between allowing her readers to develop their imagination and their
sense of humour *and* reminding them of the moral limits of this
freedom.[3] Although other texts for children published at the time Jane
was writing also reflect this tension, one of the main differences
between these and Jane's texts is the way in which her whole
pedagogical project was driven and encompassed by her understanding
of 'love'. This word can be found throughout her writing; for example,
it appears 53 times in the lesson cards, second only to the word 'good',
which appears 82 times. Most of these references are to the love of, or
love for, God but love is also mentioned in more earthly contexts,
particularly as the bond between parents and children.

Jane made her moral priorities clear to her children: the worst
consequence of not being 'good' was God's anger, but it was also the
withdrawal of maternal love. In Jane's story, which we will discuss
below, naughty Tommy is punished by God's angels for his
wrongdoing and dies because he feels he is not loved as much as the
other children in the story. In a letter to Robert from 1755 this same
message comes across: 'Give Miss Prue a Kiss for me, & tell her I
Love her dearly, because I believe she is a very good girl, for I don't
Love anybody that is not good.' At the same time she signs off with 'I
Love you Dearly, & your Happiness is the constant wishes [sic] of Jane
Johnson'.[4]

Throughout this chapter we would like to imagine how her children
may have responded to Jane's texts and therefore to the tension in her

writing. Although we cannot know the answers, these questions invite us to view children's texts from a different perspective: What did the children make of their mother's didactic messages? Did they enjoy all types of text equally, reading difficulties set aside? Did they prefer the more playful ones? What aspects of her story did they like best? Did they find maxims and religious advice dull or comfortingly familiar? How did they place themselves in her story?[5]

A Very Pretty Story for Children

Jane's knowledge, beliefs and character all come together in her children's story of 1744. At that time her two eldest children were four and six years old. A note at the end informs the reader that 'This Story was made in the Year 1744 on purpose to tell Miss Barbara Johnson & her Brother Master George William Johnson, who took Vast Delight in hearing it told over & over again a vast many times by Jane Johnson'.[6] While it is a moralistic tale heavily influenced by conduct literature, the story contains many appealing descriptive passages and uses elements of fairy stories to provoke a delighted response in the children.

Briefly, the story is about four children, two of them are Bab and George Allworthy. The other two are Lucy and Tommy Manly.[7] The surnames are typical of the allegorical names used in children's literature, a tradition that has its origins in Bunyan and continues throughout the eighteenth and nineteenth centuries such as in Charles Kingsley's *Water Babies*.[8] The children are the best of friends, so when Tommy and Lucy lose their parents and become destitute, they are taken in by the Allworthys, 'a fine Gentleman and a fine Lady [who] lived in a fine House'.[9] The children are good and happy until the day when a fair comes to the town. On their way there, they come upon a group of ragged boys and girls in bare feet to whom all the children except Tommy give sixpence. Having spent all his money on sweets and still wanting a toy horse, Tommy steals from his friend George and blames Molly 'the Cook-Maid'. The most extraordinary part of the story comes next, extraordinary in terms of the plot itself but also in terms of the evocative and imaginative detail of the fantastical occurrences. The day after the theft, the parlour door opens and into the room comes

> ... a fine Chariot all over Gold & Diamonds; & it was drawn by six fine White Lambs, dress'd all over with flowers & Ribbons, & the

most beautiful little Boy that ever Eyes beheld seated on the coach-box, & two Charming pretty little Angels Rode on two Charming fine Lambs by the Chariot side.[10]

This chariot takes the three good children to the 'Castle of pleasure and Delights', but Tommy is taken in the 'stinking arms' of 'a little ugly man all over stinking Dirt' and put into a little dirty black chariot dragged along by two black hogs who grunt all the way to a great hogsty where Tom is locked up with them.[11]

Although Tom is eventually allowed back to the house and is forgiven, he feels no one loves him as before, so he sickens and dies. The others, however, grow up to marry rich, handsome and good partners and

> ... God Almighty granted their Prayers & did Bless them in everything, because they were very good, & said their Prayers, & went to Church and behaved themselves Handsomely there, & were very good to poor people, & to everybody, so they all Lived very happy, & loved one another Dearly till they were very Old Men & Women & then they all Died & went to Heaven to live with God Almighty & all the Good Angels for ever and ever. Amen.[12]

The story clearly appeals to children's sense of justice as the 'good' children get their just rewards in this world and the next. Another aspect of the story is that two of the main characters - good ones of course - are named after Bab and George. The act of frequently re-telling or re-reading a text which includes her own children's names and which juxtaposes the familiar and the fantastic suggests a belief in the power of literacy to change lives, not just through grim example, but through empathy, imagination and enjoyment. The fact that Jane stipulates the age of her audience and that the events in the story happen when characters are slightly older - eight or nine - shows how much she was in tune with their interests (and desires) and aware of their developmental stages. The message of the story is serious; the consequences of greed, theft and lies are no laughing matter, but as we shall see, there is plenty of evidence that Jane was happy to create a text that would please her listeners as well as help them to grow in virtue.

Historians of children's literature such as Alderson (1999), Avery (2001) and Watson (1997) have all remarked on the originality of this mother's tale even though they have also pointed out how Jane builds her story on the existing literary traditions of her day such as the Puritan moral tale, the fairy tale and the early novel.[13] They have confirmed that this story is one of the earliest known narratives for young children, causing Alderson to call Jane 'the first lady of children's literature'. According to Alderson, the originality of what he calls this 'short secular novel' lies in three elements for which there are no 'obvious precedents' in English children's books before 1744:

> First, she casts her own children, Master George and Miss Bab, as characters in the story [...] Second, she plots the story as a full-length tale rather than as a cautionary anecdote or dramatic incident [...] and third, she interpolates into the everyday comings and goings of her characters passages of symbolic fantasy ... (Alderson, 1999: 184)

Because Jane was not writing for commercial purposes she had the freedom to insert references into the story which meant more to her particular audience. She included allusions to her children's everyday life, such as their dancing lessons and their play. She inserted events such as going to the fair, with all its symbolic suggestions of a place which arouses greed and uncontrollable desire. She also includes a 'paradise' for children, full of 'pretty' trinkets and pets as well as biscuits and other treats, and she has her characters choose what were probably their favourite toys and activities in real life:

> Miss Bab and Miss Lucy chose to play at making dinners for their dolls, and Master George chose to ride upon the rocking-horses, and to shoot with a bow and arrow, and to play at marbles.[14]

As Alderson reminds us, early children's fiction usually took the form of short anecdotes, most of them with a simple plot (or without one at all, as the nursery story Richardson has Pamela tell her children) which involved illustrating some kind of moral lesson. Even Sarah Fielding's *The Governess, Or, the Little Female Academy* (1749), which is considered the first novel-length work of fiction for children, is composed of several tales albeit within the larger framework of a story about a girls' school. In this tradition, the message is the point of the text and Jane's story is no exception but her lessons on charity and honesty are interwoven throughout an enjoyable tale, rather than simply thrust at the reader.

Flights of fancy

The other reason Jane's 'lessons' make more of an impact is because of those 'passages of symbolic fantasy', in other words, the intrusion of the imaginary in the form of magical chariots, angels and 'devils'. There could not be a starker contrast between the extraordinary locations, the 'Castle of Pleasure and Delights' and the 'hogstye': on one hand, a heavenly vision, on the other, the stuff of nightmares. While these symbolic places had been a part of books that taught moral and religious values to children, particularly the extremely popular *Pilgrim's Progress*, neither Locke and his followers, nor the late eighteenth-century rationalists, would have approved of involving imaginary beings. Watts, for example, urged parents not to terrify children with 'dismal stories of witches and ghosts, of devils and evil spirits of fairies and bugbears' which would make them fearful and superstitious (Watts, 1859: 336).

English tales such as 'Tom Thumb' and 'Jack the Giant Killer', along with the tales of Charles Perrault and Mme D'Aulnoy, were well known in England in this period. Until the end of the seventeenth century, most of these tales, especially fairy tales, were considered a waste of time, but it was when Locke pointed out their potential moral and psychological dangers that they began to be attacked. As the development of a rational capacity in a child became important, the tales that they were exposed to (even though they were not meant specifically for them) become subject to scrutiny. Robert Bator contends that in the first half of the century they were tolerated as long as their moral lesson was clearly stated, but by 1750 Lord Chesterfield is writing to his son that fairy tales and other 'idle frivolous stuff [...] nourishes and improves the mind just as much as whipped cream would the body' (quoted in Sayle, nd: 154).

From mid-century, although fairies, giants and fantastical characters continued appearing in chapbooks, in the literature specifically written for the young they were encased within 'safe' moral structure and eventually are almost completely suppressed. For example, in Fielding's *The Governess*, mentioned above, there are two stories which contain giants and fairies. Although 'the Governess', Mrs Teachum, simply instructs the teller of these stories to make sure her audience distinguishes between fact and fancy, it is evident that she is displeased. By 1820, an edition of this book, revised by Mrs Sherwood, excludes these two tales altogether.

Despite fantasy apparently being relegated to the popular and the vulgar, in the attempts to disentangle it from the imagination and its 'legitimate' pleasures, the debate continued and the lines were not always as clearly drawn. William and Cluer Dicey, for example, predecessors of the printer John Marshall (who also printed for the Cheap Repository Tract Movement) seem to have attempted to please the critics of popular literature and yet defend the 'old songs' by adding the following note to their broadsides:

> Note: As the use of these Old Songs is very great, in respect that many Children never would have learn'd to Read, had they not took a Delight in poring over Jane Shore, or Robin Hood, &c. which has insensibly stole into them a Curiosity and Desire of Reading [...] till they have improv'd themselves more in a short time than perhaps they would have done in some Years at School: In order to make them still more useful, I premise to affix an Introduction, in which I shall point out what is Fact and what is Fiction in each Song; which will (as may be readily Suppos'd) give not only Children, but persons of more ripe Years, an insight into the Reality, Intent and Design ... (quoted in Deacon, 2002: 35)

Bator suggests that 'the moralizing of the fairy tale leads naturally into the moral tale which appears in full bloom after 1744' (Bator, 1971: 8). From this point of view, Jane's story is placed at a crucial point of development. However, other critics suggest a less distinctive line should be drawn between these two genres; for example, a recent study on fairy tales, which looks at chapbooks and the work of Fielding and Mme de Beaumont, shows how 'fairy tales existed simultaneously as the didactic and the fantastic in two different literary fields' (Wanning Harris, 2001: 80). There is no sense that Jane wants to prevent her children's exposure to the world of the imaginary. Indeed, in a letter from 1755 to fourteen-year old Henrietta Ingram, a friend of the family, Jane mentions the 'History of the man in the moon' and expresses her affection for the young girl with lines that reflect no discomfort with a mention of imaginary beings:

> ... you have never been a day together out of my thoughts, for whenever I am at leisure to regale them with any thing that is

agreeable, you pop into them with as much vivacity as a Fairy through a Key-hole.[15]

In his close study of Jane's story, Watson has written in detail about the fairy tale elements it contains, comparing them in particular to those in Mme d'Aulnoy's tales (a collection of her stories in three volumes was published in 1720, when Jane would have been fourteen, although the first English translation appeared in 1699). Watson shows the similarities between the magical passages in *A Very Pretty Story* and Mme d'Aulnoy's rococo imagery, with its vivid descriptions of clothes, jewellery and landscape. Magical chariots and fantastical animals are common features of these fairy stories. Jane has taken the bright and colourful imagery used in these tales such as descriptions of ornamental details and made these particularly appealing (and more suitable) for her young audience with the appearance of birds, horses, peacocks, Chinese swings and other playthings, as well as gay decorations. The images have a strong resemblance to those that appear on her lesson cards, where exotic landscapes and oriental motifs are common. One of the images for example, shows a lady driven by a footman on an extraordinary looking sledge with a mythical bird's head as a kind of mast-head. In front of the woman, either as part of the sled or some sort of symbolic presence, is a little cupid waving a piece of cloth. A gaily decorated prancing horse draws the sledge.

Figure 17. Set 14, item 31. Courtesy of the Lilly Library, Indiana University, Bloomington, Indiana.

Why does Jane, who must have been aware of the misgivings surrounding fantasy, include these passages? Maybe it was because, as a keen reader of the *Spectator*, Jane was familiar with Addison's essay on 'Taste and the Pleasures of the Imagination' (*Spectator,* 1712), one of the key works on this subject in the early eighteenth century. Addison wants to find a place in rational life for a 'polite imagination' and writes of the 'pleasurable terror' experienced by readers in fiction. Summerfield, who writes on fantasy and reason in eighteenth-century children's literature, says that 'In canvassing and endorsing - promoting, indeed - the legitimacy of the imaginations' pleasures, Addison was unwittingly offering a coherent and persuasive legitimating of the child's delight in fantasy' (Summerfield, 1984: 13). It looks like Jane knew she could make use of the potential of the imagination to captivate her audience, but she is careful to describe the fabulous Castle of Pleasure and Delights as a reward from angels rather than fairies. Also, it is only 'about five miles from the house', a safe distance, close to rational and watchful parents.

Whatever her views on fairy tales, *A Very Pretty Story* strikes an even balance between the fantastic and the moral, as well as between the unbelievably good and 'real' children. There are also pragmatic moments, in the same way that some of the precepts of the lesson cards are concerned with the nature of wealth and project a vision of middle-class expectations. For example, the two girls, now 'Ladys', marry

> ... two of the Richest and Handsomest of the little Masters as they used to play with at the Castle of Pleasure and Delights; & Master George was married to a Little Miss that had the best sense, & the most good nature of any one there, & her that he admired the most the first time he went there. And Mr. and Mrs. Allworthy kept all their Weddings in a Very genteel & Handsome manner ...[16]

As well as being wealthy and good looking, we know for certain that the future spouses had been good children as well.

The Language of childhood

While the fictional child characters are clearly meant to illustrate social and moral conduct, the 'real' child emerges in the way that the story is told. Watson describes the 'child-centred rhetoric' of the story, which includes not only the shared family jokes but also a language that conveys the excitement of childhood dreams come true. One of the ways in which Jane transmits the reality of childhood experiences is through accumulation: the use of the conjunctions, especially 'and', with few pauses all of which convey the energy of childhood activities and echo the 'breathless' manner of children's speech:

> Then away they went & gather'd flowers & made Garlands, & nosegays, & then they went up stairs & dress'd their Bird-cages, & their Rocking-Horses, & their Dolls all over flowers, & they Danced, & jump'd & play'd about, & was as merry & as happy as possible.[17]

Another language feature is repetition of certain words such as 'little' and 'pretty'. The diminutive, as Watson points out, is also present in Mme. D'Aulnoy's texts. Finally we also have the small details of childhood which bring the characters to life and stem from Jane's acute observation of her children, such as in the following examples:

> Oh! Madam says Miss Bab. (almost out of Breath with Runing [sic] so fast) ...[18]

> ... why then says Miss Bab. & Master George (both speaking at once) ...[19]

> ... but he was Dull & out of humour because he could not have the Ivory Horse, he talk'd of nothing else all day, & in the night he could not sleep he so much Long'd for it ...[20]

The story that Richardson has Pamela tell at the end of the second volume of the novel of that name provides a point of comparison with *A Very Pretty Story* and highlights the differences between a tale composed by a male author (and put in the mouth of a female one) for publication with a tale told by a mother in a domestic situation. According to Pamela's letter where she transcribes the story, it is a 'little specimen' of one her *nursery tales* and *stories*'. In fact, she tells what are actually two unrelated accounts in response to her children's pleas:

> "Dear Madam, a pretty story," now cries Miss: "and dear mamma, tell me of good boys, and of naughty boys," cries Billy. (Richardson, 1984: 461)

As Watson notes, Jane was probably familiar with this novel (first published in 1740) and may have used it as a model. The beginning of the first 'story' is very similar: 'a story of two little boys, and two little girls, the children of a fine gentleman and a fine lady' (Richardson, 1984: 462). However, rather than a developed narrative, Pamela's first story turns out to be 'an inventory of righteousness' as Watson describes it, while the second one is an inventory of 'naughtiness' and its consequences: 'as they grew up, they grew worse and worse, and more and more stupid and ignorant' (Richardson, 1984: 463). In Pamela's stories there is no action, the characters simply function as examples to illustrate a lesson which reflects Pamela's virtues as a mother. The sentimental language is of a different strain to that of Jane's story, where it is possible to hear the story-teller's voice coming through: 'Most important of all, and totally missing from Richardson's rather self-conscious account, is the inimitable *oral* character in the language, its intimate and loving child-centred rhetoric' (Watson, 1997: 44).

Interestingly, Richardson provides us with the response of one of Pamela's children to her tale of a widow driven to her death because of her children's bad behaviour. All the listeners shed tears and one boy cries 'Poor, poor widow woman!' (Richardson, 1984: 464), thus showing the reader that Pamela has cultivated a sense of pity and sensibility in her offspring. One wonders what the reaction to naughty Master Tommy's death would have been in the Johnson household. It is not unlikely that it was his stay in the hogsty and everlasting ban from the Castle of Delights, rather than his death, which might have impressed the children. Pamela's education of her children is meant to set an example for women readers in mid-eighteenth century, not only in terms of her approach to their learning but also in terms of what sort of texts they should come to know. Jane's story, while following some of Richardson's precepts, reflected a more responsive approach to children's interests and paints a more accurate picture of their childhood activities.

Pretty readers

As far as we know, *A Very Pretty Story* is the longest text Jane wrote for her children, and through this exemplary tale she not only introduces her audience to narrative conventions but also allows them a glimpse of the fantastic, turning the tension between the didactic and the entertaining into a smooth-running vehicle for her own specific purposes. While the reader can indulge in the imaginary through fantastical events, there are always mechanisms of control which contain this freedom of the imagination and clearly mark it as an experience of childhood.

One of these markers is found in the title which clearly indicates its intended audience by including the word 'pretty'. Linked to the idea of the miniature, of the 'littleness' of children, is the idea of 'prettiness'. A surprising number of titles for children during the eighteenth and nineteenth century contain the word 'pretty', for example, *Nancy-Cock's Pretty Song Book* (first advertised in 1744), *Tom Thumb's Pretty Song Book* (circa 1744). It is so common that perhaps we overlook its significance in the frequent appearance in Jane's lesson cards as well as in her story.

In the *Oxford English Dictionary*, the most common definition corresponds to 'fine', 'nice' and 'pleasing', emphasising something that is 'agreeable' to the 'mind, feelings or senses'. But there are other ways in which 'pretty' has been and is still used. Firstly, though less common nowadays, it has developed from being associated with 'tricky', 'cunning' and 'clever'. Then, there is the sense in which it applies to 'having the proper appearance, manners or qualities of a man', as in a 'pretty fellow' which by the end of the eighteenth century became a derogatory sense of a 'fop'. Jane includes the following line in one of her cards: 'How pretty this Man looks, with Sword, Hat, and Cane' (Set 21, item 2), applying the term to a genteel looking man and his fashion accessories. Finally there is the condescending tone associated with the word, as the *Oxford English Dictionary* says, we grant something is 'pretty' (for example, to say 'pretty things' or a 'pretty child') while 'beauty' is 'imperious and commands our acknowledgement'.

All of these senses can be found in eighteenth-century texts for children where the word 'pretty' appears. There is a negative connotation in desiring 'pretty things' (naughty Tommy wants the 'pretty' horse) or in its association with 'fine' or luxurious clothes. However, it can also be positively associated with a modest, clean appearance in contrast with dirty or slovenly appearance. There are also different connotations of the word when used in terms of money, such as 'a pretty penny' and when it is used ironically such as 'a pretty kettle of fish'. So titles which include 'little' and 'pretty' do have that sense of adults trying to appeal to children, even trying to 'trick' children into reading which brings us back to Locke, with his idea of 'cheating' children into learning with, perhaps, a 'little pretty' book. Jane was not only trying to attract her readers with the use of the word 'pretty', but also providing them with lessons in aesthetics, in other words, she was moulding their expectations for enjoyment and appreciation of the qualities of a literary text.

Religion and morality in Jane's writing for children

As a child Jane must have read the sterner religious and moral texts written by Puritans in the seventeenth century, yet her own teaching reflects the changes in the view of childhood and is more concerned with the promise of Heaven for the virtuous than with the threats of Hell-fire and damnation for sinners. However, Jane's writing for children does fall within an all-encompassing religious and didactic intent, and if we want to widen our understanding of eighteenth-century writing for children and of the cultural experience it implied for the reader, we need to look more closely at the moral dimensions of her own project.

Some seventeenth-century writers did offer more benign paths to salvation. Bunyan's simple rhymes in *Divine Emblems* (1686) are about homely objects and country sights that children would know about. Later, Watts' *Divine Songs* (1715) attempted to tie 'delight and profit together' in the teaching of religion. Watts believed 'that making children literate would also make them good and that poetry was a means of teaching virtue' (quoted in Styles, 1998: 14). It is very likely that Jane would have known these two books from her own childhood and read them to her children. Both books remained in print during the eighteenth century; *Divine Songs* was the best selling book of poetry in Britain for 150 years.

Conduct and guide books, dating back to the middle ages, were one of the most popular genres for adults in Western literature.[21] They were written from different perspectives - religious, social and political - but as Hunter writes, 'they agree in a basic worry about contemporary principles to ignore higher principles and indulge individual appetites' (Hunter, 1990: 252). They also assumed literacy was an effective tool for shaping the individual toward a future role (e.g. the 'ideal' wife). In his seminal account of childhood in the eighteenth century, Plumb stresses the change in education from religious to social: 'Morality is still uppermost, but it is a social morality with which parents and teachers are concerned...' (Plumb, 1983: 290). This change was reflected in new texts for children and youth which emphasised proper conduct and attacked vices like drinking, swearing and gambling. They also advised on what and how to read.

It is possible to see how stories for younger children emerged from this popular tradition, incorporating these types of lessons through examples within some kind of narrative (compare Hunter's point on didactic literature as an antecedent of the novel). These books also had an influence on Jane's moral views. Her advice on proper behaviour, found throughout her writing, is meant to ensure her children's moral development *and* social advancement. It is also inseparably linked to her lessons in literacy.

In Jane's lesson cards there is a clear attempt to teach not only reading but also religion and morals. Out of 187 lesson cards that contain text rather than simply lists of syllables or words (and without counting one repeated set of religious maxims), approximately 100 are straightforward religious precepts or moral lessons (most of these can be found in Sets 22 and 23). She does however, always try to make religious and moral topics accessible to her children. Her descriptions of the paths to salvation, while earnest, are made more compelling by her use of language and metaphors. The first of the next two examples is from one of the lesson cards; the second is an expanded version of the first, written in her commonplace book and probably intended for her children at an older age:

> Hea-ven is such a Fine place,
> it is worth ta-king a great deal
> of pains to go there. (Set 22, item 37)

> Strive to enter in at the Strait Gate, that is, take a Great deal of Pains to go to Heaven, for we must not expect to be carried there Lolling at our Ease in a four Wheel'd Post Chaise hung upon springs, but provided we get there at last, it is very well, even tho' we are jolted through the Cart Ruts in a Dung-Cart.[22]

As we have already mentioned, there are the lesson cards with light-hearted images which belie the pious instruction.

Jane's God is an ever-present figure in her writing and most of her letters and poems include some mention of Him (see Chapter 1). In the lesson cards, the word 'God' or 'Lord' (in the religious sense) appears 145 times. They present us with a hierarchy where God is at the top, followed by 'Pappa and Mamma'. Other religious precepts follow which paraphrase the fourth of the Ten Commandment, for example:

> Ho-nour thy Father and thy
> Mo-ther both in word and
> Deed that a blessing may come
> up-on thee from the Most High. (Set 22, item 39)

Despite God's love being even greater than that of parents, the last picture in George's little book is a very fine coloured image of a little girl swaddling a baby closely watched by her mother. However, the final text is a reminder to the child that parents will not be around forever to guide children in the correct path and provides Jesus Christ's summing up of Christian practice: 'My son, so long as you live never forget the following Rule Always do unto every one as you would they should do unto you. Remember this when I am dead and Gone.' (Set 11)

Death, which is never far away, brings no fear to those who have behaved righteously because of the belief in God's love and the joys of Heaven. One of the lesson cards makes this clear: 'You ought to be more a-fraid/ of Sin than Death' (Set 22, item 36). Death and the afterlife are very present in all of Jane's writing and there is no shielding the children from their inevitability. However, the various lesson cards that refer to the death of a child usually make it a joyous event involving angels. Also, in *A Very Pretty Story*, Miss Lucy doesn't cry much for her dead parents because 'they are gone to Heaven, & are much Happier than they could be in this World'.[23] This belief must have been of some help to the Johnson children at the early death of their father (particularly Charles and Robert, who were then only 8 and 11) and, three years later, of their mother. It must have also been a comfort to know that their parents' many virtues would have ensured them a place in Heaven.

Lessons in vices and virtues

The particular themes which appear in Jane's writing are obviously rooted in her religious beliefs. There is a stark division between, on the one hand, virtue and happiness and on the other, vice, sinfulness, wickedness and punishment. Most texts focus on one or another particular vice while the virtues are simply gathered under the often-repeated term 'good'. Jane uses strong words and images to impress upon her readers the urgency of her message: the first example is from her commonplace book; the second, from the lesson cards:

> Flee from sin as from the face of a serpent; for it is better to die than to do any wicked thing.[24]

> It is wicked to get
> drunk, to swear, lye, or
> steal.
> And those that do such
> things will Hell Torments feel. (Set 17, item 25)

Figure 18. Courtesy of the Lilly Library, University of Indiana, Bloomington, Indiana.

Once a sin is committed, punishment cannot be avoided because although parents may be deceived, God is all-knowing. In George's book we find several reminders to the effect that 'The eyes of God are always upon you, and you cannot go out of his sight' (Set 11). In a letter to Robert when he was 10 years old Jane writes: 'Be sure to remember God wherever you are & whatever you do, for his Eyes are always upon you'.[25] This is the harsh lesson Tommy learns in *A Very Pretty Story* when an angel says:

> Sure you forgot that God Almighty sees every thing that is done, & that he saw you when you put your hand in Master George's pocket and stole two shillings, and that he heard you when you told Lyes ...[26]

Dishonesty in children, in the form of lying or stealing was considered as one of the worst vices of all, not only by Jane, who mentions them nearly 40 times in her lesson cards, but also by other children's writers during the second half of the century. In his book, *Moral Instruction and Fiction for Children 1749-1820*, Samuel Pickering (1993) has a whole chapter on books about liars which show how lying is the beginning of the road to Hell, leading to drink and financial ruination along the way. Like Tommy, these characters are subject to severe punishments and, like him, most of them never recover. In 1754 Jane writes from Olney to her son Charles (then 7) who is staying with his cousins at Milton Bryant:

> I write the following line for you to learn by heart and I pray always remember to speak the Truth upon all occasions and then God will love you and so will everybody and particularly Jane Johnson
>
> The better soul abhors the Liar's part
> Wise is thy voice - and noble is thy heart.
> This is the Truth and Oh Ye Powers on high!
> Forbid that Want should sink me to a Lye.
> Whom want itself can force untruths to tell,
> My Soul detests him as the Gates of Hell.
> Pope's Homer[27]

Another vice, perhaps even more loathed by Jane, was drinking spirits. We have speculated that her strong condemnation may have been a result of an alcoholic family member, perhaps her own father. It may also be a result of the gin drinking craze in the early eighteenth century and her coming into contact with the consequences of it during her life in London. According to Hunter (1990), in some parishes every fifth house in London sold sprits. 'Gin Lane' is also famously depicted in Hogarth's print from 1751. We find mention of drink in George's book and in the lesson cards: 'My Son, if you wou'd have/ good health, drink no wine/ without water in it, till you/ are thirty years old' (Set 22, item

53). We also find it in her commonplace book, which she writes a decade later, at a time when her sons were in most danger of acquiring the habit: 'I pray God my sons may have the Grace to be sober and chaste in an age when 'tis the fashion to get Drunk' and 'Neither Fornicators, Adulterers nor Drunkards &c: shall inherit Eternal Life.' Finally, there is the "Note" at the end of *A Very Pretty Story* which blames drink for the 'riotous' life and the eventual demise of some young gentlemen.[28]

Swearing also comes high on Jane's list of vices. We find mention of it in George's little book, 'My Son use not thy mouth to swear, nor thy tongue to name the Name of God in vain' (Set 11) and it appears 14 times in the lesson cards. She also sends a very clear message in the letter to Robert from 1755:

> ... mind who amongst the Workmen are Idle & who work hard, & be sure if you hear any body swear tell them it is very wicked & remind them that they should never swear but when they are in a place where God can't hear them.[29]

Idleness, extravagance and meanness are some of the other vices mentioned. The latter is put in opposition to being charitable, a virtue that appears in George's book and the lesson cards: 'Stretch out thine hand to help the poor, and God will bless thee in all thy ways' (Set 11). There are reminders of poverty and begging in the lesson cards and in *A Very Pretty Story*, Tommy's first crime is meanness, as he won't contribute sixpence for the poor gypsy children to buy shoes. On the other hand, money is not to be parted with foolishly. Although surely a charitable woman, Jane would be the first to make sure it was a worthy cause and she was keen to instil a sense of thrift. George's book and the lesson cards contain some well known proverbs and other maxims (some of them appear in Newbery's *A Little Pretty Pocket-Book* and in Cooper's *Child's New Play-thing*) on the management of money. In her hierarchy of values, 'being good' is at the top, but it is followed closely by health and wealth:

> Health is bet-ter than
> Rich-es, but to be good
> is bet-ter than both. (Set 22, item 52)

> In the first place, take

> care to be good; and in
> the next, take care to be
> Rich. (Set 22, item 54)

Around the time Newbery died, in 1767, even as various successors continued publishing 'pleasant' books, his texts came under attack from the moral reformists and educationalists who distrusted his more light-hearted approach to children's books. As Jackson writes:

> Like many of us today, the reformers preferred to ban ugly facts from pictures of child life, to soften them, or to feature them as evils that bad youngsters brought upon themselves but from while repentant were rescued by adults. In contrast, Newbery's ironic instructive laughter tempered the harsh facts of life. Satire and humour were conscripted for his paramount task: to show the young how to become successful adults - honest, shrewd, industrious, and happy. (Jackson, 1989: 99)

This trait became more pronounced as the century drew to a close with threats of revolutions. For these and other reasons Jane's texts are closer to Newbery's than to the reformist writing that followed. She does not soften or exclude 'ugly' facts of life but like Newbery she uses humour to balance them. Although she does not relinquish control to her child readers, and in *A Very Pretty Story* the loving and sensible adults are always present in the background, there are instances of fallible and even foolish adults in many of her lesson cards, a characteristic of Newbery-like texts which was thought by the late eighteenth-century moralists to encourage anti-authoritarianism.

Robert, the father of seven children between the years of 1773 and 1788, would have probably come into contact with reformist literature. However, despite his religious profession, it seems unlikely that he would have been much impressed by these more rational books and he may have continued purchasing diverting publications such as *Mother Goose's Melody* (first published in 1760) or *Nancy Cock's Pretty Song Book* (published around 1780). As we shall see in Chapter 6, Robert and his wife followed Jane's footsteps in terms of their affectionate involvement with their children, but with a more relaxed moral discipline.

Notes

1. Manuscript Nursery Library, Lilly Library, Indiana University, Bloomington, Indiana, (Set 22, item 2). There is also a similar card which reads: 'A good Boy will be a good man. Love to learn your book.' (Set 1, item 47) All the lesson cards quoted in this section are from the Nursery Library.

2. Oxford, Bodleian Library, MS.Don.d.198: 20.

3. It is a tension that can be sensed in her other writing, where she seems to be constantly appealing to reason and morality to keep her own feelings and desires under control.

4. Uppingham School Archives.

5. Hunter argues that modern readers find it difficult to understand the eighteenth century's 'cultural devotion to didacticism' (Hunter, 1990: 228). He suggests that readers at that time actually enjoyed moral and didactic texts and cites their huge print runs as evidence.

6. Oxford, Bodleian Library, MS.Don.d.198: 42.

7. Lucy was the name of Jane's mother and also of her sister who died in her twenties. The young Lucy's husband was called Thomas Pulleine and there is some evidence that Jane fell out with him.

8. The name Allworthy is generally denotes a character with positive traits (such as in Henry Fielding's *Tom Jones*). In this case 'Manly' does not, although it does so in other books such as in Mary Pilkington's *Henry; or, the Foundling* (1801).

9. MS.Don.d.198: 19.

10. MS.Don.d.198: 31.

11. MS.Don.d.198: 33.

12. MS.Don.d.198: 41.

13. Immel (2002) takes issue with Watson's hypothesis that publishers like Newbery may have borrowed from domestic nursery culture rather than attributing the creation of children's literature to the book trade. Although the book trade and educational philosophies were responsible for some of kinds of texts that were being written, it seems to us that oral culture from the nursery, including stories about good and bad children, would have found their way into print at this time.

14. Oxford, Bodleian Library, MS.Don.d.198: 36. With this bow and arrow George could shoot at birds, mice and butterflies without missing. Kindness to animals, as opposed to cruelty, became an important theme in children's literature later in the century.

15. August 5, 1755. Oxford, Bodleian Library, MS.Don.c.190, fols. 23-24. There is a note by Barbara attached to this letter about the long friendship between the Johnson and the Ingram families which resulted from Henrietta's first visit to Olney. Henrietta's sister Catherine married Michael Wodhull (see Chapter 6).

16. Oxford, Bodleian Library, MS.Don.d.198: 41.

17. Oxford, Bodleian Library, MS.Don.d.198: 25.

18. Oxford, Bodleian Library, MS.Don.d.198: 23.

19. ibid

20. Oxford, Bodleian Library, MS.Don.d.198: 28.

21. See Armstrong 1987 and Hunter 1990.

22. Oxford, Bodleian Library, MS.Don.c.190, fols. 72-102.

23. Oxford, Bodleian Library, MS.Don.d.198: 22.

24. Oxford, Bodleian Library, MS.Don.c.190, fols. 72-102.

25. July 15, 1755. Uppingham School Archives.

26. Oxford, Bodleian Library, MS.Don.d.198: 32.

27. Lincolnshire Archives, Johnson I/2, p.71.

28. Oxford, Bodleian Library, MS.Don.d.198: 42.

29. July 15, 1755. Uppingham School archives.

Chapter 5

Women as Readers: Jane Johnson's Commonplace Book

> Read Homer once, & you need Read no more,
> For all things else appear so mean & Poor
> Verse will seem Prose, yet often on him look
> You will hardly need another Book.
> Jane Johnson (Commonplace Book) [1]

In 1711 Joseph Addison recommended *The Spectator* to members of 'the female World, who aspired to 'move in an exalted Sphere of Knowledge and Virtue' (*Spectator* 10). Between 1755 and 1756, Jane included 43 extracts from this periodical in her commonplace book. Her purpose is clear:

> He [sic] that with attention Reads one Spectator, Guardian, or Tatler every Day of his Life, can't be ignorant of any useful Knowledge; can't fail being an Philosopher, thinking justly, Talking, & writing Elegantly.

From her other entries and what we know about her life, Jane constantly endeavoured to enter into Addison's 'exalted Sphere', merging it with her domestic roles as loving companion to her husband and affectionate mother/teacher to her children. One of the principal ways in which Jane succeeded in this, as the entry above suggests, was through her reading and other literate practices. While becoming less direct, Jane's role as a mother pedagogue did not end as her children left behind their early years; in fact, in some ways it became even more encompassing after, and no doubt, as a result of, her husband's death. In this chapter we shall see how reading and writing provided her with intellectual and moral strength but also consoled her and allowed her to vent her feelings.

In her mid-life, from the safety of her rural estate, but with the experience of having lived in London as a young woman behind her, Jane observed the world and meditated on what she saw through the exemplary thoughts she found in her reading. She may well have seen herself as part of Addison's 'Fraternity of Spectators' which included 'everyone that considers the World as Theatre, and desires to form a right Judgement of those who are the Actors in it' (*Spectator,* 10). Her comments and chosen extracts seem to help her arrive at the 'right' thoughts and judgements about what she saw, both in others and in herself. In his chapter on eighteenth-century studies of reading, Peter de Bolla points out that:

> ... the important thing to note is the perceived relationship of the type of reading matter to the gender of the reader. To read [...] is to make a series of claims for oneself within the contemporary network of social and sexual codes of behaviour'
> (de Bolla, 1989: 236).

We would argue that Jane used the tools of language, humour, irony and satire, both her own and that of others, to fashion herself as the virtuous woman she was expected and wanted to be.

Jane's commonplace book stands at the intersection of three different histories: the history of reading, gender and eighteenth-century culture. It is thus a rich source of information, not only on Jane's specific literate practices, but also because it suggests ways in which this genre allowed women in similar social situations to make sense of texts, themselves and the world around them.

The Commonplace book genre and Jane's notebooks

The practice of keeping commonplace books was revived as a result of humanist education in the sixteenth century by Erasmus and Vives.[2] The primary objective was to imitate the Classic writers and, in the process, to make the text one's own. It was a common practice well into the eighteenth century and, like diaries and letterbooks, commonplace books formed 'an inner library by which identity was shaped through memory and writing.' Kenneth Lockridge points out that this practice is curiously post-modern in the sense that 'while each commonplace book is an effort to assemble culture out of scrap-like bits towards a synthesis of standard moral and social knowledge, each is also unique' (Lockridge, 1992: 2). Later, the practice was endorsed and regulated by Locke (*New Method of a Common-Place-Book,* 1706) and in the eighteenth-century collections of extracts or 'places' were published, as well as personal ones.

Lockridge describes individual commonplace books as 'instruments of self-fashioning' of 'personal identity and even of personal self-justification' (Lockridge, 1992: 4). He describes the genre as very varied, embracing paraphrases, transcriptions, critical commentaries, original compositions and accounts, but mainly reproducing passages from other works. There were several objectives involved in keeping a commonplace book, such as using it for moral guidance, as a memory aid or as a rhetorical exercise in imitating the classics; however, in the end, the process of selection made the text one's own. Entries are linked to other entries, they are used for supporting an argument in both oral and written forms and, most importantly, they help shape the transcriber's view of the world.

Some of the historical readers mentioned in Chapter 2 kept commonplace books, albeit in different forms. In his analysis of Drake's commonplace books from the seventeenth century, for example, Sharpe (2000) distinguishes three genres - proverbs, fables and emblems - through which Drake worked out his personal and political values and then used them as rhetorical tools. Vehicles of ideology, all three genres were considered to impart rules of moral and civil life and were a source of learning for the transcriber. Also from the seventeenth century but more unusual because it was compiled by a woman, is Bowyer's manuscript commonplace book. As we have noted before, Bowyer makes the extracts more personally relevant by altering or omitting words (Burke, 2001). The majority of the quotations are, like Jane's, sententious in nature and like Jane she does not organise them under different headings.

Children probably also compiled commonplace books as a method of learning, although Sharpe (2000) suggests its value as a pedagogic method had declined by the eighteenth century. In 1712 Mather gave his younger children blank notebooks in which 'they were to transcribe passages from their reading that has "most affected" them' (Monaghan, 1991: 356). An example of a nineteenth-century commonplace book is that of Hester Thrale who, as we have mentioned (see Introduction), was also thoroughly involved in the education of her children. She kept a notebook entitled *New Commonplace Book* from 1809 to 1820. James Clifford describes its contents as having descriptions of books and writers but also witty stories and 'a strange jumble of jeux d'esprit, aphorisms, bits of doggerel written by herself and her friends, and shrewd comments on the state of the nation' (Clifford, 1987: 438).[3]

There are two commonplace books in the Jane Johnson archive. The shorter one (with 22 leaves) probably dates from the mid-1730s, around the time of her marriage. We have already discussed some aspects of this booklet (see Chapter 1), beginning with the sentences in code. There are three extracts taken from other texts: *Publius Lentulus's Letter to the Sennate [sic] of Rome conserning [sic] Jesus Christ*; *The Creed of Pope Gregory the Great*; and *Veni Creator Spiritus Translated in Paraphrase by Mr Dryden*. As we mentioned before, the rest of this pocketbook contains what appear to be original compositions which reveal deeply held religious beliefs and take the form of prayers and rather severe self-analysis of moral conduct - not unusual in the young - such as the following:

> 'Examination'
> ... Have I been guilty of Evil-Speaking: have I aggravated it by Speaking ill of my Parents or Governours in Church or State: or of my Neighbour. Have I divulged any Ill I know of them, when neither justice nor Charity required it? have I in my Anger uttered injurious Words ...[4]

Maxims have been inserted at different periods (judging by the ink and handwriting) wherever there was a blank space. There is also a clue as to what Jane saw as the purpose behind her reading:

> When I read, O Lord, Strengthen my Memory,
> That I may always retain those Things that
> May most contribute to my Increase in the
> Knowledge and Love of Thee ...[5]

The second notebook (with 30 folios), which is the commonplace book we shall be focussing on in this chapter, is divided into two sections, headed 1755 and 1756, and contains mainly two kinds of content: transcriptions and her own original compositions, bridged by some paraphrases of original sources. There are approximately 360 entries, written one after the other without much spacing in between, on quarto size sheets beginning with a sheet of paper entitled 'Extracts by my mother' in Barbara Johnson's handwriting. There are 185 entries with a reference, either to a title or to an author. Another 88 are marked with a cross (+) sign and in the margin is a declaration that 'All the Paragraphs marked thus + are my own Jane Johnson 1756'. The remainder have neither reference nor cross mark. Some are probably

Jane's as well (she was not entirely methodical in her referencing) and, while we have been able to trace some to their original sources, others are still unattributed (see Appendix ii for a complete list of references). On some pages, all the entries are marked with the cross, while others contain only copied extracts; out of the last 50 entries, for example, 30 are her own.

Jane turned 50 in 1755; by then her children were growing up and her role as teacher during their early years had ended. With her husband's death in 1756 and her parents and only sister dead, it is not surprising that despite her strength of character, thoughts of her own death (with some premonition?) and a pessimistic view of the state of the world can be seen behind many of her entries, both those extracts copied from others and those she authored. In many of them she appears to console herself by writing and meditating upon virtue, such as in the following example:

> Who would think any Labour too Hard
> When Heaven is to be the wages. Mr Hurd's Sermon 1756.

And she also takes advice, in this case rather severe, from her reading:

> Learn to have no need of other people's help. Turkey Spy. [6]

In her study of the commonplace tradition, Lechner emphasises the importance of moral maxims or commonplaces in educational writings aimed at teaching how to live virtuously, particularly in the sixteenth and seventeenth centuries. This led to

> ...[t]he student's mentality [being] so conditioned by the habit of conceiving of everyone and everything in terms of virtue or vice that when he reached manhood [...] he continued viewing life through the telescope of the commonplace tradition which was focused on virtuous living. (1962: 225)

It is the same sort of 'telescopic vision' that Jane reflects in her writing, in her first notebook from the 1730s to the commonplace book from the 1750s, and including her lesson cards for her children from the 1740s. All these texts are firmly focused on the opposition between virtue and vice. Many of the entries in the commonplace book from 1755-56 in particular explore aspects of these polarities such as reason versus passion, modesty versus vanity, truth versus falsehood etc. Selecting texts that fitted in with this dichotomous view of the world not only reinforced Jane's own moral position, but also almost certainly served to reinforce the moral and religious education of her children as they entered adulthood. Her worries about her children, particularly her sons who were coming of age in a world 'drown'd in Wickedness' and 'Set on Fire with Sin', are evident: [7]

> With what difficulty shall they that have Riches inherit Eternal Life! The Force of Custom, the Charms of Women, Wine, & Gay Company are very strong; Pray God Preserve my sons from the common Vices of a Gentleman's Life …+

Some of the moral positions that are explored can be seen in the prevalent themes that run through the commonplace book. As we have mentioned elsewhere, one of Jane's themes is love. On the positive side there is, above all, the love of and for God, and also the love for her husband and children, both of which were so important in her life. The negative side is the 'passion' of love which only causes trouble:

> I am more & more convinced that there is something criminal in the Passion of Love as well as all other Passions, otherwise it would not be attended with so great anxietys. +

Reaffirming one's beliefs, acquiring knowledge and keeping abreast of current events helped people to think, talk and write in ways that made for an 'agreeable' participation in a society. In the eighteenth century this refinement and sense of gentility are contrasted to the unbridled passions which have the power to sway the best of men and women and need to be regulated by reason, a persistent theme of educational treatises and conduct books. Jane's commonplace book is a form of self-regulation where unreasonable appetites can be checked. Her frequent choice of entries that emphasise using Reason to control Passion, hint at a woman who sought reinforcement from the established (male) authorities in order to do so, but who then took their meaning and made it her own. It might also suggest a woman for whom deep passion was an issue in her own life. A close look at the passages reveals how some extracts are used for supporting personal arguments

Figure 23 page 192

Figure 24 page 193

Figure 25 page 198

Figure 26 page 199

Figure 27 page 207

Figure 17 page 103

Figure 18 page 111

Figure 19 page 183

Figure 20 page 185

Figure 21 page 187

Figure 22 page 189

All illustrations reproduced with the kind permission of the Lilly Library, Indiana University, Bloomington, Indiana

Figure 10 page 81

Figure 12 page 83

Figure 13 page 86

Figure 14 page 88

Figure 15 page 89

Figure 16 page 91

Figure 3 page 4

Figure 5 page 51

Figure 6 page 70

Figure 7 page 76

Figure 8 page 77

Figure 9 page 80

or beliefs;

> The Strength of the Passions will never be accepted as an excuse for Complying with them. Spec. [The Spectator]

> If we had not Passions we could have not Virtue, for all Virtue consists in conquering our Passions, & approving of whatever God permits to happen to us. +

Lockridge suggests that there are moments where a personal crisis can be 'working itself out through the medium of entering bits of print culture into a commonplace book' (Lockridge, 1992: 4). Such seems to be happening at some stages in Jane's writing, particularly when Woolsey died. About a month before his death she writes the only dated entry (followed by lines which are, tantalisingly, crossed out and therefore illegible):

> March 6. 1756
> I [show'd] gave a strong proof of my Courage, made a Bold stand against Vice, but my forces were weak, & the Enemy soon got the better & drove me out of the Field. May Virtue for the future have a more powerful, & more successful Advocate.+

The rest of the world does not interest her, in so far as it does not relate to her personal life or to a particular tragedy like her husband's death. Even her handwriting changes around this period and her unusually sharp, uneven strokes seem to indicate a distressed frame of mind. These entries cannot but be read in this context and probably afforded her some consolation. A few pages after a personal epitaph for Woolsey, she writes:

> Doubtless Woolsey is immortal & happy, let us congratulate the Time of his Decease as the Day of his Nativity ...

The last entry in the notebook, is a poignant indication of her state of mind:

> The sight of you will Clear the Spirits, & Serene the Heart that is clouded with sadness. Turkey Spy

Some entries must have pleased her love of language as well as providing moral support, such as the long poetical quotations from

Homer and Milton. Other entries are less serious and clearly appealed to her sense of humour and her penchant for social satire such as in the following examples:

> What would you give for a Good Husband? More than I would for a bad One. Miss Gukie[sic?]

> The Goddess of Persuasion with all her Charms dwells on his Lips. Labelle Letters[8]

When creating her own entries Jane often uses her wit with the same playful use of language that is found in her lesson cards.

> To be Great and Wicked, is to be Greatly Wicked. +
> To a man that wish'd I would Ride to Hell, No, I assure you that's the last place I'll ever choose to go, because 'tis the <u>most</u> likely one to meet with you again.

> Miss-Conduct, Miss-Behaviour, Miss-Demeanour, Miss-Carriage, Miss-Chiveous, & Miss-Fortune are half a Dozen young Ladies that commonly keep company with each other.[9]

Original sources for Jane's commonplace book

The extracts in Jane's commonplace book are taken from a wide range of text sources including the Bible, theological books, sermons, newspapers, epitaphs, periodicals, the Classics and English and French verse and prose fiction. Although the reading is as varied and 'extensive' as that of most women in her social situation (see Brewer, 1996, Vickery, 1998), she does seem to have read each of the texts carefully, in an 'intensive' manner.[10] As a married woman, mother of four children and household manager, the time Jane had for her own reading would have been more limited and much of it was probably often done in parallel with the books her husband or her children were reading. She probably combined the reading of various genres and read them 'intermittently' over several months as other female readers did (Tadmor, 1996).[11] But despite all her other activities, it does seem clear that reading continued to play a great part in her life judging by the amount and the variety of books she read, or returned to, and which are quoted in her commonplace book.

The most often quoted book is *The Eight Volumes of Letters Writ by a Turkish Spy Who Liv'd Five and Forty Years Undiscovered at Paris*, first published in 1684 by Giovanni Marana and abbreviated by Jane to 'Turkey Spy'. Popular in the late seventeenth and eighteenth centuries, it has been largely neglected since. Through these fictional letters, the author comments satirically on everyday life in France (and European culture in general) from 1637 to 1682, including politics, religion, philosophy, education and science. In her pioneering book, Martha Conant (1908) considers Marana's satire to be the prelude to the 'pseudo-oriental' fiction written in England from the early eighteenth century which saw the first English version of the Arabian Nights as well as introduction of fantastic elements from fairy tales from France. It is the first series of letters written by a 'foreigner' about the country he is visiting and in this case it is a Muslim who makes the more enlightened, and in some cases more liberal, remarks on what he observes. The forty extracts from this book that Jane copies, scattered throughout her commonplace book, are evidence that the volumes were close companions for at least those two years.

Like other fashionable readers of the period, Jane was interested in the oriental and exotic, perhaps again for the way these mirrored her own culture. Lyttleton's *Letters from a Persian* are the first English collection written in imitation of Montesquieu's *Letters Persanes* (1721), where the exotic is used as a vehicle for social and political satire. Conant also suggests that the popularity of this genre was also due to its 'romantic character' and the way it brought to the reader 'something of the magical atmosphere and strange glamour of the East' (Conant, 1908: 247). Brilliant imagery and descriptive language are often used in this genre, as in the passage Jane transcribes from The Spectator (no. 545) which is purported to be a 'A Letter from the Emperor of China to the Pope'. In it, the Emperor is the 'Highest above the Highest under the sun & moon, who sits on a Throne of Emerald' and 'writes with a Quill of a Virgin Ostrich'. The imagery, detail and humour remind us of Jane's own fantastic descriptions in *A Very Pretty Story* and of the scraps she selected from 'lottery sheets' to illustrate her lesson cards.

The 'Turkey Spy' extracts signal her enjoyment of the fictive narrative device which allows satirical social comment, a device also used by Addison and Steele and by at least two of the other writers she quotes from, George Lyttelton (*Letters from a Persian in England*, 1735) and Frank Coventry (*Pompey the Little: or, the Life and Adventures of a Lap-Dog,* 1751). Another example of this form of satire is found in the *Tatler* no. 257, which Jane deems 'excellent' in a marginal note (but doesn't quote, presumably because of its length). It is a description of a supposed travelling show seen in Germany in which waxworks, some of them automated, represent the different religious sects in England at the time (Popery, Jewry, Presbytery, Quakerism etc.) by means of their dress and gesture. This represents another of the themes that runs through the commonplace book: the hypocrisy and corruption of the Christian religions, both Catholic and Puritan, from the moral standpoint of her own Anglicanism. Jane has little sympathy for zealotry or theological quibbles:

> In this canting Enthusiastick age, one may sooner find an hundred saints, than one Honest person.
>
> It is to be wonder'd that the Papists never disputed about what sort of Wood the Cross was made off. +

After the 'Turkey Spy', the most quoted source is *The Spectator*, with 43 mentions in the commonplace book. The *Tatler* gets six mentions and the *Rambler*, one. Jane's affinity with Steele and Addison's views is not surprising given their recognition of female readers and, as Kathryn Shevelow points out, the way in which their literary style draws on the 'virtually homogenous background of female social conditioning' in which the paternal voice of the popular conduct books is 'activated in the very process of reading' (Shevelow, 1986: 121). Needless to say, Jane's reading is dominated by this paternal voice, a voice which places her in a subordinate social position and reinforces conservative values about women's roles and behaviour.[12] However, even though she does not set out to confront them, the fact that Jane sets her voice alongside the male authors suggests a self-confidence that subverts the expected, passive, female response of the time.

Not surprisingly, another large group of extracts comes from the Latin and Greek classics, particularly Juvenal but also Horace, Martial, Plutarch, Plato, Pericles, Plautus and Cato; Pope's translation of Homer's *Iliad* and *Odyssey* is quoted several times and Homer is even the occasion of a verse almost certainly of her own composition (see quote at the beginning of this chapter). Her enthusiasm for Homer can also be found in a rhetorical question inserted after the transcription of a long passage from Pope's translation of *The Iliad*: 'Can any man of sense be tired with reading Homer?'. Jane also attempted her own translation of some of these Classics, perhaps, as we have said, as a result of having to improve herself in subjects such as Latin. In the translation of the following lines from Horace, Jane has taken considerable licence and forfeits fidelity for the rhyme scheme:

Commend not a man 'till He's thoroughly known;
By Praising a Rascal, his Faults are your own.

Commend not, 'till the Man is thoroughly known;
A Rascal prais'd, you make his Faults your own.
Horace 18 Epistle

The rest of the passages appear to be mainly from the Augustan period and from other popular literature of her time, including philosophical and theological treatises, sermons and religious writings, letters and poetry. As we know, her educational methods and materials were influenced by Locke, and in the commonplace book she quotes from *An essay concerning human understanding*. She also takes extracts from Owen Felltham, William Nelson and Moses Browne. Some of the passages are from sermons she may have heard 'live', such as 'Mr Hurd's Sermon' on October 17, 1756.[13] She quotes from published letters, such as one of Lord Bolingbroke's letters to Swift.[14] As for poetry, although less quoted than other genres, there are extracts from Milton, Pope, Swift, Thomson and Young.

There are very few extracts from the increasingly popular genre of the novel; she probably considered most of them 'only for Diversion', but she does quote from Richardson's *Charles Grandison*. There is at least one extract from a play, *The Mourning Bride,* by William Congreve (1697); she may well have seen it performed. Although Jane shows an inclination to read for improvement rather than for entertainment, it may be that at this particular time of her life when she kept the commonplace book there was less room for fiction. Also, considering the eight volumes of 'Turkey Spy' and the length of *Charles Grandison* - as well as all her other duties - there cannot have been much time for other novels. The fact that she took something from them, however, indicates her willingness to give them the same status as more openly didactic texts in terms of what they can teach the reader.

Jane's original compositions

Jane was clearly a deeply religious woman who felt God beside her in all her multiple tasks, including the act of writing itself. Diaries, journals and spiritual autobiographies were commonly kept by genteel women, and many of them also wrote poetry, however, Jane mixes both of them in her notebooks. The following extract - one of the few in the commonplace book that uses the first person and allows us a glimpse into a more intimate experience - places her as both author and 'enactor' of her own lines:

> I have experienced that it is good & profitable to begin & end everything we do & say with the Name of God, he that doth otherwise will either fail in the progress or the end of his Design. There-fore before I begin any action I always say the following Lines

> Since I no Labour Dare begin
> Till Heaven I first Adore,
> Thy Blessing on the Work, O God
> And Workman I implore.

Her shorter moral verse (several examples of which are found in the commonplace book and the lesson cards) is calculated to be easily memorised by her children and was perhaps included in her letters to them at school:

> You may tell a fine Tale
> But the Truth will prevail.

> Do your Best, & for the Rest,
> Trust in God & you'll be Blest.

At other times Jane makes her point through stark, powerful images and does not hesitate to use strong language:

> When Old Batchelors Die they will be changed into Jack-Asses to carry the Whores to Hell. +

She experiments with analogy, simile and metaphor and includes everyday objects and common experiences, perhaps with the intention of using them with her children.

To regard what people say of us is, to just as much purpose as to fret at the swarms of flies in summer. 'tis best to get out to the noise [crossed out: '& hearing of'] of their Buzzing.

Knowledge of God without a suitable Practice (or Faith without Works) is like a Bell without a clapper: The Bell may be as good a Bell as ever artist made, but for any use it is of, it might as well have remain'd in the Bowels of the Earth. +

Always be upon your Guard when you meet with people that are unaccountable civil. For under the Fairest Grass often times Lurks the most venomous Snake. +

The following example is one of several cases where two and even three versions of one particular idea follow each other on the page (emphasis not in the original):

To have a Right Judgment in all things *is only to be* expected *from* Angels.

We ought always to Labour for *perfection* but must *never expect* to attain it.

To have a *Right Judgment in all things* is too great a privilege, and *perfection* for a *mortal*.

In other cases, Jane adds her own comments to a copied extract:

Of all the Evils under the Sun, that of making Vice commendable is the Greatest.
Tat[ler] 191
of this fault every Lady is guilty, that admires & commends a man for being a Rake. +

Like Anne Bowyer, she also adds and changes the ending of Thomson's *Winter* poem, transforming it into a short prayer (her additions are in italics - see footnote):

Father of Light & Life thou Good Supreme!
O! teach me what is Good; teach me thy Self.
Save me from folly, Vanity, & Vice,
From every Low pursuit, feed my Soul
With Knowledge, Peace & Virtue, & preserve
my body in Health, in Ease & cheerfulness.

for Jesus Christ his sake Amen.[15]

In a sense it is not necessary to know which are Jane's original compositions and which are not, given that she makes all the texts her own as she captures them in her notebook. They reveal a knowledge both of the word and of the world which is put into the service of affirming beliefs to herself and transmitting them to her children. Her beliefs are obviously linked to her Anglicanism, but they are also part of the world view of other 'genteel' women who are able to reflect on their position as women, and also as readers. Although Jane does not gloss or cross-reference her entries as some other commonplace book-keepers did, as she interposes her own aphorisms, verses, observations and prayers among the published texts, these become a kind of critical comment, a very personal and intimate kind of reader response. This practice supports Sharpe's conclusion that 'the commonplace method made every educated Englishman or woman into a reader who very much made his or her own meaning.' (Sharpe, 2000: 41)

Reading like Jane: Pedagogue, spectator, actress and interpreter

As a woman, wife and mother Jane could not be merely a spectator: she was also a 'performer' on the 'world stage', and in the theatre of the eighteenth century, her role as a genteel female 'actress' was meant to be even more virtuous than that of her fellow players. Like Christian in *Pilgrim's Progress* she must engage in dialogues with the likes of Vanity, Modesty, Idleness and Honesty and win her arguments through the perceived wisdom of the texts that are available to her and through her own reflections:

> ... what can be more comfortable to the mind than Calmness? What more troublesome than Passion? What more at rest than Clemency? What so full of Business as cruelty? Modesty & Chastity enjoy a perfect Leisure, whilst Lust is ever lived with Laborious pursuits.

However, she is not just content to learn her lines by rote; she makes them her own through her selective process and in the ways she links them. She appropriates and rearranges language so that she is not simply taking the meanings intended by the authors, but applying them to her own situation. For example, the following extracts appear one after another in a logical line of thought that connects female beauty with virtue and situates them both within the private, domestic sphere:

> I love to find Virtue in a fair Lodging. (Sr. Philip Sidney)
> It is an old saying that the woman of good Reputation is she that has nothing said of her.
>
> There is no charm in the Fair Sex that can supply the Place of Virtue. Spec[tator]
>
> Female Virtues are of a Domestick turn, the Family is the proper province for private women, to Shine in, aspire after those virtues only that are peculiar to your sex, follow your native modesty, & think it your highest commendation, not to be talk'd off one way or other. Pericles's Oration

When it came to women's conduct, Jane was quick to pick out those extracts that reflected her own critical observations. Her wit matched the sharpness of her eye for detail, and the two were often paired in her satirical comments on vain, idle and empty-headed woman. According to Michael Ketchum, in *The Spectator* 'Steele shows the social world to be a continual process of acting, observing, and evaluating, an intricate process of measuring other people according to their behaviour and adjusting our responses to them' (Ketchum, 1985: 52). Jane does this as she reflects on women and the fashionable world and customs such as painting one's face or on affectation, for example:

> She smiles so impertinently, & affects to please so sillily that you see the simpleton from Head to Foot.

In comparison to diaries and journals which are usually seen as private, self-conscious sites where the individual can display agency, the commonplace book appears to have little space for individual acts. However, in Jane's case, the selection and interweaving of her own compositions with the extracts creates both intra-textual and inter-textual dialogues on the level with the mainly male-authored texts. As Sharpe argues, 'far from a retreat into private space, the commonplace book is the site of successive conversations between text and reader and text and society' (Sharpe, 2000: 281).

From the Renaissance onwards there was a recognition that readers had an independent role to play in the interpretation of texts, and authors either encouraged or tried to restrict this freedom. For example, in the section entitled 'to the reader' in Owen Felltham's *Resolves divine, moral, political* (1677) - also quoted by Jane - the author appeals 'to every man's just liberty, to approve or dislike as he pleases' (quoted in Sharpe, 2000: 337). This 'liberty', however, was not without its risks, as women also had the power to 'reconstruct the poem or use it for their own purposes, a power that sometimes causes anxiety in male poets but is sometimes actively solicited by them' (Pearson, 1996: 87).[16] This was particularly true for female readers engaged in solitary reading. The 'text-fear', as de Bolla calls eighteenth-century reading theories' increasing obsession with what and how women read, was mainly about novel-reading, but it was also about readers finding unintended meanings in the text. Given they were meant to reproduce received (patriarchal) wisdom, commonplace books could ostensibly provide a more secure space for observation and reflection as opposed to private diaries where unchecked emotions could be impulsively set down.

Although Jane does not comment critically on the books she reads or the texts she copies in the commonplace book, she does mention one of her contemporary's response to Richardson's *Clarissa* in a letter from 1749. She makes it clear that she thinks this negative response has to do with this reader's personal experience and character rather than with the novel itself:

> ... Mrs Hackshaw's Fine Taste & Judgement [...] possibly may be very good, tho' she does not approve of Miss Clarissa Harlow, for perhaps her dislike of that story may proceed from a consciousness of its reproaching her own conduct [...] Any person who after they have read it quite through, & do not commend it, but I shall conclude that they have either a bad heart, or a bad head, or both, for in such case the fault must be some where & I am sure there is none in the Book.[17]

As we have shown in Chapter 3, she regarded comprehension and the ability to make informed judgements as a part of reading and was critical of those who read without becoming any the wiser:

> Such a One is acquainted with the Surface of things, & has Read just enough to make him impertinent. Spec[tator].

In Jane's commonplace book, there are two entries where she does engage with questions of the construction of meaning and interpretation. In both cases, the text in question is scripture. The first one (which is unreferenced, but the underlining suggests it is her words and emphasis) is a gloss of one of the commandments and implies an exploration of the meaning of the term 'love' within this particular context:

> That saying of our Saviours in which he commands us to Love our neighbour as ourselves seems, not so fitly to be interpreted of the Degree of Love, as of the Truth & Sincerity of it.

While some interpretations of scripture may be more 'fit' than others, different possibilities of interpretation do not however apply to this text. As we can see from the following comment, the meaning itself is 'Plain', and it is not for the reader to 'guess' at meaning. The reader has no control over what will be mysteriously revealed or when this revelation may happen:

> The Scripture are not set forth as a Riddle for every one to Guess at, but every thing that is necessary for any one to Believe, & Practice, is so Plain, that those that Run may Read it, & a Way-Faring man tho' a Fool shall not Err herein. Therefore those parts that are mysterious to any one, don't relate to them, but were wrote for different Persons, or different Times, & by those Persons, & at those Times were, or will be, well understood. + [18]

If Jane had any criticism of her readings, she did not set it down on paper. However, through the act of inclusion and exclusion of texts, she makes her preferences and her judgements clear.

A wise and virtuous woman

Jane's case study poses the same problems and questions that are applied to readers in other historical periods. To understand what she read, how she read and what it meant to her is to understand how she thought (Darnton, 1984: 210). This applies to Jane, not only as a reader and writer (as well as author, illustrator and editor of hand-made primers and other learning materials for her children), but also as a teacher, mother and social woman. The commonplace book raises many questions we cannot hope to answer, questions which would help us understand her many acts of reading. For example: Did she keep notebooks during other periods of her life? (It seems to us extremely likely that she did.) Did her reading change before and after marriage? Did Woolsey make suggestions or intervene in her reading choices? Did she share the notebook with him or with her children?[19] How often did she come back to her books and her notebooks - if indeed she did?

Finally, why did Jane choose to read the particular texts from which she took the extracts, and how did they come to be in her possession?

Jane did not read or write in order to publish or to stand out in the public domain by making brilliant and witty conversation. She and other genteel ladies read to improve themselves, to become better companions for their spouses and more knowledgeable teachers for their children. However, Jane's private writing, in particular her notebooks and letters, reveal the extent to which an eighteenth-century woman was able to construct herself through her reading, through seeing herself as a reader, through selecting particular messages and ignoring others and through modifying and appropriating particular codes. For example, in the 'Clarissa' letter mentioned above, before commencing her own moral 'story', she wishes for 'Rhetorick & Eloquence to put my sentiments in proper light'.[20] Language is thus linked to improvement, as wisdom is linked to virtue. Jane writes:

> To be wise is to be Good, & to be Good is to be wise, for Wisdom is Goodness, & Goodness is Wisdom.

and

> If you would be perfectly wise, study the Bible, the Universe, & Learn to know thyself.

As we have seen, Jane's 'goodness' was inextricably linked to her 'thinking justly, talking eloquently and writing elegantly' but also to a knowledge of herself. That she managed to encourage these same virtues and skills in her children is evident from their own literate practices as adults, discussed in the next chapter.

Notes

1. Unless otherwise stated, all the following references to Jane's texts are from Oxford, Bodleian Library, MS.Don.c.190, fols. 72-102. We have left Jane's original spelling in all transcriptions from her notebooks.

2. Sister Johan Marie Lechner's (1962) detailed study of the concept of the commonplace goes back to the Graeco-Roman classical writers and to its links with rhetorical training and moral instruction.

3.   As far as we were able to find out, there are no other commonplace books that have survived by women in roughly the same period as Jane's.

4.   Oxford, Bodleian Library, Ms.Don.e.193.

5.   ibid

6.   From Giovanni Marana's *Letters Writ by a Turkish Spy* (1684). We are indebted to Victor Watson for identifying this reference.

7.   Jane writes that this vision of a corrupt world 'is the exact picture of Great Britain at the present time Anno Domi 1755.'

8.   We were unable to find any information on either of these two references.

9.   These young ladies are reminiscent of those that appear in Pamela's story for Miss Goodwin: Coquetilla, Prudiana, Profusiana and Prudentia (*Pamela* vol. II).

10.   The distinction between reading 'extensively' and 'intensively' which was proposed by Rolf Engelsing refers to the period up to around 1750. Darnton disagrees with this simplistic division and Jane's is a case in point, as we could argue that she read both ways. See Darnton 1986: 12.

11.   The repetition of a couple of quotations in different places in the notebook suggests she went back to these particular texts after some time and forgot she had already transcribed them.

12.   There do not appear to be any extracts from women authors.

13.   That she probably read other theological works by Hurd is possible given his enthusiastic praise of Milton, Spenser and Richardson (Young, 2001), all quoted in the commonplace book.

14.   This particular letter (from 1723) was published as a postscript to a letter to Pope from Swift in Mr Pope's Literary Correspondence vol. 5, for E. Curll in 1737.

15.   *Father of Light, and Life! Thou Good Supreme!*
      O! teach me what is Good! teach me thy self!
      Save me from Folly, Vanity and Vice,
      From every low Pursuit! and feed my Soul,
      With Knowledge, conscious Peace, and Vertue pure,
      Sacred, substantial, never-fading Bliss!
      James Thomson (Winter)

16.   As Pearson shows, just a century earlier, women's reading was associated with disease, madness, rebellion and 'transgression of the boundaries of acceptable femininity' (Pearson, 1996: 86).

17.   Oxford, Bodleian Library, MS.Don.c.190, fols. 11-12.

18. Mandelbrote points out that children of different denominations were taught to read the Bible in particular ways and that 'the Church of England was most prescriptive in urging that certain parts of the Bible, notably prophecy, were unsuitable reading for ordinary people' (Mandelbrote, 2001: 46) He uses this same quote by Jane Johnson to illustrate this point.

19. Sharpe (2000) points to another difference between diaries and commonplace books: the latter were often lent and borrowed. We have no evidence that anyone else except Jane's daughter Barbara read her commonplace book, and this reading took place, in all likelihood, after her mother's death.

20. Oxford, Bodleian Library, MS.Don.c.190, fols. 11-12.

Chapter 6

Reading the World of Adults: The Letters and Journals of Robert and Barbara Johnson

'I am at present for grave reading deeply engaged in Paley's moral philosophy [...] for afternoons [...] Boswell's *Life of Johnson* furnishes abundance of amusements ...
Robert Augustus[1] Johnson to Barbara Johnson[2]

Reading the past

The past is a foreign country.[3] It is impossible for those of us writing in the early twenty-first century to imagine life as it might have been more than two hundred years ago. As Porter puts it, 'nothing could be sillier than to tightlace the dead into today's conceptual corsets. The most we can hope is to understand them...' (Porter, 2000: xxiii). Sharpe and Zwicker also remind us that reading has a history with forms and practices from a past that is 'neither universal nor natural but culturally specific and culturally constructed' (Sharpe and Zwicker, 2003: 1). Even so, Sharpe makes the case for richly textured case studies of readers from the past in order to better understand the history of reading. He explains that whereas 'until recently the reader was perhaps the most neglected element in the framework of literary communication, the shift from concentration on authors' intentions to the performances of texts led obviously to readers' (Sharpe, 2000: 34).

In this chapter we follow Sharpe's advice by embracing 'the reader as central actor (who) newly opens and extends the text in all the interpretive communities and exegetical circumstances of its unfolding history' (Sharpe and Zwicker, 2003: 25). Darnton also suggests that it should be possible to discover the social dimensions of thought and to tease meaning from documents by relating them to the surrounding world of significance, passing from text to context and back again until he [sic] has cleared a way through a foreign mental world (Darnton, 1985: 14).

Reading, along with its surrounding artefacts, activities and attitudes, amounts to a substantial portion of family legacies. From generation to generation, what is passed on by reading and writing becomes very much part of inherited culture and values. It also becomes a source for others to place and 'understand' a particular family and its history. We attempt, therefore, to investigate a slice of eighteenth-century English cultural history in the 'ethnographic grain' by examining the books and ideas discussed and quoted in the letters and journals of Jane's children when they reached adulthood.[4] Robert and Barbara are our chosen subjects whom we illustrate by setting out their thematic interests, favourite genres, and comparative contexts for analysis. We also show how gender and reading interact, and how life stages determine the what, when, and how of reading, as well as the interactions generated and sustained by reading. Mostly, however, we allow the voices of our writers to speak for themselves, believing that the Johnson family texts give us a point of entry into the way people read, wrote and thought in the eighteenth century.

Jane's children as literate adults

Jane was clearly an affectionate mother who tried to steer her children in the direction of a happy, moral and well informed adulthood through the reading matter she provided for them and by the example she set. We have shown elsewhere how Jane's enlightened views on education offered her children aesthetically attractive reading lessons which incorporated storytelling and poetry, as well as many references to the arts, wider society and the everyday world of ordinary folk. In this chapter, we try to investigate what reading meant to her family as they grew up and how their childhood and education might have influenced the literate adults they were to become.

We follow the Johnson children into adulthood through their reading and writing. We know about aspects of their young lives from Jane's letters to them and others, from what we can learn about their schooling and from the evidence at our disposal to imagine their responses to their mother's reading materials and *A Very Pretty Story*. Much of this is using conjecture from the indications available, as well as our knowledge of children, texts and reading in the eighteenth century. But once the children became adults, we have first hand accounts of their lives through the letters they assiduously wrote to each other, through their wills and family documents, and through the journals Robert kept.

Although Jane's children led rather different lives, the tone of their letters suggests they were extremely fond of one another and gained satisfaction from keeping closely in touch with what everyone was doing, reading and thinking. Indeed, Jane's adult offspring and their close friends could almost be described as forming an unofficial reading group, certainly a community of readers, for the second half of the eighteenth century, as they regularly recommended, loaned, acquired and discussed books among themselves.

Reading in England during the Enlightenment

Before we explore the particularities of the Johnsons' literary diet, we need to refer the reader back to what has gone before in this book, where we examine the context and nature of reading in the eighteenth century. The Johnsons lived at a time of change when certainties that had been taken for granted were being thrown up in the air. Take religion: as Porter puts it, 'many of Europe's greatest minds concluded that, in the search for truth, neither implicit faith in the Bible nor automatic reliance on the Ancients would any more suffice' (Porter, 2000: 52). Ideas on education were in a similar state of flux, particularly after the publication of Rousseau's *Émile* (1762) which brought the author Europe-wide celebrity. Hume and other influential voices argued against learning being 'shut up in colleges and cells', while Dr Johnson praised Addison as 'the first great media man', bringing 'Philosophy out of Closets and Libraries, Schools and Colleges, to dwell in Clubs and Asssemblies, at Tea-Tables and in Coffee-Houses' (Porter, 2000: 88).

Moreover, as we have indicated elsewhere, print culture in England was undergoing a revolution and becoming less expensive, so relatively cheap sets of popular novels and English poets appeared on the market and were made available to a much wider readership. Book clubs and circulating libraries spread like wildfire, so that Dr Johnson was able to describe England as 'a nation of readers' by the middle of the eighteenth century (Porter, 2000: 94). His own *Dictionary*, which was published in 1755, was sold in weekly sections at sixpence as well as in a handsome book version. Porter argues that 'reading became second nature to a major swathe of the nation [... proffering] an admission ticket into the cultural magic circle [...] Indeed, the key polarity in Georgian England was that between those swimming in the metropolitan culture pool created by print and those excluded' (Porter, 2000: 77). Reading itself had been seen as a source of empowerment by enlightened thinkers for some time: Pope advocated reading in his poetry; Cobbett's inspiration for his *Rural Rides* stem from his early reading; while Edward Gibbon (one of Robert's favourite authors) talks of his 'invincible' love of reading which 'I would not exchange for the treasures of India' (Gibbon, 1796: 36).

The rest of this chapter is devoted to examples from the siblings' journals and letters. We have tried to situate Barbara and Robert within the context of their time, but whether we have managed to *understand* them, in Porter's terms, is open to question.

Reading Robert Johnson's private writing

Robert kept a journal intermittently between 1771 and 1777, between the ages of 26 and 32. He begins as a well-to-do young man and his journals cease at a point where he has become a devoted husband and father of two children, still enjoying life, but having had to face poor health and the loss of a baby son. They also tell of his busy social life with many friends who include baronets and peers, but also embrace the lads with whom he lays bets, the local doctor, and older married women he gossips with. Although his marriage involved a step of upward mobility, Robert gained easy acceptance into the bosom of his wife's family - Nan was the sister of William, the sixth Lord Craven.[5] Yet his regular trips to Witham tell of his closeness and loyalty to his family of origin. Robert makes regular reference to all kinds of literature in his diaries, frequently copying quotes from his favourite authors. A list of the sources of his reading is provided in Appendix iii.

The Culture of politeness

Robert is quintessentially the 'polite' gentleman. The culture of 'politeness' in the eighteenth century was related to good breeding and inner moral virtue made manifest in society through the cultivation of refined manners and expression.[6] Robert's willingness to reveal his emotions openly without being afraid of being judged weak or effeminate is another sign that he was part of 'polite culture'.

Robert's journals showcase his polite credentials - including a love of learning, while avoiding heavy erudition. On the one hand, Robert is clearly something of an intellectual, eager for knowledge, keen to discuss ideas, interested in philosophy, history and the big ideas of his time. On the other hand, Robert is not averse to enjoying himself and he is often engaged in shooting, at the races, dancing at balls, and playing cards. He gives attention to the arts - painting, sculpture, music, theatre, architecture and poetry all delight him and demand his attention. We also find him writing in his journal about subjects as various as the cost of being a student at a Scottish university and details of Latin American history, all based on texts he had been reading at the time. Although being a polite gentleman included many refinements which helped to distinguish the gentry from the 'lower' classes, it also involved an obligation to be courteous to those of other ranks. Like many another genteel gentleman of the late eighteenth century, Robert pursued moderate, rational pleasures which allowed him to mix decorously in society with his own sex and with the ladies. However, he was never impervious to a pair of sparkling eyes.

26 Sept 1775
Lady Craven's business with Harborne was concluded, set off immediately with Charles for Astrop Goose Feast. Got there as they were beginning to dance. Danc'd two dances with Kitty.[7] Am engaged to dance with her next Goose Feast. The lovely dancer has the most beautiful eyes in the world. Miss Hervey agreeable. Miss Sheppard handsome.[8]

Like other diarists of the eighteenth century, Robert also used his journals to explore the emotional lifts and setbacks that cannot easily be voiced to others. As Julia Martin shows in some of the diaries she studies, these narratives 'served a purpose in analysing and classifying personal experience, not so that it stood out as unique, but so that it conformed to a pleasing, unified pattern' (Martin 2002: 202). In doing this, Robert was also reflecting on how to conduct himself in his relationships with others. Some of these examples echo Jane's firm resolve to subdue unruly passions.

2 Jan 1772
How very difficult it is at all times to command our tempers, even on trifling occasions, but tho' it may not be in our power to prevent feeling disagreeable sensations, we may at all times be able to keep them to ourselves. How comfortable is the sensation afterwards that arises from not having given way to expressions dictated by passion.[9]

7 June 1772
When we speak in commendation of our friends we ought to be very careful to praise them only for qualifications they really possess, and not for those they have not; a fault that an overstrained partiality frequently leads to.[10]

Robert in love

Some of the most moving entries in the journals document Robert's state of mind as he falls in love with Nan. Robert isn't one to wear his heart on his sleeve, but a few comments and quotations that crop up in the middle of accounts of travel, sporting and social events, hint at his growing attachment. (Sadly, the journal of his marriage year is missing.) Interestingly, it wasn't always poetry or personal writing which inspired Robert to thoughts of love, though he is clearly enraptured (like half of Europe) with Rousseau's *La Nouvelle Heloise*. In the example which follows, Robert considers the anguish as well as the joy of love after reading Adam Ferguson's essay on the history of civil society.

17 June 1771
The company of a beloved object may increase our affection to a degree we before thought ourselves incapable of.

Happiness is not that state of repose, or that imaginary freedom from care, which at a distance seems so desirable but with its approach brings a tedium or a langour more unsupportable than pain itself.
(from Ferguson's *An Essay on the History of Civil Society* Section viii 'On Happiness')

A week later, we find Robert reflecting judiciously on love and human nature.

24 June 1771
When our affections are centred on one object, we look on the whole world beside with an eye of indifference scarce to be conceived but by those who have felt it. Great part of our happiness arises from being deceived, true philosophy then consists in our agreeably deceiving ourselves. A great deal of our happiness or misery is in our own power.[11]

The final entry in this section sees Robert anticipating connubial happiness:

> 1 Jan 1773
> *At Witham with my brothers. That every year may bring with it as*
> *pleasing prospects as seventy-two, is the happiest wish I can form for*
> *myself.[12]*

Indeed, Robert married Nan on 21 January 1773 at St. Andrews Church in Ogbourn, Wiltshire. The relationship between them went on to fulfil Wrightson's description of late eighteenth-century couples viewing marriage 'as a practical and emotional partnership' (Vickery, 1998: 86).

A Family man in Georgian England

> 19 April 1775
> *Nan went upstairs to bed at ten in perfect health without a complaint.*
> *Soon after she had some slight pains and was seized with a shivering*
> *fit, we immediately sent for Holyoake who came in an hour and*
> *quarter (though he was in Bed and fast asleep at the time George got*
> *to Warwick, and George had the horse to saddle when he went from*
> *hence). Nan's pains came on very quick between eleven and twelve,*
> *and a quarter of an hour after one o'clock on Thursday morning April*
> *20th she was deliver'd of a Boy, and in a little more than half an hour*
> *afterwards of a girl. They were baptised the same day by the names of*
> *Robert Augustus[13] and Maria. The Boy is the largest child, but they*
> *are both well and hearty, though neither of them are so brisk, so large,*
> *or so stout as Harriet when she was born.[14]*

While it is easy to imagine Robert writing the passage quoted above in an excited letter to a close sibling or friend, it does raise the question as to why he felt the need to write in such detail for a private journal at such a busy time in his life. Did he expect to share that journal entry with someone else? Did he wish to remind himself about that evening at a later date? Did he feel that writing it down would help him come to terms with a momentous event in his life? Did he write in the white heat of the moment in order to copy out later to others in letters? We can only speculate.

For his time, Robert seems to have been unusually involved in the intimacies of family life. For example, he documents the birth of his twins in excited detail and recounts that the breast-feeding[15] was going well. He is close to his eldest daughter, Harriet, noting everything from her first tooth and first steps, to her emerging personality. All the indications suggest that he and Nan kept a happy if slightly chaotic household. The extracts which follow show Robert's engagement with his children[16] - no remote father here. The little down-to-earth touches are reminiscent of Jane's letters.

25 April 1775
We trusted Harriet for the first time alone on the grass plot, she walked very well. She has got three double teeth and six single ones, but does not yet attempt to talk.[17]

Sometimes for no apparent reason (unlike Pepys who used bad French to hide sexual indiscretions in his famous diary), Robert breaks into French for several pages at a time, making occasional grammatical and idiomatic mistakes.

30 March 1771
Le plus heureuse jour de ma vie.[18]

10 Jan 1775
Little Harriet [...] I think that she will be bien vive, on peut en voir a present bien less commencement ...[19]

8 Jan 1776
Nan and myself returned to Bath. Snow on the ground - 5 and a half hours by Chippenham [...] The children at H/B are very good - they are kept remarkably quiet and silent & seem dull and heavy, mine are constantly talk'd to, are riotous and troublesome [...] Neither Nan or myself have a good knack at bringing up prettily behaved children, I own I like children much better than formal, premature men and women.[20]

With his happy disposition, Robert counts his blessings and makes the best of the troubles that come his way. We are in little doubt that he prefers his children 'riotous and troublesome' to 'silent & dull'. In fact, the final sentence speaks volumes about Robert's liberal views on childhood.

Observations of nature

Robert's journals also highlight his reflections on the visual world. Eighteenth century poets and writers presented their readers with sublime visions of nature through detailed descriptions - the particular leading to reflections on the infinite. Scientific learning and knowledge was also considered to begin with close observation of the natural world. As a child, Robert had been guided by his mother's lessons to notice even the smallest animals and plants, to note what seasons they appear in, where they can be found, and their colours and sizes. These observations not only encouraged an appreciation of the beauty of God's world, but also the acquisition of knowledge about land and farming. Robert is close to his mother but also close to later observers, such as Dorothy Wordsworth, who also wrote about nature in simple, direct, yet evocative language.

13 May 1775
Saw a field of rye in ear near the oaks going to Stoneleigh. But Dr Wilmot tells me the field of rye on the right hand going to Wootton was in ear the sixth of the month. The Mulberry tree in Mrs Bird's garden is now budding, the buds look green, and there is one leaf full out.[21]

6 July 1775
Rode with my brothers to see the ruins of Crowland Abbey. It is about 16 miles from Witham across the Fen which was this summer remarkably dry. The variety of birds you see constantly flying about in the fen have a pretty appearance.[22]

Also like Dorothy Wordsworth, Robert's accounts of the natural world are often interlinked with informal observations of people, especially children.

1 March 1775
The spring is uncommonly forward. I have seen violets, some apricots with blossom full out, some hawthorns cover'ed with leaves and the ground enameld with daisys and primroses.[23]

30 April 1775
*Saw today two or three bushes of whitethorn in bloom. The two little ones thrive apace, probably owing to Nan's having milk enough for them both.*24

24 March 1777
Harriet gathered a cowslip in the field ...[25]

Social engagements

Although he adored his family, Robert enjoyed a full and active social life. Social events provided a space for meeting with friends and making the acquaintance of politicians, artists and members of the aristocracy. It also provided an opportunity for observing human nature. Robert often makes shrewd comments on the character of people he encounters.

21 April 1771
Went with Webb to Bromley rerturn'd in the evening and at eleven o'clock set out for Exeter in the post coach, lay at Blandford. Miss Hilliard of Warminster a pretty, sweetly good humoured girl. Good humour never fails to please. Set off again at four o'clock. Got to Exeter in the evening without being greatly fatigued. A fine open country from Dorchester to Bridport, but more rich and beautiful from B to Ex, particularly so about Charmouth to Honiton vale.[26]

30 Sept 1775
Came with the Wodhulls from Astrop at five in the morning, got home as the sun rose, slept two hours and got up perfectly well and in good spirits. Russell dined at Thenford. The most agreeable man I know, clever v sensible, Charles Bathhurst v clever. Charles Willes has great drollery. Whitmore an eccentric Bore.[27]

21 March 1777
I played whist and was miserably beat at the Rev Mr Martyns.[28]

In the following extract, Robert details a fortnight's social activities in Bath during the Autumn of October 7 - 16, 1775.

Rode to preach with Russell at Somerton, a good fine country.
Wrote to Mrs Williams. We all drank tea and play'd at cards at Mrs Wards [...]
General charity sermon for Bath Hospital [...] Mrs Napier dined and supped here - most agreeable woman.
I at the Ball - much crowded 805 people - danced with Miss Burgess
All at the play - the West Indian with Irish Widow - Mrs Didier great at the latter[29]
Mrs Craven and Madam Ann[30] at Fishers concert, a good one- 736 people
Madam Ann had around 100 people room too full.
A Fast on account of the American War which we did not keep.
At a route at Mrs Easton's, play'd whist.
Went with Mr Weston to see Mr Charles Hamilton's pictures. Inside views of St Peter's, St Paul's and the Pantheon - capital. A landscape- Rocks - good[31]

It is interesting to look more closely at what is presumably a typical fortnight in Bath during the season. There is a strong sense of business, bustle and jostling crowds in Robert's hectic social calendar. (How did he come up with such exact numbers, too large to count - 736 at concert; 805 at the ball?) Mixing in polite society with its dances, dinners, conversations and card games was part of the regular fabric of his life. Significant time was also taken up with the arts - music, theatre, painting and poetry (see below) which are generally commented on, albeit briefly. Nor is the more serious side of life ignored as Robert's diary includes charitable work, preaching and politics. One wonders whether they did not keep the fast 'on account of the American War' because they did not believe Britain's stance was the right one, or because they were not prepared to do without their supper.

In sickness and in health

Robert and his brothers suffered various ailments as the years went on, usually without much fuss, though Charles writes at some length about his gout and hearing loss. Robert's winter move to Bath was probably as much for health as social reasons. His children catch the usual childish illnesses of their time and it is moving to note his anxiety for their recovery (see also Letters section below). Although the family is quite well to do, it is clear that the parents themselves minister to the children when they are sick. The women seem to take illness in their stride, or were lucky in their constitutions, as there is very little reference to poor health for Nan or Barbara, except that the latter complains about her eyes as she gets older.[32]

In the journal entries that follow, Robert's recent illness makes him mindful of thanking God for his blessings. Despite his optimism, he had to spend another miserable winter in Bath trying out various remedies such as cold baths.

> 1 Jan 1775
> *Comfortably settled in our house at Bath, began this year with every pleasing prospect. My having my health and hearing perfectly restored to me which I have every reason to hope from a return of the warm weather, will leave me hardly anything to wish for that this World can bestow. Let me not forget the gratitude due to the Almighty hand that has so plentifully showered down his blessings on me, but remember to*

look up with love and reverence to the author of all good and obey by
properly enjoying the bounties his benificent hand has provided.[33]

1 August 1776
... my two little girls come on apace, though poor Harriet is still
plagued with her teeth, but Maria with the form of a fairy has the good
luck to enjoy the constitution of a Hercules ...[34]

3 June 1777
Wrenched the cartilage of my knee by turning myself in bed. Holyoak
worked it about and applied a cold poultice of Port wine and oatmeal
with a v little spirits of Wine in it, bound it on and desired me to wet it
two or three times with port wine and lie on the bed all day. I could
not stir my leg at first without its giving me violent pain, but in the
evening the inflammation was gone and I could move it a little, and the
next morning I was able to walk about with a stick.[35]

Like many men at that time, Robert was interested in his health,
observant about his body and kept an eye on developments in
medicine. He kept annual accounts of how much he and his brothers
weighed with or 'without anything in pockets'. Although he is
energetic, Robert is clearly the smallest and slightest of the three
brothers who all weigh significantly less than equivalent men of their
age today.

4 July 1775
Set out to go to Witham. Lay at Uppingham and got to W to dinner
next day.
 Weighed in this morning in shoes without anything in pockets
Brother 11..4..13 and a half ounces
Charles 11..9..14 ounces
Robert   9..6..12 and a half ounces[36]

Travellers' tales

Whatever the difficulties of travel in the eighteenth century, Robert gets
about a lot, concentrating on the areas around his homes and those of
his family and friends. On his journeys he tells us about the weather,
nature, the state of the roads: we know the inns he slept in, the number
of miles he travelled and many of the interesting examples of
architecture, landscapes, gardens, manor houses, churches, castles (and
their history) along the way. Early in the journals, we encounter him as
a single young man, out and about on his horse, in a carriage or the
post coach.

23 May 1771

*Mr Waters of B capable of being made a very fine place, but at present
every object convinces you of the more than Gothic ignorance of the
owner.*[37]

5 July 1771

*Drove Mr Curteis to Richmond. The prospect from the Star and
Garten very rich in wood. Nothing can be finer than the water, but the
country is too flat. In the views to the left from the park toward
Hampstead and Highgate the ground lies much better [...] Jacob's
contrivance for turning carriages in a small space excellent ...*[38]

15 Sept 1773

*Left Kenilworth. To Swan, Warwick To George, Shipstone 17m .a
small market town. To Chappel House 10 m. To Woodstock 10 m.
(Black Bear) not a v large town. remarkable only as being so near
Blenheim. The country from Warwick to Long Compton v. rich and
fine [...] From the top of Edge Hill beyond Long Compton it is more
open, some v extensive views. Walked into Blenheim gate. The
entrance of the park most noble. Bear 8 m. So Oxford the country
nothing striking. Met Kitty and my sister here. To London in the post
coach.*[39]

March 1775

*Rode with Rooper to Bristol, went the lower road 13 miles pass a
large old house of the Duke of Chandos's at Kynsham. Bristol a large
dirty irregular built city, large ships can unload at the Quay. The
Exchange a handsome modern built ediface, perhaps the inside too
heavy. The Isles of the cathedral in a singular style of Gothic
architecture. Some good openings and good streets. Returned home by
the upper road to dinner. At Bath all is gaiety and elegance, at Bristol
all business and bustle. perhaps so total a change of scene is not to be
met with anywhere within so short a distance ...*[40]

25 June 1775

*Rode to Atterby the Duke of Buccleugh's. A large irregular pile of a
building. a tolerable good gallery. a fine bust of Julius Caesar which
cost a thousand pounds. The garden tolerably pretty, a piece of water
made by the present Duke. Affectation most disgusting. But if people
will be affected, it is odd they won't affect rather a pleasing than a
troublesome character...*[41]

> 27 June 1775
> *Returned to Thenford. Nothing can amuse after leaving those we love.*
> *Pass a pretty good place of Sir Charles Cotterel's laid out by the*
> *famous Kent. The style seems much like Brown's.*[42]

Robert and Barbara's keen interest in travel (albeit vicarious, in Barbara's case, see below) was linked to late eighteenth-century enthusiasm for novelty, curiosity and the exotic. A desire for knowledge of the world spurred many to travel, as did reading traveller's accounts of their adventures. Detailed descriptions of distant places with their natural wonders, strange customs and artefacts allowed reflection and comparisons with one's own culture. Before the 1790s, travel writing usually integrated 'anecdotal personal narrative' with 'curious' or 'precise observation' (Leask, 2002: 7). Even while travelling within Great Britain, Robert's brief but detailed comments on the places he has visited (with his careful notations of distance and time), follow this tradition of writing, and his observation of the natural world, buildings or cities is often inextricably linked to personal opinions about those he meets or those who own the properties he visits. They provide a point of comparison with his own life, as he almost 'measures' himself alongside others in terms of his politics, aesthetics, intellect and even manners.

Maxims to live by

The majority of quotations in the journals show Robert to be his mother's son. Although his behaviour accords with what would be expected in 'polite' society, Robert held his own astute view of human nature and used his reflective journal to help him grapple with the moral ambiguities and compromises of adult life. It is clear throughout the journals that Robert is doing more than writing down trite aphorisms, so popular in Georgian England. He actively engages with the ideas he is copying out of books and can be seen to be reflecting on them. These reading conversations seem in some cases to be 'rehearsals' for his actual talk with others about books and ideas. Some of Robert's most prolific entries could be described as maxims to live by.

> 23 April 1771
> *To feel much for others and little for ourselves, to restrain our selfish,*
> *to indulge our benevolent affections, constitutes the perfection of*
> *human nature.*

(from Adam Smith's Theory of Moral Verisimilitude in Theory of
Moral Sentiments[43]*)*

Sometimes the journal entry before the quotation shows the way his
mind is working. In the following example, one assumes Robert is
unimpressed with one of the guests seated round Mr Craven's dinner
table.

> 4 Sept 1771
> *Dined at Barton Court, Mr Craven's. Hampstead a fine looking park.*
> *400 acres. How often do we see great ostentation and great meanness*
> *in the same person. The man whose happiness entirely depends on the*
> *casual approbation of others is not likely to have too much of it.*
> *How little do we consult our own happiness when we are inattentive to*
> *that of others.*[44]

Note Robert's canny speculations on money versus merit, so like his
mother's, quoting from Rousseau on this theme:

> *They who are wealthy prefer gold to merit. In setting money against*
> *services, they find that the latter never balances the former, and they*
> *think there is an overplus due to them, even after a life spent in serving*
> *them for a bare subsistence.*
> (from Rousseau's *Emilius* ... translated by W. Kenrick, 1763)[45]

Religious musings

Robert's reading and his embracing of Enlightenment culture must
have caused him some anxieties in terms of the religious beliefs he had
been brought up with. The philosophies of Locke and Hume with their
emphasis on observation and reason, the religious turmoil of the age,
and the emerging discourse of humanism with its belief in an
autonomous, secular self, led to questioning the idea of an omnipotent
God as well as the authority of 'the Divine Word'. Journal writing in
this period, as Martin (2002) suggests, provided a place for dealing
with new ideas and exploring or confirming one's own beliefs,
allowing diarists to attach themselves to a 'collective identity' that was
coming to terms with new ways of being and believing. Robert's
entries show him looking to his everyday life and the natural world as
manifestations of God's existence, while at the same time using reason
and logic to search for the truth.

Although there is not the amount of religious discussion one might expect from a clergyman (indeed, there are only passing references to preaching in the journals), Robert displays a sure belief in a loving God evidenced both in his own writing and that of others. It is interesting how he is just as likely to draw religious ideas from a book on travel, as an explicitly devotional work, and how he can be seen to be using his reading to underpin his thinking. His religious views tend to be kind, open, and much less severe than his mamma's. For example, Robert found Haye's *Religious Philosophy* most instructive and openly approves its 'most liberal way of thinking' and the author's 'thorough good heart'. Jane would have had reservations about the former and commended the latter. In the same entry, Robert praises Prideaux's discussion of the old and new testaments.

> 2 January 1772
> *A book that tends by enlarging our conceptions of goodness and power of God in the creation, to increase in us that universal love and benevolence so much insisted on in the gospel. Some few of his notions seem built on no firmer ground than an hypothesis of his own raising, but the general tenets are very instructive, show a thorough good heart, and a most liberal way of thinking...*

> [Prideaux] *wrote with a candour that pleases the more as one rarely meets with it in writers of history. His details are now and then tedious, and his explications sometimes frivolous, but as they arrive from his wishing to make himself universally understood, they are easily forgiven. He seems to have no other aim in view than being serviceable to his fellow creatures by giving them a view of a very interesting period of history, and showing how remarkably the prophecies of Daniel were fulfilled, particularly the famous one of the coming of the Messiah.*[46]

A Man of his time

It is not insignificant that most of the authors quoted in Robert's journals feature in Porter's recent book on the Enlightenment (2000). In other words, a large part of his reading diet was by contemporary authors who turned out to be some of the key voices of the Enlightenment. (This is even clearer in the later section in this chapter on reading exchanges.) Robert writes, of course, about his reading (new books are listed with their prices), often showing how he is thinking about some of the most serious issues of his time. He gives the ideas he is considering his own particular 'spin', and there is no doubt that here is a man who knew his own mind.

27 Nov 1771
That you may take a truer prospect of my act, place yourself in your imagination beyond it, suppose it already done, and then see how it looks.
(from Wollaston's *Religion of Nature Delineated* from section VIII 'Truths concerning Families and Relations)[47]

7 April 1772
Jealousy is the fear of apprehension of superiority; envy our uneasiness under it.
(from *The works, in Verse and Prose, of William Shenstone* 1776, section 'On Men and Manners')[48]

Robert is a typical late Enlightenment person in other respects - he is humane, and as far as we can ascertain, a Whig sympathiser. Although he undoubtedly enjoyed the 'good life', we are also aware of his liberal credentials in his actions. We sometimes find him attending committees that gave money to pauper schemes. (For example, Robert belonged to a group which met regularly at the Bear Inn for the Benefit of Pauper Charity in Bath.) Like Ranson in Darnton's study[49] (Darnton, 1985), Robert's reading choices affect the way he views the world; they also demonstrate his determination to take an ethical, fair-minded stance on most matters. Robert's interest in history and world affairs is wide-ranging and not at all narrowly nationalistic. For example, several pages of his journals written in French are devoted to a radical history of French monarchs. He is interested in international events and takes a strongly moral line on the more conspicuous forms of oppression, especially slavery, wherever he encounters it. In the following entry he is clearly impressed by the history of Latin America, a popular topic at the time:

26 Jan 1776
Las Casas the Mexican friend of humanity and the Indians; struck with their mildness and simplicity, became their advocate with the court of Spain & with infinite pains after having proved that the Spaniards had destroyed 15 million of them, obtained some alleviation to their sufferings, by laws to prevent their being wantonly oppressed, but which are too frequently abused. Before this numbers were destroyed through wanton cruelty, which the Priests tolerated if they did not promote, but still far greater were the numbers swept away by the

most babarous slavery, which forced to labour in the mines and other employment, beyond what human nature was able to support. One Spaniard in the island of Hispaniola made a vow to sacrifice daily 12 Indian infidels, in honour of the twelve apostles; they hunted them with dogs which they trained to devour them. By their cruel means about one million of inhabitants are vanished from the face of the earth in that Island alone ...[50]

Erudition and chit-chat

One of the most fascinating things about Robert's journals is that his writing demonstrates an eclectic mix of erudition and chit-chat. The latter includes recipes for ailments; lists of presents at Christmas; gossip (never unpleasant); wagers with the lads. In the following extracts from his early marriage, Robert notes the purchase of candles, mentions a family event and carefully documents his manservant's (Rooper) recipe for hair cream. It is details like these which bring the everyday experience of this social stratum in the eighteenth century so vividly to life.

1 March 1775
... Mrs Craven lays me half a crown that Mr Gooch is not married to Miss Villarea before the first of January 1776 ... We had six dozen of mould candles from Wheble the beg of the month...
Pomatum to thicken the hair - Rooper
Put beef marrow into water and change the water every day for a week, melt it over a slow fire and as it cools beat into it a sufficient quantity of oil of sweet almonds to make it of the consistence you like.[51]

28 August 1775
Call'd on Mr Wise the Priory appears a sweet place. Mrs Craven had ten of her grandchildren dined with her, Miss C [daughter of Lord Craven] the eldest not eight years old. Lid's[52] *daughter Mary-Ann makes in all 11 grandchildren. Miss Craven has sweet eyes and promises to be v handsome, so does Georgiana [another daughter of Lord Craven].*[53]

25 March 1777
So warm we had no fire all day upstairs for two or three days till Good Friday...[54]

July 29 1777
Little mare dropped a fole.[55]

The overall tone of the journals which reveal Robert's inner voice is informal, down to earth and affectionate. They remind us of Jane's letters, though, disappointingly, Robert never mentions his mother. In fact, in a letter to Barbara on 16 Jan 1777, he tells her that 'I recollect so few circumstances that happen'd when we lived at Olney...'[56] Most of all, Robert's journals reveal the conversations he was having with himself.

Reading Robert Johnson's public writing[57]

In 1777, the same year as the journals end, Robert kept a dated list of all the letters he sent and received. There is no reason to believe that it was an unusual year, so we are reasonably safe in assuming that this pattern of correspondence was typical of Robert as a young family man of his day. According to his record, Robert wrote between five and ten letters to friends and acquaintances each month of the year, the greatest number in December; he received roughly the same number in return. Although he spent time with his sister and brothers during the year, he also sent and received letters to and from Barbara, at least once each month and most months to his brothers. Some of the letters were quite long with every inch of the paper filled with writing.

Brotherly love

Letters are part of the social and personal adhesive of family relationships. In Robert's case, they demonstrate his self-chosen role (one which Barbara also takes on) in linking his siblings across time, space and mutual interests. We begin with an extract from Robert's letter to George announcing the birth of his first child which exemplifies the closeness of the brothers.

> Oct 1773
> I have the pleasure of informing you that my dear little woman was last night brought to bed of a daughter [...] I need not tell you how happy this event has made me, your own good heart will conceive what I felt better than I can describe it. I will say I never felt so many pleasing sensations before...[58]

While we note Robert's proud patriarchal voice, the genuine joy in his first child and love for his wife shines through. Soon further babies appeared.

Robert in Kenilworth to George at Witham 21 April 1775

> I shall have a noble family if we go on at this rate, but I heartily subscribe to the good old maxim the more the merrier [...] I have my hand pretty full of employment at present.[59]

Robert continues to update his brother on the progress of his children throughout their lives. He shares his anxieties about the children as well as his delight in them with George, though Robert is even more confiding with his sister (see below).

Robert at Kenilworth to George at Perth Postoffice, Scotland 24 July 1777

> I see by the papers that the Duke of Argyle is since dead, I think [...] that a man surrounded with such a tribe of physical folks had little chance to recover [...] our two little girls escape the small pox still.[60]

Robert at Coombe Abbey to George at Witham, Sun 12 Sept 1779

> We are engaged in the business of innoculating our three eldest children [...] Lord Craven has been so kind to lend us this house on the occasion which is a charming place for the purpose as there is such ample room for them to run about it.[61]

A letter from Robert on 30 March 1780 talks of Harriet unwell 'in a dangerous state' with a high fever, bad ulcers in her throat and mouth, her 'tongue covered in smaller ones' which they treat with gargles and medicines. His other two little ones were well, but 'Mrs Johnson almost wrung out with anxiety and constantly attending on poor Harriet'.[62]

In the next extract, Robert welcomes the fact that George is coming back to England the following summer, gives him family news of Charles (whom Robert teasingly calls 'the Doctor', Charles having recently received his doctorate) and Barbara who was visiting friends in Buckinghamshire.

Robert in Bath to George chez Mons Giovanni Lepri Rome 2 Feb 1779

> Little William now runs about every where, and will be quite a fine fellow by the time you return. It is lucky he is so soon able to shift for himself that he may make way for another youngster who we expect to make his appearance in a few months [...] I have a little scheme in contemplation to visit the Lakes next summer and perhaps stretch a little way into Scotland.[63]

In a letter to George at Stamford on 27 June 1781, Robert describes Maria being seized with fever, William attacked next, then Harriet very ill. 'I should feel quite uncomfortable to leave her till she is quite well.' Harriet wouldn't take her medicines and 'Mrs J stands almost as much in need of assistance as Harriet herself.'

Robert's letters to George often chase the latter on his travels all over northern England, Scotland, Wales and Europe. As a family man, Robert has to be content with imagining sights he longed to experience first hand.

> 2 February 1779
> I should like above all thing to accompany you through Italy, it is the country next to America I most wish to see, but alas! matrimony though it has many roses, has some few thorns and with a wife and family one must be content with making home comfortable and agreeable without thinking of jaunting about and making tours to the continent ... [64]

Robert is solicitous about his elder brother: he helps him run the Witham estate; he takes care of things for George when he is on his travels; he procures books on his behalf (see below); and he tries to boost George's spirits and encourage him more into society. In one letter, Robert gently urges his reclusive brother to visit the family at Kenilworth. Another time, when he learns that George has become a vegetarian, he immediately suggests trying the diet with him when they next meet.

> *Robert at Kenilworth to George at Witham 21 January 1774*
> My sister tells me you are become quite a Pythagorean and live entirely on vegetables. How do you find it agrees with you? If you will give me leave I may possible make a trial of it with you for a short time in the spring ...[65]

> *Robert to George 7 Nov 1774*
> Settled in house at Bath [...] whole country round this place is beautiful beyond description. The Town too is very neat, and the regularity of the new part of it has a most pleasing effect. The Crescent is now completed and is really one of the most striking things I ever saw in my life [...] Do come and take a peep at us, I wish I could prevail on you to shift the scene from your study and retirement to ye gaities and amusements of Bath for a few months this winter. We

should be most heartily rejoiced to see you and when you had once got
here I am sure you would like it.[66]

In the next, Robert has received a letter from George in the Orkneys.
He thanks George for his description of Scotland which he desires to
visit himself.

64 Robert at Kenilworth to George at Perth Postoffice, Scotland 24 July 1777
   ... in books people are so apt to embellish their descriptions that one
   hardly knows what to rely on [...] I am sorry you find our name a
   disadvantage, but I concluded you would, Johnston's tour is wrote in a
   stile that must disgust a people so national and united as the Scotch,
   your visit will convince them that the Johnston's and Johnson's are not
   more different in family than in disposition. I long to hear your
   account of Staffa, Bank's views of Fingal's cave and the different parts
   of that wonderful Island lead one to form the most romantic ideas of
   it.[67]

Reading exchanges

The serious texts Robert refers to in his letters and journals include the
key literature for the intelligentsia of that period which encompassed
the American War of Independence and lead up to the French
Revolution. Whether it is Montesquieu on politics, Du Bois on painting
or Chesterfield's pithy sayings, Robert selects mostly contemporary
texts that are typical of the well-read liberal minded people of his day.
Influential French intellectuals form the heart of Robert's reading -
Rousseau, Montesquieu, Molière - whom he reads in French rather than
in translation, alongside contemporary English writers, such as
Ferguson, Hume and Paine. Robert also read German authors, probably
in translation, some Latin and he wished he knew Italian: 'for my
being entirely unacquainted with the Italian language puts it absolutely
out of my power'.[68] Of course, his letters also reveal the exchange of
ideas through reading within an intellectual family. We find a hint that
this exchange included his wife and at least one of his children[69] in a
paragraph in Robert's Will:

   I give unto my Son Robert Henry twenty pounds as a mark of my
   affection for him his being already otherwise provided for I likewise
   give unto my said Son Robert Henry all my Books except such of
   them as my Wife Anna Rebecca shall chuse to keep for her own use
   and amusement and reserving the use of all my said Books to my said

Wife Anna Rebecca till my said Son Robert Henry shall go into Holy Orders. (1797)[70]

Robert mentions the books he is excited by and learning from in letters both to Barbara and to George, and it is clear he values his sister's views on literature as much as his brother's. His letters show that he was not only reading philosophy, history and biography by Burke, Gibbon and Johnson, but commentaries on each - Paine on Burke (which he urged Barbara to read - 'it is excellent'), Watson on Gibbon and Boswell on Johnson. Although the catalogue of Robert's serious reading demonstrated an ease and expertise with literature across a range of genres, it also included popular fiction alongside high culture. For example, in an undated letter to Barbara from Bath, Robert confides his current reading habits.

> I assure you I read with partiality every book you recommend, and rarely have found you mistaken in what you thought I should like. But I have not so much time for reading as I would wish, various avocations break in upon any regular plan, and a work of any length is not to be read to advantage by bits and scraps. Therefore, during my winter's sojourn in Bath, I deal principally in little Brochures or any light reading I meet with.[71]

Robert's quick sketches of people he meets often make reference to their reading. In May, 1778, he writes approvingly to Barbara that Lord Huntingdon has added to his 'polished exterior [...] all that can be derived from great reading, deep reflection and a thorough knowledge of the world.'[72] One reason for this judgement might be that he shared Lord Huntingdon's good opinion of Chesterfield's letters which Robert described as 'the most useful lesson for the instruction of young men yet offered to the public.'[73]

Robert is solicitous about getting reading matter to George while he is away from home; he also looks out for titles and editions he knows will interest George when he visits London. Some of the brothers' correspondence amounts to a bulletin of texts in print, plus a wish-list of books too costly to purchase or hard to get hold of. It also shows them to be erudite bibliophiles, eagerly scrutinising catalogues of forthcoming books, as the list in the appendix will show. The lengthy extracts from the letters which follow are worth quoting, as they offer a taste of the brothers' bookish conversations on paper. It is also interesting to have a letter around the same time to George from one of his booksellers, Elmsley. While we cannot be sure which edition of any book they actually bought and read, because of the references to Payne's catalogue it is possible to track some likely editions (see accompanying footnotes).

from Robert at Berkeley Square to George at Wytham 1772[?] (enclosing Johnson's dictionary)

... it is the first edition which is reckoned to be the best printed though the other sells for more. Homer, there is another edition of it printed about two years ago on a larger paper that sells for seven guineas, but as the one I have sent you is really a handsome book and costs not quite half the money I thought you would prefer it. Robertson's *Charles the Fifth* and Chaucer, which is the only modern edition so I sent it to you tho' a folio. You should at the same time have had Chambers' supplement but the price nine guineas startled me so much I thought it better to ask you if you wish to have at that rate. The new edition of Chambers won't be out of some years, which has raised the price of the supplement so enormously. Benvenuto Cellini[74] was sold before I went to Paynes. You will see in his catalogue some other old Italian books, the prices of which are not put down...they are all very dear [...] Orlando di Berni[75] [...] Rollin's Belles Lettres,[76] Smollet's continuation, Farquhar's works in duo and Baskerville's Congreve[77] as it is the only octavo edition [...] *Le Dictionaire de l'Academie* in Quarto [...] He has a quarto edition of Racine[78], but Mr Wodhull told me the octavo one like your Corneille was much the best so I thought it better to wait. There will be likewise an edition of Moliere[79] come out in March on the same plan, do you chuse to wait for it or have the Quarto? Voltaire has just published a complete edition of his works in 10 vol quarto (price about 10 or 11 guineas) which I am told is likely to be the standard edition as he made considerable alterations and additions [...] The first edition (a history of France) in 3 V folio is greatly prefer'd as it is wrote with a spirit of freedom, the French court thought it necessary to soften in the subsequent editions. There is a handsome copy in Payne's sale at six guineas. Elmsley has one he said he could let you have for five but the leaves are very much stain'd. Daniel's History comes farther down but is not as generally liked. Le Dictionaire de l'Academie in folio, Fontenelle, La Fontaine, Boileau, Franco Sacchetti [...] Elmsely says he shall be able to send you very soon. But for the Cento Novelle [?] they are only to be picked up by accident at book auctions and are so enormously dear three or four guineas a volume that he will not get them without your farther orders [...] I have sent you the catalogue of Mr Smith's books (West's catalogue is not yet out) [...] if I am in town I will attend the auction for you with great pleasure [...] Il convivio di Dante is a very indifferent thing in imitation of Plato...[80]

Robert to George early 1773 [?]

I was sorry to find on the unpacking of Elmsley's books there were so few come of those you wanted. Fontenelle and Boileau are the only ones that are yet arrived [...] D'Anville's maps I have done everything in my power to procure, but there is really not a complete set to be got in London [...] Moliere and the residue of Voltaire are not yet out [...] These four articles are all I have kept on my list, for as I found it in vain to endeavour to get any of the old Italian romances I have given over thinking of them [...] Elmsley [...] has got two fine editions of Contes de la Fontaine, octavo with cuts, the one five guineas, the other four and a half.[81]

From P Elmsley to George Sep 10 1773

Sir,

I plead guilty in not answering your Letters. I have however try'd London for your Spanish books and have applied to Madrid for what I could not get here. What the Person you have applied to has furnished as many as he can get for you I shall be much obliged for an order for what you may not get, and by that time I hope to have received news from Spain. I have received the new 8 vo Edition of Moliere, D'Anville Atlas, and expect Barre[82] in a few days & also

Obras de Feijoo 14 vol Small vol 4to
Ulloa & Juan's voyage to So. America[83]
Parnasse Español 8 vol/in the manner of Dodsley's Poems
Comedies [sic] de Calderon 12 vol. Small 4o.
Dict: de l'academie [sic] de Madrid 6 vol fol.
Reflexiones militares de Santa Cruz 12 vol. Small
L'Auracana. D'Ercilla fol. A famous Epic Poem

If you should like to have either, you shall not wait for them, & if you will be so good as to excuse this one disappointment for which I have not better reason to give than that of having more business at present that I perhaps deserve. I engage to be more punctual for the time to come, & that henceforth you shall have not reason to complain of

Your most obedient & most humble Servant

P. Elmsley[84]

These letters seem to indicate that Robert regularly purchased a great number of books and that his reading is closely tied to exchanges with his sister, brothers and friends. Robert clearly views books as beautiful objects as well as reading matter; the significance of the size, shape, print, binding, general condition of books is seen as highly significant. Even so, he took account of the cost of books and tried not to be too extravagant, though George was clearly willing to spend a small fortune on acquiring the right publications. The best / latest editions of key books are a concern to Robert, so that decisions have to be made about whether to get the best available versions of the moment or wait for the complete edition. The sheer range of authors with whom Robert, George and Barbara have easy familiarity is impressive and takes in reference works, as well as fiction and plays. Robert makes regular attendance at book auctions and knows his way around books - his comments on books are discriminating and he is up-to-date with publication dates and titles. He also enjoys a close familiarity with booksellers and collectors.

Before we leave Robert and turn our attention to Barbara, it is worth digressing to the topic of poetry, a genre of literature that was important to both of them.

Lady Miller's Muse

As we have seen, Robert enjoyed poetry, mentioning Shakespeare, Shenstone, Akinside, Homer and other poets in his journals and letters, and discussing particular editions, translations and volumes of verse. For example, while he appreciates Addison's version of the twenty-third psalm, he also notes that 'it is not in the power of our language to convey in other words that sublime idea of the Valley of the shadow of Death'.[85]

He also spends considerable time while he winters in Bath at evening gatherings which included the reading, writing and discussion of poetry. Many of these poetry soirees, at which Robert seems to have been a regular if ambivalent attendee, were hosted by Lady Anna Miller who appears to have been a somewhat pretentious literary lady. Mrs Miller clearly both amused and irritated him. In an undated letter to his sister, he remarks: '... I have talked enough about this silly woman, who everybody laughs at, yet everybody follows'.[86] Mrs Miller's literary salon is described as follows in the Dictionary of National Biography:

> She invited all persons of wit and fashion in Bath to meet once a fortnight at her house. An antique vase that had been purchased in Italy [...] was placed on a modern altar decorated with laurel, and each guest was invited to place in the urn an original composition in verse. A

committee was appointed to determine the best three productions, and their authors were then crowned by Lady Miller with wreaths of myrtle. (DNB, 1995)

On 25 November, 1780, Robert writes to Barbara about the latest shenanigans at Bath-Easton - 'a most miserable piece of business' - where the hostess appears to be more interested in the poems that praise her than in literary merit. Robert often tells Barbara entertaining anecdotes about aspiring 'bards' competing to win the poetry prize, secure in the knowledge that she would sympathise with his views. On more than one occasion, he submits a poem by Barbara which wins the laurel wreath: 'I assure you your Ode bore off the prize from twelve competitors with universal applause'.[87] As we have mentioned, Barbara was the poet of the family and Robert often sought her help in his penmanship for the Bath-Easton poetry evenings.

Horace Walpole seems to have shared Robert's misgivings about the influential but somewhat ridiculous Lady Miller. In a letter, Walpole remarks that he was glad his correspondent had 'escaped' Mrs Miller's follies at Bath-Easton and described her book, *Political Amusements at a Villa near Bath* (1775) as 'a bouquet of artificial flowers, and ten degrees duller than a magazine.'[88] Be that as it may, it included poems by eminent persons such as Lord Palmerston, Lord Carlisle, David Garrick and Anna Seward, so Robert is mixing with the political and literary elite on a regular basis. The following quotes from Robert's diary and letters chart his increasing frustration with Mrs Miller.

5 December 1775
*We at Mrs Miller's subject music several copies of execrable verses.-
some fine lines of Dryden's overlook'd.*[89]

From Robèrt at Bath to Barbara 16 Jan 1777
Easton tired to death with hearing verses on physiognom [...] vile set [...] stupid beyond conception [...] Mr Temple read 20 quarto pages on this subject, they had merit, & he would have deserved the prize he gain'd, had they been comprized in 100 instead of 600 lines. The subject given out for Thursday sennight is the rise & progress of the British Theatre. do you feel inspired? If you do, you may send us a few stanzas, but if they don't flow quite spontaneously don't give yourself much trouble about them, as the vase is now always filled with such a quantity of trash, & merit has so little chance of being discriminated,

that it really is not worth while to take pains about any one means to put in it .[90]

Barbara might well have been 'inspired' as the theatre which thrived during the Regency period was one of her many passions, as we will see.

Fashion, Fiction and 'An Elegant Mind': Reading Barbara Johnson's Album and Letters

March 12 1776
I think you will like to take one farewell look at Garrick before he entirely quits the stage which he will do after this season.

12 December 1778
The players have been here these four months. I have attended them very often. They acted the *School for Scandal* very well which I think a most excellent play. I suppose you saw it in Town.

October 16 1781
I have been at two private concerts here lately, which I enjoyed very much. I don't believe anybody is as fond of music as I am.

October 20th 1803
If you go to any of the plays pray let me have an account of them.

Barbara was clearly a lady of wit and intellect. Her brothers' warm regard for her is clearly shared by others as she boasts many devoted friends and is adored by her nephews and nieces. For example, Robert reports in an undated letter to Barbara in London that an acquaintance spoke of her 'in the highest terms, and says he never met with anyone with a more elegant or better-informed mind'.[91] Barbara's letters give a lie to Lawrence Stone's dated, but much quoted, demeaning description of late eighteenth-century women of the mid and upper classes as 'increasingly idle drones ... [passing their time in] novel-reading, theatre-going, card-playing and formal visits...' (Stone, 1977: 396-7). Barbara may have spent some time in these pursuits, but she was certainly neither idle nor superficial. (Indeed, if either of the siblings could be described as an idle drone {and we would *not* wish to do so}, it was Robert rather than Barbara who spent more time at the races, playing cards etc.) Most of all, like her mother before her, Barbara is a keeper of the family archive, carefully hoarding documents and annotating for clarity where necessary.

It is much more useful to comply with Tadmor's admonition that we should be 'cautious before re-inscribing as history the eighteenth-century fantasy of supine femininity induced by reading' (Tadmor, 1996: 174). Indeed, in *The Gentleman's Daughter,* Vickery argues that women's reading in the eighteenth century could be just as eclectic, but also as serious as that of men, as Barbara's correspondence indicates.

> The female reader could study sermons preaching domesticity in one mood and philosophies praising active citizenship in another [...] We should not presume without evidence that women (or men) mindlessly absorbed a single didactic lesson like so many pieces of unresisting blotting-paper (Vickery, 1998: 7).

Vickery goes on to suggest that 'it was in their tireless writing no less than in their ravenous reading that genteel women embraced a world far beyond the boundaries of the parish [...] The pious soul-searching that inspired most seventeenth century diarists is a distinctly muted theme in many eighteenth-century women's journals' (Vickery, 1998: 287). We don't know if Barbara kept a journal, but her letters provide plenty of evidence to support Vickery's thesis.

We do not, unfortunately, have as much information on Barbara[92], as Robert, and that is why we are unable to discuss her reading and writing quite as fully as we would wish. However, one of the points we wish to emphasise in this chapter is that despite Robert's prestigious Public School education, and Barbara's home schooling, there was an equal intellectual and literary exchange between the siblings throughout their adult lives. Part of the foundation for this may have been the excellent educational grounding they both received from their mother in the shape of her nursery library.

A Lady goes dancing

from Barbara at Thenford to George at Witham, Feb 25 1773

Northampton was extremely gay last week, there was a very good Concert on Tuesday at which most of the Neighbouring Familys attended. Mr I was so good as to take me in his coach, the room was a full as it could hold, after the concert there was a Ball. Mrs Bouverie and Mrs Crewe danc'd with two of the Officers here, they are the two most beautiful Women I ever saw except Lady Craven who I think superior to everybody. Two days after the Concert there was another assembly at which I danc'd till past one in the Morning [...] I suppose these gayeties will be over when this Regt. Leaves the town which will be next Month.[93]

This could almost be the breathless account of one of the sisters in Jane Austen's *Pride and Prejudice*. Although Barbara does not include descriptions of the rooms or the dresses, she does conjure up colourful and dynamic scenes for her reader, such as in the following case where there is a theatrical effect to her words:

Barbara to George at Stamford Weds March 21 1781
> We had great rejoicings here for the taking St. Eustaphia [sic]. The whole Town was Illuminated and the next Morning the Militia was drawn up on the Market-Hill with the Music Playing, Colours flying, Bells ringing, and everybody shouting for Joy. They let off the Cannon, which broke some Windows, but the Officers very handsomly paid for their being repaired. The Officers likewise sent Cards of Invitation to most of the Neighbouring Gentlemen to dine at the Peacock and drink Sir George Rodney's health.[94]

Barbara mainly set up home with one of her dearest friends, Catherine (Kitty) Ingram (1744-1808), who married the liberal intellectual, Michael Wodhull (1740-1816). He was a writer, translator, book collector, printer, publisher and poet. Wodhull is described as 'a keen Whig, ardent for the spread of civil and religious liberty, and his poems show him sympathetic to the views of Rousseau' (DNB, 1995), views which we know Barbara (and Robert) shared. Among other things, Wodhull translated and published nineteen tragedies of Euripides, wrote critical works on the classics, composed poetry, including an 'Ode to Liberty', and contributed regularly to the *Gentleman's Magazine*. Barbara spent much of her life living harmoniously with this couple, though she always paid her own way. Robert was also on excellent terms with the Wodhull family which suggests that they were likely to have been of similar persuasions both intellectually and politically.

One gets a sense of the more relaxed and familiar side of Michael Wodhull and his relationships with the women in his life from a teasing letter he wrote to Barbara. The allusion to his secretary is, of course, his wife, Kitty.

From Mr Wodhull at Berkeley Square to Miss Johnson Feb 26 1774

Mary was in town but a fortnight, however like all Country ladies She made the most of her time, rose at eight, the friseur waiting for her drest for the day, consequently durst not stir but in a coach or a chair out to breakfast, the rest of the morning making visits, dined out in the eveing the Opera, out to supper & returned about two in the morning ...

... the Ridicule of dress is carried to such a length that Public places are disgusting to the greatest degree, you can conceive nothing so sickening, as the present set of fine Gentlemen [...] No one appears but with his delicate white hands enfolded in a muff ornamented with the richest lace, I believe the Ladies in general look upon them with the greatest contempt, but my Secretary assures me that I am mistaken, & that though I may look down on a Coat of the Richest Gold Stuff lined with Ermine, with triple ruffles on the wrists of our Beaux, yet they have their weight...

I suppose you are charmed with your little niece, May She inherit the virtues that adorn the mind of her Aunt with whom my Secretary laments that He is only acquainted by Fame that loudly blazons forth her praise ...[95]

There is also a great deal of warmth and fun in exchanges between Robert and Barbara who seem to have inherited Jane's sense of humour. What follows is an amusing letter from Robert to Barbara when bad weather stops him from visiting her one new year. The 'Thenfordians', of course, refer to Barbara and the Wodhulls who lived in Thenford.

Thinking the intentions of the Thenfordians as unalterable as the laws of the Persians, I had wrote to you at Northampton [...] Had I a sledge from Lapland, I should be tempted to break into your retirement. It would give me that greatest pleasure to flatter myself (as you have no Beau), that my company would not be unacceptable. But alas as neither of these conveniences nor Fortunatus' wishing cap are now to be obtained, I must content myself with visiting you in idea. I see you all surrounding a cheerfully blazing Fire, Kitty with some sound Divine in her hand, by turns attentive and distrait, and now looking out at window & deeply commiserating the miseries many of her fellow creatures suffer from the inclemency of the weather.[96]

Emotional bonds

There is no doubt that Robert readily confides in Barbara, appears to trust her judgement in most matters, and shares private feelings with her. Barbara clearly adored Robert's children and their letters to her as young women show that affection was reciprocated.[97] She reveals herself as a fond aunt in a letter to George which served the double purpose of attempting to persuade him to give up his solitary state and visit Robert's family.[98]

> I wish you could see them all, for I think they are the most engaging children I ever saw in my life, which is not altogether the partiality of an old aunt, for others are of the same opinion.[99]

More than twenty years later, we encounter Robert as an emotional father of his grown up children, first with Harriet on the morning of her wedding where his grief at 'losing' a daughter is obvious, despite the good sense of the match. The second extract occurs when Robert learns that his eldest son, William Augustus (who made his career in the army), is to be stationed in the West Indies; a trip to Aberystwyth is cut short and Robert's anxiety is unmistakable.

From Robert to Barbara at No 1 Kensington Square, Middlesex Tuesday noon
> Poor Harriet was greatly affected & so indeed were we all, & I can by no means express to you what I now feel, I will however strive against it and endeavour to recollect that it is for my dear Harriet's happiness and that the loss is ours alone, and that she will reap the advantage. At least she seems to have a fair prospect of happiness, as mutual affection, & worth in the man she has married, can bestow [...] the indissoluble knot is tied.[100]

From Robert at Wistanstow to Barbara at Thenford from R Sunday night
> ... very unpleasant information of our Dear William's regiment being ordered to go to the West Indies, which I own was a stroke I did not expect, and was not prepared to bear with the fortitude I ought. I am assured that the yellow fever is abated, that the troops are going out at the best possible season of the year, and that the prodigious force we are sending will make the Duty still less severe that heretofore [...] but still my heart sinks within me whenever it comes across in my mind.[101]

Barbara stays at home

In her correspondence, Barbara keeps up with politics and enjoys society with its fashion, balls, dinners and, one imagines, animated conversations. However, there are limits to what Barbara was able to do, though it is not entirely clear whether they were self-imposed limitations or genuine difficulties put in the way of women or at least those of relatively limited means. One of the things Barbara denied herself was travel beyond the hearths of places she could almost call second homes. She loved nature, longed to visit cities she had read about in history texts, desired first hand experience of art treasures and craved dramatic landscapes. There is a wistful quality to these comments in her letters to George, though she seems to have compensated by reading every possible account of travel she could get her hands on.

9 July 1776
I am delighted with your account of those Romantic scenes (George is on a Cumbrian tour) and often wish myself with you upon those cloud-capped mountains. I have not yet met with Mr Wyndam's tour but will be glad to read it at the first opportunity [...] I am now reading Goldsmith's Animated Nature[102] which entertains me extremely. I have not met with a book to please me so much a great while.[103]

17 August 1776 (asking George if he kept a travel journal)
I dare say you could not go so far and see so many places without making memorandums and observations which it would give me great pleasure to see. I was often looking over maps to trace the parts I supposed you might be in.[104]

13 February 1777
I should like vastly to see the Tour you went last year through Wales and as you mention Wyndham having described it I wish you would be so good as to lend it me to read ...[105]

26 May 1778
I very often wish myself with you particularly when you describe the Antiquities and curiosities of Rome ...[106]

12 December 1778
I thank you for wishing I could pass conveniently into Italy or France. I assure you there is nothing I should enjoy so much, and was I a Man would certainly set out directly, but you know Women are helpless Animals and not calculated to launch out so far as their inclinations would carry them.[107]

We believe Barbara's tone to be somewhat ironic. Adventurous though admittedly exceptional women like Mary Wollstonecraft set off to

Europe alone, even to France during the revolution, just ten years later. Like many other women of her wealth and station, it is likely that Barbara would have seen her brothers' letters, along with her book reading, as a way of satisfying her desire for all kinds of knowledge. Even more trivial details, such as descriptions of current fashions in London which revealed the desire for novelty in an increasingly consumer-oriented society, could be turned into a moral reflection on the ridiculous lengths to which consumers could go to make themselves uncomfortable (a point also made by Jane).

A Lady of science

I like the best to wait on the Philosopher
Who each Hypothesis with ease can toss over
And doubts resolve, or at least seem to gloss over.
He Lectures reads on Optics, Hydrostatics,
Magnets, Astronomy and eke Pneumatics,
He leads us through the Starry wide Expanse
Where Comets roll and all the Planets dance,
He treats too of the swift Electric fluid
Unknown in Ancient times to British Druid.
The Ladies all attend these learned Lectures
At which some stare, others form strange conjectures.
(A verse letter from Barbara to Kitty Wodhull, May 1778)[108]

As her poem shows, Barbara was also interested in science, but her tone also reveals a certain scepticism in the power of science to explain everything. She pokes gentle fun at the audience for whom the event is presumably just another fashionable activity. However, she was a keen observer and was likely to have attended a series of lectures organised by the Philosophical Society of Northampton while she was living there (one of several such societies which were formed due to the new enthusiasm for Newtonian science). As well as attending public lectures, Barbara may well have read scientific journals for women. She also kept up with philosophy, politics and current affairs.

17 August 1776
Pray did you see the eclipse of the moon in your tour? I believe the whole town sat up to look at it, it was very curious and well worth sitting up for.[109]

21 March 1781
*I am obliged to Charles for sending Lord George Gordon's trial which
I will take care to return as soon as I have read it ...[110]*

16 October 1781
*I wish I had been with you to see Mr Lunardi ascend in his Balloon
[...] I should like of all things to see him descend.[111]*

A Lady of fashion *and* literature

In one undated letter, Robert asks Barbara if Dr Johnson is in the
Brackley Book Club. This suggests that she was member of this book
club which was based in Northamptonshire and was known as the
Brackley Book Society from about 1780.[112] We believe that Barbara's
closeness with her brothers was strongly based on their shared taste and
appetite for reading, as well, of course, as familial affection. By the
mid 1770s, newspapers, magazines and periodicals have also made a
big impact on the Johnsons' reading diet as she explains to George.

12 December 1778
*I wish I could send you some newspapers. They are full of debates of
the house, where they attack each other very smartly: and with great
wit and humour [...] I conclude you have visited the respectable
mansion of the great Rousseau, late citizen of Geneva. I should have
had a great veneration for the habitation of so wonderful a genius, and
wish he was alive now that you might see and converse with him. Is he
not mentioned with great respect by all his fellow citizens?[113]*

3 February 1776
*I have been much entertained by Lord Chesterfield's Letters [...] I
suppose you have read them both. We were amused with no less than
<u>nine</u> different magazines last month and two reviews.[114]*

12 March 1776
*Have you read Lady Luxborough's Letters? You may see a criticism
upon them by an acquaintance of yours in the St James Chronicle of
January 20 sign'd Clara Quid-Nunc ...[115]*

12 December 1778
*I suppose you can get books of all sorts at Geneva, and as you are now
well settled I imagine you have a good deal of time for reading.[116]*

Barbara's album of fashions and fabrics means she will be
immortalised chiefly by her collecting habit. Not surprisingly,

Barbara's letters show a healthy interest in the latest fashions of her day, particularly letters to and from her nieces not included here. But she is interested in far more than passing fads and fancies. When her Aunt Williams dies, her money, plate and jewellery are divided amongst the rest of the family, but it is *Barbara* who inherits her bookcase and books. What we have tried to show is that Barbara was a lady of letters as well as fashion, a voracious and cultured reader of the key texts of the Enlightenment period, and an astute and affectionate writer within the domestic sphere, like her mother before her.

Robert and Barbara as readers

So what have we learned of Robert and Barbara as readers? Has their mother's determination to expose them to the written word from their earliest nursery years paid off? How have her imaginative yet rigorous reading lessons at home affected the adult readers they became?

The question of cause and effect cannot, of course, be answered with total confidence, but it is clear, as we have shown, that Robert *and Barbara* turned out to be confident, knowledgeable, insatiable, critical readers of a diverse variety of texts, as well as diligent and lively writers. Their education and their mother's influence appears to have equipped them to trust their judgement and find their own ways into the texts that mattered to them. The siblings are also typical, liberal readers of their time, keen to keep up-to-date with newly published literature - from newspapers to scholarly works. The books they read taught them about the world they lived in and their interests were wide-ranging and international rather than narrow and parochial. They were also flexible readers, using texts for a variety of purposes - from knowledge acquisition and escapism, to personal nourishment and light relief.

In terms of the education of women in this period, although she did not go to school, we believe that Barbara is every bit as well read and sharp as her brother. There is no sense of Robert driving Barbara's reading. Indeed, the literary exchanges between them are those of equals. A letter from Robert reprimanding Barbara for recommending something she had not actually read herself shows the intellectual level of the siblings' intercourse.

> Who recommended Histoire Philosophique des Establisments &c to you. I am told it is very clever but there is a mixture of true & false in

it I don't much admire [...] You would not have recommended it had you read it yourself, there are many scenes too hightly colour'd.[117]

We hope the extracts from letters and journals quoted above offer further evidence for the Enlightenment as the age of reading as well as reason.

Notes

1. We have given Robert his middle name here to distinguish him from other family members, such as Archdeacon Johnson. Elsewhere in this chapter, we simply refer to him as Robert Johnson.

2. Oxford, Bodleian Library, MS.Don.c.191, fol. 41.

3. This much quoted remark is actually the opening sentence of *The Go-Between* by L. P. Hartley.

4. There is more data available for Robert Johnson (6 journals as well as many letters) than any of the other siblings, so we give him priority in this chapter; as there is less information about, and writing by, Charles, we have largely neglected him in this chapter.

5. Lord Craven VI was married to the notorious Elizabeth Anspach (1750-1828) who left him in 1783 and later married the Margrave of Brandenburg. She wrote plays, many of which were performed during her lifetime. There are references to their separation, and later to his death, in Robert's letters.

6. For more detailed studies on eighteenth century politeness, see Klein (1994), Cohen (1996) and Carter (2001).

7. This might be Kitty Wodhull with whom Barbara spent much of her time.

8. Oxford, Bodleian Library, MS.Don.e.196, p. 57.

9. Oxford, Bodleian Library, MS.Don.e.195, p. 2.

10. Oxford, Bodleian Library, MS.Don.e.195, p. 14.

11. Oxford, Bodleian Library, MS.Don.e.194, p. 9.

12. Oxford, Bodleian Library, MS.Don.e.195, p. 2.

13. Sadly, baby Robert died a few months later.

14. Oxford, Bodleian Library, MS.Don.e.196, pp 23-24.

15. Locke and Rousseau both recommended breastfeeding which is discussed in some detail in Richardson's *Pamela*.

16. Robert and Nan went on to have seven healthy children.

17. Oxford, Bodleian Library, MS.Don.e.196, p. 22.

18. Oxford, Bodleian Library, MS.Don.e.194, p. 3.

19. Oxford, Bodleian Library, MS.Don.e.196, p. 6.

20. Oxford, Bodleian Library, MS.Don.e.197, p. 24.

21. Oxford, Bodleian Library, MS.Don.e.196, p. 28.

22. Oxford, Bodleian Library, MS.Don.e.196, p. 35.

23. Oxford, Bodleian Library, MS.Don.e.196, p.12.

24. Oxford, Bodleian Library, MS.Don.e.196, p. 22.

25. Oxford, Bodleian Library, MS.Don.e.198, p. 27.

26. Oxford, Bodleian Library, MS.Don.e.194, p. 4.

27. Oxford, Bodleian Library, MS.Don.e.196, p. 55.

28. Oxford, Bodleian Library, MS.Don.e.198, p.27.

29. *The Irish Widow* was by David Garrick; *The West Indian*, first performed in 1771, was a comedy by Richard Cumberland.

30. This is an affectionate reference to his wife.

31. Oxford, Bodleian Library, MS.Don.e.196, p. 7.

32. In letter to George she says that inflammation of her eyes prevents her from writing too much (Oxford, Bodleian Library, Ms.Don.c.193, fol. 41)

33. Oxford, Bodleian Library, MS.Don.e.196, p. 1.

34. Oxford, Bodleian Library, MS.Don.c.191, fols. 3-4.

35. Oxford, Bodleian Library, MS.Don.e.198 p. 38-9.

36. Oxford, Bodleian Library, MS.Don.e.196, p. 33.

37. Oxford, Bodleian Library, MS.Don.e.194, p. 7.

38. Oxford, Bodleian Library, MS.Don.e.194, p. 13.

39. Oxford, Bodleian Library, MS.Don.e.195, pp 21-22.

40. Oxford, Bodleian Library, MS.Don.e.196, p. 35.

41. Oxford, Bodleian Library, MS.Don.e.196, p. 10.

42. Capability Brown started work on Coombe Abbey Sept 1771; he was paid £7000 by Lord Craven 6th for his work on the garden which was finished by 1774 (Oxford, Bodleian Library, MS.Don.e.196, p. 11).

43. Oxford, Bodleian Library, MS.Don.e.194 , p. 8.

44. Oxford, Bodleian Library, MS.Don.e.194, p. 17.

45. Oxford, Bodleian Library, MS.Don.e.196, p. 29.

46. Oxford, Bodleian Library, MS.Don.e.195, p. 5.

47. Oxford, Bodleian Library, MS.Don.e.194, p. 18.

48. Oxford, Bodleian Library, MS.Don.e.195, p. 12.

49. See Chapter 2.

50. Oxford, Bodleian Library, Ms.Don.e.197, pp 12-13.

51. Oxford, Bodleian Library, MS.Don.e.196, p.14.

52. Lid was the Rev. William Liddiard who was married to Jane, Lord Craven's sister.

53. Oxford, Bodleian Library, Ms.Don.e.196, p.45.

54. Oxford, Bodleian Library, MS.Don.e.198,p. 27.

55. Oxford, Bodleian Library, MS.Don.e.198, p. 40.

56. Oxford, Bodleian Library, MS.Don.c.191, fols. 9-10.

57. We have provided the reader with all the information at our disposal regarding letters among Jane's children as adults. We have normally given dates, names and places when they are known.

58. Oxford, Bodleian Library, MS.Don.c.193, fol. 50-1.

59. Oxford, Bodleian Library, MS.Don.c.193, fol. 59.

60. Oxford, Bodleian Library, MS.Don.c.193, fol. 64-5.

61. Oxford, Bodleian Library, MS.Don.c.193, fol. 92-3.

62. Oxford, Bodleian Library, MS.Don.c.193, fol. 96-7.

63. Oxford, Bodleian Library, MS.Don.c.193, fols. 85.

64. Oxford, Bodleian Library, MS.Don.c.193, fols. 83-4.

65. Oxford, Bodleian Library, MS.Don.c.193, fol. 56-7.

66. Oxford, Bodleian Library, MS.Don.c.193, fol. 58

67. Oxford, Bodleian Library, MS.Don.c.193, fols. 64-5.

68. Oxford, Bodleian Library, MS.Don.c.193, fol. 44-5.

69. There is also a letter from his daughter Harriet to Barbara in 1816 in which she describes *Tales of my Landlord* (by Walter Scott) and discusses the gossip which attributes this and Scott's other novels to his brother.

70. Oxford, Bodleian Library, MS.Don.c.195, fols. 1-2.

71. Oxford, Bodleian Library, MS.Don.c.191, fols. 20-1.

72. Oxford, Bodleian Library, MS.Don.c.191, fols. 27-8.

73. Oxford, Bodleian Library, MS.Don.c.191, fols. 27-8.

74. Probably *The life of Benvenuto Cellini* [...] *written by himself in the Tuscan language and translated from the original by Thomas Nugent* (1771).

75. Berni, Francesco *Orlando in amorato* and other burlesque operas by Berni.

76. Rollin, Charles (1732) *De la maniere d'enseigner d'etudier les Belles-Lettres*

77. *Works of William Congreve* (1773)

78. Racine, Jean (1760) *Oeuvres*

79. Voltaire, & Bet, A.M. (1773) *Ouevres de Molière*

80. Oxford, Bodleian Library, MS.Don.c.193, fols. 46-7.

81. Oxford, Bodleian Library, MS.Don.c.193, fols. 48-9.

82. Could refer to *The Authentic Memoirs of the Countess de Barre*, the French king's mistress by Sir Francis N-, which had just been published in 1771.

83. Probably Antonio de Ulloa's *A Voyage to South America* (3rd. ed. 1772)

84. Oxford, Bodleian Library, MS.Don.c.194, fol. 26.

85. Oxford, Bodleian Library, MS.Don.c.191, fol. 22.

86. Oxford, Bodleian Library, MS.Don.c.191, fols. 7-8.

87. Oxford, Bodleian Library, MS.Don.c.191, fols. 23-4.

88. Horace Walpole's letter was to Hon H S Conway

89. Oxford, Bodleian Library, MS.Don.e.197, p. 5.

90. Oxford, Bodleian Library, MS.Don.c.191, fols. 9-10.

91. Oxford, Bodleian Library, MS.Don.c.191, fols. 45-6.

92. There are only 22 letters from Barbara extant.

93. Oxford, Bodleian Library, MS.Don.c.193, fols. 1-2.

94. Barbara recounts in vivid detail an occasion of celebration when St. Eustasius, a Caribbean island which then belonged to the Dutch West Indies, was captured by Admiral Sir George Rodney to prevent its supporting the French and American armies by supplying them with guns and ammunition during the American War of Independence. Oxford, Bodleian Library, MS.Don.c.193, fols. 33-4.

95. Oxford, Bodleian Library, MS.Don.c.191, fols. 81-5.

96. Oxford, Bodleian Library, MS.Don.c.191, fols. 15-16.

97. Letters indicate she regularly sent them gifts. There are letters from her nieces thanking her for toy snakes, dolls and a stool.

98. It is interesting that as a single woman Barbara did not choose to live with her unmarried brother who had the space and means to provide for her. One can only speculate what the reasons might be. Despite her strong affection for George, Barbara had an independent spirit and she might have found his solitary ways unconducive to her taste for society.

99. Oxford, Bodleian Library, MS. Don.c.193, fols. 27-8.

100. Oxford, Bodleian Library, MS.Don.c.191, fols. 43-44.

101. Oxford, Bodleian Library, MS.Don.c.191, fols. 53-4.

102. Goldsmith, O. (1774) *History of the Earth and Animated Nature*.

103. Oxford, Bodleian Library, MS.Don.c.193, fols. 17-18.

104. Oxford, Bodleian Library, MS.Don.c.193, fols. 19-20.

105. Oxford, Bodleian Library, MS.Don.c.193, fol. 21.

106. Oxford, Bodleian Library, MS.Don.c.193, fols. 27-8.

107. Oxford, Bodleian Library, MS.Don.c.193, fols. 25-6.

108. The philosopher she refers to in the poem might be Thomas Yeoman, an engineer and itinerant lecturer. Oxford, Bodleian Library, MS.Don.c.191, fol. 92.

109. Oxford, Bodleian Library, MS.Don.c.193, fols. 19-20.

110. Oxford, Bodleian Library, MS.Don.c.193, fols. 33-4.

111. Oxford, Bodleian Library, MS.Don.c.193, fols. 37-8.

112. Oxford, Bodleian Library, MS.Don.c.191, fol. 41.

113. Oxford, Bodleian Library, MS.Don.c.193, fols. 25-6.

114. Oxford, Bodleian Library, MS.Don.c.193, fols. 11-12.

115. This suggests that the 'criticism' was written by Barbara herself under her pen name (see Chapter 2, note 7. Oxford, Bodleian Library, MS. Don.c.193, fols. 15-16).

116. Oxford, Bodleian Library, MS.Don.c.193, fols. 25-6.

117. Oxford, Bodleian Library, MS.Don.c.191, fols. 18-19.

Chapter 7[1]

Child's Play for Private and Public Life

Shirley Brice Heath

> These letters were but the vehicle for gallantry and trick. It was a child's play, chosen to conceal a deeper game...
> Jane Austen (1815: 319).

From the Middle Ages forward, cultures whose political systems depend upon socio-economic and social-intellectual hierarchies have placed high value on familial possession of material ephemera. Though such an emphasis certainly does not override the valuation placed on land ownership and possession of high-cost material goods, such as jewellery, houses, or furniture, ephemera, often involving little or no cash expenditure, seem essential within socially stratified societies. Often, these ephemera systemise the habits surrounding their use into games, playful routines, and other organised leisure-time pursuits. Ball games and their physical accoutrements, as well as card and board games (and their contemporary counterparts in electronic game gadgets), amount to ephemera - continuously acquired but not taken seriously as property to be maintained and preserved.

Rarely do earlier societies leave us their ephemera, for such goods are made to be replaced; moreover, they must continuously reflect in their construction something of the styles and technological possibilities of the time of their production. Consider the changing texture of the paper used for cards of card games, as well as the shifting features of folding game boards and their storage of small items needed in their play.

The ephemera of child's play consistently compel the young to link their actions, thoughts, and deeds to narratives beyond the game or activity at hand. Most obvious are the age-old narratives re-enacted in every game: winning and losing, gaining or falling behind, separating and connecting. Every game or playful routine that goes forward does so through a mutually understood set of rules. Embedded within these rules are meta-narratives that have to do with what it means to win or lose and how the game of the moment relates to life lessons of discipline, sportsmanship, fairness, and cheating or lying. Each game re-enacts narratives of past generations; every newly created move within the rules lines the individual up as a strong or weak player, able to bring imagination and wit to the habituated familiar. All play and games of children in societies of hierarchical economic and political arrangements encompass fundamental ideological values. These help prepare children in private for following through on the norms and practices essential in the public social fabric held together by adults as workers, family builders, bearers of political and religious ideologies, and members of the civic and cultural commons.

This chapter draws across the Johnson family materials and their interpretations offered in prior chapters to reveal some core values related to the Johnson children's transitions from the private to the public realm, from the relatively closed roles of child to the comparatively open choices of adults. Three primary features mark the materials of the play and games of the children in their transitions. Along with the rich historical evidence from the early eighteenth century, these materials tell us much about the contexts and practices surrounding their uses and values in the Johnson home.

A central feature evidenced in the materials is the imperative of linking the cognitive and the social. A second feature relates to the integration of scientific observation and mathematical understanding with language and literacy. The final characteristic demonstrates the point that verbal fluency must go hand-in-hand with attention to the visual and the dramatic. We cannot claim absolute uniqueness for either Jane's nursery library and short story or the philosophical and personal underpinnings behind her elaborate handcrafted pieces. Yet we are compelled to reflect on what they illustrate about mental processes that went into preparing the young for moving from the privacy and intimacy of the home and family to the public spheres of school and professional life in the first half of the eighteenth century.

Building the cognitive through the social

Long-term and close-up familiarity with the Johnson family materials, particularly those created by Jane for the nursery library, allows some curious juxtapositions to emerge. Much discussed in this volume have been her wit and humour, along with her deep religious devotion. She, like others of her day, did not wish the heaviness of moral instruction to cover the joy, delight, and personal rewards of a life of learning. In this feature, Jane was no particular exception to others creating games of play related to literacy.

But, taken as a whole, Jane's body of work employs unexpected disjunctures and twists and turns. One such twist comes in her infusions of the seemingly trivial and idiosyncratic within deeply cognitive lesson-like materials. She compels children to puzzle through the simultaneities of close-up and distant, fantastic and factual, sacred and profane. Her game materials for literacy bring the children and their neighbours together with animals and angels, all in the presence of Biblical and philosophical quotations and illustrations from the Roman Empire. To be sure, in some sets, she includes only Biblical references, though selected and often paraphrased to meet a child's understanding. Within other sets, she mixes vernacular renderings of sacred scriptural messages with accounts of local events, such as country fairs and market days. She includes pictures of well-known farm animals as well as strange creatures; she portrays singing, dancing, juggling, pantomime, and harlequinades - all part of the stage effects of the life of fairgrounds and other ad hoc playing spaces of provincial theatres that spread throughout England in the early eighteenth century.[2] These juxtapositions and mixtures within the nursery materials would have ensured some narrative recall of direct entertainment experiences as well as laughter over details of the movements, dress, attitudes, and activities of the bawdry, haughty, and ordinary.

Attention to detail, recall of experiences, and comparison across what appeared to be samenesses as well as differences must have accompanied use of the materials. These sociocognitive behaviours surely would have been foreshadowed in Jane's mind as she created the materials. Keep alert; pay attention; say what you see; interpret illustration and text; see that life embraces the spiritual and the secular. These thought-provoking prompts lie embedded within the elements of construction, as well as within the easily accessible content of the card sets. The playful routines that attended games the Johnson children played with these sets must surely have been conversationally interactive occasions. On these occasions, the ephemera brought about not only the repeated practices that support lifelong literate habits, but also patterns of text-based and life-referenced conversation that mark adults who take their place in the civic and cultural common.

Jane's fascination with puzzles and disjunctures are often underscored through her use of visual illustrations as well as her textual challenges to children to imagine visually what they have never seen. Some illustrative materials extend meanings possibly inherent in their accompanying written texts, while others bear no discernible relationship at all to their accompanying words and sentences. Distant events, such as beheadings or hangings come along with alphabet rhymes and portrayals of quirky or unseasonable appearances in nature. Within mini-narratives of the card sets, as well as in *A Very Pretty Story,* surprising juxtapositions spring up to catch the attention and draw the young into puzzlement as well as laughter and pleasure. In this, her longest text for children, Jane ties what must have been a local spectator event in a country fair with an impossible chariot ride. She blends the real theatrical spectacles of the fair, rich in the thrills of acrobats and harlequins, with the magic of a visually rich imaginative journey to faraway places.

During the first half of the eighteenth century, combinations of spectacles stretched beyond urban areas such as Lincoln to smaller towns. The Johnson children surely witnessed markets (mentioned in several card sets Jane created) that took place in regional towns. To these markets came theatrical diversions along with dramatic performances that included intermissions of spectacular stunts, displays of strange animals, and outrageously costumed pantomime artists. Included in several sets are characters such as a female tight-rope walker (figure 18), male in Oriental costume, male playing a long flute, dancing couples, drunkards, a 'monkey-man,' and a monstrous 'strange' bird 'ugly enough to fright little Misses'.[3]

Figure 19. Set 21 item 6. Courtesy of the Lilly Library, University of Indiana, Bloomington, Indiana.

Thomas Boreman's volume, *A Description of a Great Variety of Animals and Vegetables Extracted from the most considerable Writers of Natural History; and Adapted to the Use of all Capacities, especially for the Entertainment of Youth* (1736) was a supplement to an earlier volume, *A Description of Three Hundred Animals*. Along with sections on plants, fruits, and flowers, are 'four-footed beasts,' birds, fishes, and insects. But within each of these categories, certain 'strange creatures' appear. Figure 7 is of 'The Man-Tiger,' described as

> a Beast that participates [sic] much of the subtle and mischievous Nature of Apes and Baboons; but much more bold and fierce. Some Writers have confidently asserted, that some of these Creatures have had the boldness to attack the Chastity of Women. (Boreman, 1736: 5)

Boreman believed, as Jane no doubt did, that such descriptions would not only 'delight and please young Persons,' but would also be 'undoubtedly [...] a fresh Motive to engage their Attention' (Boreman, 1736: np). There is good evidence that Boreman, Johnson, and others of the spectator-readers of their day also endorsed the view that materials of 'natural history' represented an 'inexhaustible Subject' and served to advance learning in ways 'vastly superior to the Tales, Fables, and Stories of Love, used in Schools' (ibid). These 'natural' materials were therefore deserving of considerable attention by parents wishing both to entertain their children and to prepare them for the leisurely pursuits that would continue to be available to them as adults.

Jane includes the natural and the 'odd' in card sets that also portray such mundane activities as lying down on the ground, watching robins, commenting on the coaches of the rich, and remembering street cries of the milkmaid. Thus there is a constant back-and-forth movement, compare-and-contrast, see-and-remember quality to the game sets of Jane's materials. In one set (Set 17),[4] number 27 is of a milkmaid, while number 26 is of a linnet and thrush, and number 30 is of a peacock. In the centre of each card of this set - generally after the first two lines - is pasted one or two colour cut-outs of the central item(s) noted in the text (e.g. birds in a tree, peacock, etc.):

> A linnet, and a
> Thrush. Sitting in a Bush.
> For three Months in the Spring, They
> most sweetly do Sing. (Set 17, item 26)

> Of all the fine Birds
>   that fly in the Air,
> None can with the Peacock, for beauty
> Compare. (Set 17, item 30)

Yet number 29 takes up little George Johnson's friendship with what must have been a neighbour child:

> O! had I wings I would
> Fly like this Dove
> To Visit Miss Wrighte
> Who so dearly I Love. (Set 17, item 29)

Beneath these lines is written in carefully printed letters: George Johnson. Here with her use of the deictic (or pointing) pronoun of *this*, Jane departs from her usual pattern of third person pronouns (such as *they*) to point to details of her illustrations. Furthermore, on this card, she adds George's full name to ensure that the '*I*' of the quoted wish is clearly identified.

Along with such innocent and light-hearted friendship hopes of young children come some reminders of behaviours and characters not generally included in polite conversation. As was customary in other materials for children of the early eighteenth century, some of Jane's game sets do not sidestep the matter of defecation, body parts, unseemly sexual behaviours and characters, and cruelty to animals and children. One item of a vocabulary-development set leads off with 'breast' and ends with 'guts'. A set of rhyming sounds includes 'shit,' while another lists 'slut'. Within one set, a hungry eagle carries off a child in a cradle, and the cries and screams of the child were 'in vain, For his Life, was soon ended' (Set 16, item 1).

Figure 20. Courtesy of the Lilly Library, University of Indiana, Bloomington, Indiana.

These juxtapositions and contrasts, based on both the seen and unseen of everyday hopes and fears, signal Jane's own approach to taking care that her materials would give good exercise to the inquiring minds of her children. In Robert's journal, as well as Barbara's letters, we have ample evidence that the giggles, slight taunts, joys of entertainment, and habits of inquiry stayed with Jane's children into their adulthood. Barbara's letters as an adult indicate that she longs to know more of the foreign places to which George travels. Robert, George, and Barbara seek out books that will bring them news from afar, familiarity with the strange, and materials for deeper reflection and meditation, and even challenges to their customary ways of seeing the world.

Science and mathematics in the everyday world

Materials printed for children in the eighteenth century often urge the young to observe and know the 'natural world' through taking note of features that appear in the here-and-now and often for functional purposes. Yet the young must also be prepared to see these features within abstract shapes. Jane's eye for design reflects this dual understanding. Moreover, many of her card sets illustrate a sense that core activities of the world of science - typologising, identifying, and describing - must be habituated from an early age. She juggles triangles, squares, and their arrangements in several mobiles, making these arrangements sure prompts for counting as well as discriminating shapes, sizes, and their possible re-arrangements. She lays out lists whose items are bound by common features; she sets out definitions and identifications, illustrating the underlying grammatical principles of these core scientific practices through reference to everyday people, places, and objects known from the children's experiences and observations.

Within many of the sets, she reflects in her designs a perception of the simultaneity of the abstract and the concrete. A box is a box with many functional purposes, but it also may be a square that will, as a result of its physical features and measurements, rest in a parallel line against only objects that have at least one straight edge. Rotation of the square for parallel alignment is possible only when another object has at least one corner with a 90-degree angle. The mobiles Jane created illustrate such abstract notions of the arrangement of geometric forms, and the tiny box created to hold one set of cards each no larger than a fingernail and more than seventy in number is an almost perfect square that holds tiny rectangular bits within. Jane thus created materials that would have allowed her to illustrate through manipulation principles of alignment, size comparability, and commonalities across figures her children would later come to know in their studies of mathematics.

This sense of get-ready-for-later-learning-challenges comes as well in the fact that Jane's materials indicate to the young that curiosity about the natural world will lead to a desire to read not only more widely but also more deeply. The other value of 'natural history' and its links to the sciences and mathematics comes in the fact that core scientific principles are played out in the everyday and the common. One such principle (co-occurrence) appears in her numerous recountings of events and animals that appear in certain seasons of the year, especially Spring. She often illustrates cause-and-effect 'laws' at work in the world of nature. And she does so in her mini-narratives on the behaviour of children as well. Consider the following rhyme:

A Boy and a Girl did
eat Sugar and Plumbs
Till they made their teeth
ake, and fall from their gums;
And then they could eat,
no-thing but bread crums.
(Set 18, item 1)

Figure 21. Courtesy of the Lilly Library, University of Indiana, Bloomington, Indiana.

Certainly, many of these 'mini-lessons' also illustrate ways in which nature and natural events demonstrate not only the cause-and-effect principles of sciences and mathematics, but also the power of God and the resulting call to observers and readers to honour God for his 'works of perfection' (see the introductory materials to Boreman, 1736, for expression of these values). Jane's card sets were no exception to this idea, but once again, she adds to the power of 'natural history' the narrative appeal of personal history.

As noted earlier, she designs her materials in ways that call upon the children to be alert to the abstractions reflected in the everyday order of things. Furniture, houses, beasts and birds, foods and tools - either as wholes or in parts - reflect morphology and invite categorisation. For example, one page of the little book created for George confines itself to food and items used in setting a table: plate, dish, fork, knife, spoon, salt, meat, beef, veal, mutton, lamb, pork, bread, cheese, pudding, table, cloth, mug, cup, glass, wine. These are not random, however, for they suggest an order or sequence to their use in setting a table and taking part in a meal.

One set of twelve cards (Set 19) includes only definitions or identifications. These open the learner to understanding that one way of organising the world is to compile lists of items arranged according to their core or most defining features. For example, one such list of Jane's is of objects or items that are inanimate and have been constructed (for example, plates, glasses, bread, pudding); another is of items derived from natural or formerly animate matter (for example, meat, beef, or veal). Yet another way of managing items in the world is to offer definitions or identifications that lead to categorisation. All of Jane's cards that are definitions offer a single noun (common or proper), followed by a comma, and a definition. For example, 'A Bustard, a great sluggish Fowl that is good to eat' (Set 19, item 1). On this card, the definition appears on the front, and on the reverse is a coloured picture of a bird that could only loosely be construed as a 'bustard'.

Jane's items constructed as identifications open with the person or event (often a proper noun) to be identified; this naming is then followed by a comma and descriptive material. For example, one member of this set offers the following identification: 'Lady Margaret Mordaunt, Daughter to the Earl of Peter-Borow, in a Red Lustring [sic. intended to be Lutestring] Coat' (Set 19, item 2). Here again, Jane is not insistent that the picture on the reverse side of the card reflect precisely the detail of the identifying description; the picture accompanying Lady Mordaunt's identification is of a woman in a pink ballgown, but she wears no coat. Yet another such identification is of 'Miss Cherry Lily, dress'd in a blue Sattin Coat; walking with a Fan in her hand, to Church' (Set 19, item 5). The accompanying tiny picture is of a woman dressed in blue carrying a fan in her hand, but she wears no coat.

Figure 22. Courtesy of the Lilly Library, University of Indiana, Bloomington, Indiana.

Jane's descriptions include not only proper nouns, but also everyday items. However, all of these named in this set are specifically contextualised in spaces and often with people the children must have known. For example, the following three cards are included:

A Tulip, and a Sun-
Flower; that grew in the Dutchess of Ken-
dal's Garden, at Hickling in Nor-folk.
[pictured on the reverse are two flowers, a tulip and small sunflower]
(Set 19 item 11)

Two very pretty
Chickens, in an Or-
chard, of Thomas
Pelham's Duke of
Newcastle at Farn
in Northumberland.
[pictured on the reverse are two chickens, one yellow, one grey]
(Set 19, item 12)

One card is highly local and must have referred to a garden the children saw on their family trips to Lincoln: 'A Rabbet, and an Ash tree, in Dunnington Warren in Lincolnshire' (Set 19, item 9). Others refer to common animals, such as a cow or deer, and their identification places these in relation to named individuals as well as geographic locations. Advancing achievement in mathematics and sciences has always depended upon a learner's facility in both recognition and production of definitions and identifications. Innocent as Jane's writings appear, their design reveals an underlying systematicity that cannot be overlooked.

Jane returns again and again in the sets of her materials to the need to draw the attention of her children to ordering members of a class or set, perceiving cause and effect, and discriminating among phenomena that might, on the surface, appear to look alike. She arranges animals into groups of the familiar and the fantastic, offering different types of descriptions of each, drawing in the first case on what the children already knew and in the second on their need to have metaphors to create images of creatures they have never seen. Lists of insects include only pests and familiar animals of the household, rather than the usual alphabetical compulsion used by other authors of her day to include both the exotic and familiar in such lists.

When she writes of birds, she goes repeatedly to her local favourites - the robin, linnet, thrush, and hawk, but she illustrates their individual characteristics of appearance as well as their different capabilities. She directly and indirectly encourages her children to observe birds and animals in relation to their lives at different seasons of the year. In 1747, Jane composed the ballad inviting Barbara back from London to enjoy the countryside in early May, filled with nature's abundance of Spring. She writes:

> The Gold Finch, Linnet, and the Thrush
> Now charm our ears from every Brush:
> The shrill larks soaring to the sky,
> Most sweetly singing as they fly.
> The nightingale with tuneful song,
> Enchanting Warbles all night long.[5]

This level of detail and description mark many of the genres she produced, inciting the children to connect activities of animals and birds with seasons and specific locations. Bits of geography, local farm life, and seasonal rituals mingle in the natural history of Jane's materials with the far more abstract tasks of learning classification systems and grasping the relationship of parts to the whole in the morphology of the human anatomy.

The Verbal, visual, and dramatic

The variety of verbal means taken up in the sets of cards that Jane created offers several contrasts with the uses of language in other children's materials of her day. The list of genres reflected in her extant writings include: aphorisms, maxims, fable, short story, street cries, retelling of children's antics and familiar events, action-scripted conversational observations, moral summative statements, Biblical quotations and paraphrases of verses, as well as personal letters, letters of complaint, and, of course, her commonplace book (see earlier chapters for more detail on each of these genres). To be sure, many of these genres incorporate language in ways familiar also in the writings of her contemporaries. However, the full corpus of her texts reveals some differences that show her persistent tendency to push boundaries beyond the given from other texts written for children that she must have been reading and consulting.

Most evident is her use of complexly constructed sentences that include everyday material and direct quotations of speech. One way of thinking about her approach to syntax or combinations of ideas in grammatical form is to imagine this mother's action-scripted conversation with one or more of her children during walks through the nearby countryside or in household chores.[6] One set in particular (Set 16) touches on the descriptive or the identificational features noted above, but the cards of this set include syntactically complex sentences that combine utterances that Jane might have said to any one of her children. For example, one card notes on the front the following sentence: 'Roger Bowyer, with a Sheep that has its Legs tied together, hanging over his arm; he is going to sell it, at Colebrook Market, and as he walks along, he hears the Cuckoo Sing, which makes him lift up his hand in great surprise, it being in the month of March' (Set 16, item 5). The picture on the back of the card is of a man who carries a sheep over his arm.

Figure 23. Courtesy of the Lilly Library, University of Indiana, Bloomington, Indiana.

Though this card begins with an identification, the next portion is explanatory of the action (walking to market to sell an animal) and also of an expression of emotion (surprise at the early sign of spring). One can hear an adult answering the question of a child 'why is he carrying the sheep?' with the response 'He is going to sell it at Colebrook Market'. The child responds: 'why is he holding his hand up like that?' The adult answers 'I think he must be surprised to hear a cuckoo sing so early in the spring'. Yet the combination of this string of oral utterances into a single highly literate written sentence brings about a highly descriptive and syntactically complex description. Note that this is a narrative, for it moves action and character forward in time, but it is also an example of description in *literate* style embedded in a very simple short recount.

She often inserts a conversational interactive framework within her alphabet-patterned collections, but sometimes these are of ordinary talk and at other times of literary formal writers. After a string of observations or descriptions, she will insert a highly formal and literary line, such as 'D was a Drawer, Pray, Sir, do you call?' (Set 5, item 2).

One set of cards in particular (Set 18) lends itself to interpretation of her mixture of styles and referents of language. This set includes nine items. The cards are made of white paper, doubled with Dutch gilt paper backing, often with narrow strips of the richly coloured Dutch gilt paper also encasing the large central black and white etching, which is usually of a single figure. Lists of vocabulary items are placed along the sides and sometimes at the bottom. Some are more ornate than others and include verses at the top and bottom with the Dutch paper frame going out at each corner to a pasted corner brace made of the same type of paper. A set of green threads attached at the top indicates the cards were made for hanging. Several of these sets can be read as containing internal ironies, but one is particularly notable. The central verse reads:

> There was an old Sow, and she had but one Pig;
> And one day she gave her some grapes and a fig
> And the next day she gave her some good milk and whey
>
> [central picture is of a book with the inscription in Latin: *DOMINUS ILLUMINATIO MEA* (The lord is my Light)]
>
> And did Dress her with Flower all over gay
> Then bid her take care and keep out of the dirt
> For her ears she would box if she should prove a slut. (Set 18, item 6)

Figure 24. Courtesy of the Lilly Library, University of Indiana, Bloomington, Indiana.

The list of words that runs along one side include: King, Queen, Prince Duke, Lord, and on the other: Sir, Miss, Madam, Lady, Master. Though inferring motive for such juxtapositions must be done cautiously, it is difficult to believe that given the extraordinary care that Jane used in the construction of so many items of her nursery library, she was unaware of the ironic combination of characters and actions in the verse and word lists on this card and others of this set. All have an undertone of irreverence about them, with several picturing harlequins, circus-like figures, and entertainers. One of these includes the central illustration of a figure dancing with a battledore in the right hand; the figure is in front of what appears to be large public buildings in the background. Yet another pictures a man with a basket dancing in the street also in front of a public official building. It may simply be that these illustrations were Jane's way of indicating that the public stage in the provinces was indeed just that: highly public and open to ad hoc performances.

One of the cards of this set contains a verse that echoes the language of earlier sets in that it is a reminder to the children that the scene captured in the verse is familiar to them. Here the message may be that the animals manage their needs in complementary distribution and perhaps in a more harmonious manner than do humans.

> A Horse, and Mare,
> a Buck, and a Doe,
> Did all live in a park
> And so did a Crow;
> The Crow eat the worms
> the rest eat the grass.
> It was not far off
> where this came to pass. (Set 18, item 3)

A tone of irreverence and jabs at the foibles of humans, even those in high places, also characterised other materials written for children during the period in which Jane was composing her nursery library. But these other materials consistently make fun of those distant from the young learner and not next door, on the way to market, or down the road.[7] Her verses hit the high and the low. She calls attention to the dishonesty of the miller near the end of town, the slow pace of the cobbler at work, and the hunter who accidentally shoots his dog. She also points out the false pride and illicit passions of those of lineage and wealth.

Beyond her conversational tone in language that is by no means simplified for child listeners is her presentation of both current 'standardised' prestige forms of English and well-known regional and common forms. Here she once again shows juxtaposition - both conservation and innovation - in her literacy instruction.

Writing and its transmission through literacy acquisition are often considered as means of conserving, transmitting, and enforcing 'standard' or prestige language varieties. In Jane's case, she played the gamut from the most 'bookish' to the most colloquial. The predominant discourse and style features of published works for children of the period include, along with word lists, sing-song combinations of lines, Biblical quotations, or short moral tales. Though these features also appear in Jane's corpus, other portions indicate Jane's adoption of ordinary conversational segments (such as 'The Eagle flies high, but can't touch the sky' or 'A duck and a drake jumpt into the water, and all the young ducks did paddle in after' - from Set 17) along with lexical items that are highly regional and border on the archaic. Yet, unlike other nursery materials of her time, Jane's materials rarely include words such as *thou, shalt, thee,* or abbreviated literary forms, such as *where'e'er* or *go'st,* sure to pull children's sense of language away from ordinary conversational language within their own families. She sometimes directly quotes Biblical texts, but she also often paraphrases these, often in connection with an illustration from everyday life (see also Chapter 4).

Attention to word patterns comes through in the arrangements of items in several series. Within even the most boring bits of the English language, such as function words (prepositions, pronouns, articles, and the like), Jane manages to introduce intrigue and humour. Son George finds his name embedded within such a list: *from, most, must, take, wick, wild, which, George, good, thought, Strength, lip* (Set 17). The boy was most certainly called on to create with some of these words a short recounting of at least one of his antics. For the above list of vocabulary items, we can imagine young George creating a sentence in which he is the young actor, jumping *from* the bank in a *most wild* manner, causing his dear mother to *take* all her *Strength* to recover him (see Barbara's account of this event in Chapter 1).

Alongside her switches within the materials that help ensure attention to verbal shifts in style and conventions, Jane's cards and letters to her children also indicate her insistence on their visual attentiveness. The aesthetic qualities of the nursery library stand out as the most obvious evidence on this point. However, numerous other aspects of her work underscore her sense of not only the visual supports to the written word that come through illustrations, but also the need for 'reading' illustrations or having visual literacy. The latter relates directly to the conversational nature of many of her card sets, for the illustrations provoke conversations of interpretation that depend on seeing and linking details within the art as well as tying the entire visual illustration to the written words on the single card within the set.

Jane's writings, especially her card sets, open her perspective on children as performers in like households of the English countryside. Though filled with reminders about behavioural strictures of polite society and 'good boys and girls' (as well as 'proper' men and women), the card sets (and Jane's story) let us know some of the ways in which the Johnson children most frequently misbehaved. Lying, showing disrespect, and displaying pride and selfishness appear most frequently in her little lessons and admonitions. The downfall of the fated child in Jane's story centres around lying and selfishness, falsehood and greed, and her admonitions against lying run the gamut from parental disapproval to 'Hell's Torments'.

Noted throughout earlier chapters of this volume has been Jane's care to include within her materials references to both the wealthy and the poor. However, within her materials, and often through cards that portray either the rich or the poor, Jane also inserts in quite distinctive genres certain sub-texts that must reflect other levels of awareness she wished to pass on to her children. Primary among these is her care to reference women (and tradesmen) in their work. Tasks and obligations range from begging for one's children (illustrated in a street cry: 'Give some Bread to my Children I beg and I pray Or they will be starved having had none to day') to stopping fights in public places. Often within these cards, her sub-texts are layered. For example, in the beggar's street cry, the illustration is composed of two separate pasted cut-out pictures, one of a woman richly clothed responding in a haughty manner to a separate but facing illustration of a poorly dressed woman with two children by her side reaching out toward the woman of wealth (Set 17, item 15). Her unspoken commentary through her selection of illustrations points to the needs of wealthy women as well as those of poverty. Jane seems to be 'saying' in her illustrations: see the evidence of attitude, mental state, background, and need of these individuals.

Jane points out numerous 'occupations' of women - some vocational as well as avocational, and the roles or functions that women serve in maintaining a quality of character within the society. One card (within Set 17) includes the statement: 'How wicked these men are to Quarrel and Fight: They surely forget that they are in God's sight' (Set 17, item 19). The illustration is of a woman trying to stop a fight between two men. Living in respect for and obedience to God falls to women often in Jane's verses and illustrations. One card, for example, states: 'They that fear the Lord will obey his world [sic. for *word* must have been intended here], and they that love him will keep his Laws' (Set 15, item 3). The illustration is of a woman standing by a tree and staring into the distance. Other verses of this type, such as those reminding readers to 'love the Lord' or acknowledge all wisdom from Him, come in association with illustrations only of women. To be sure, some illustrations are of males, but most often those asserting goodness come with portrayals of women, and often with women attempting to halt or call attention to the misdeeds of men.

Jane also seemed eager to point out the hard labour that many women had to endure. One set of cards (Set 17) includes several cards devoted to the occupations of women (as well as tradesmen) and their diligent work. One reads:

> At a house by a Gate,
> Did live without state
> A little old woman
> and man.
>
> [central illustration of a woman and a man, each with a garden tool, pictured on a background farm scene]
>
> They did work for
> their bread, And were
> very well fed, and the
> old woman's name, it
> was Nan. (Set 17, item2)

Another card in this set illustrates again Jane's contempt for wealthy women who appear to disdain those in need or who must work hard.

Good Girl make
haste and have
done with your broom

[pasted in the centre are two separate pictures; one is of a girl with a broom, and the other is of a mistress clad in rich-looking garments and bearing a haughty manner]

Of all things I hate
such a dust in the
Room. (Set 17, item 16)

Figure 25. Courtesy of the Lilly Library, University of Indiana, Bloomington, Indiana.

Street cries appear in contemporary materials for children of Jane's time, but once again, her personal concerns and interests are reflected in her patterned selection of these. All her women provide the most sustaining of foods - milk and fruit - for their buyers (for discussion of street cries in children's literature, see Gumuchian, 1941). One card pictures a woman with two large milk pails, each at the end of a bar laid across her shoulders; the woman cries out:

> Maids will you
> buy any Milk, will
> you have some or
> no, Unless you
> come quickly, away
> I must go. (Set 17, item 27)

Another is of a woman with a cart of oranges, issuing the familiar cry of 'Two for a penny, Oranges, all sound and sweet; come try them and buy them of me in the street' (Set 17, item 41).

Figure 26. Courtesy of the Lilly Library, University of Indiana, Bloomington, Indiana.

Language always works as a primary force to indicate not only our intended meanings, but our unspoken and unrealised subtexts as well. Jane's materials reflect this truism in many ways. Pious, observant, dedicated mother and wife, as she must surely have been, she had views and talents of her own that she chose to insert judiciously and discretely into a set of literacy materials that appear to parallel many other literacy materials of her day. Yet by reading closely and comparatively across this rich set of Jane's ephemera, we learn more than she might think we as distant outsiders could possibly know of how her mind worked and what her aspirations were for the types of adults she wished her children to become.

So what?

At the end of any process of historical research, arduously and painstakingly carried out, often over thousands of miles and through piles of correspondence, the ultimate question of 'so what?' has to be asked. Those 'possessed' in the process of historical inquiry understand perfectly well why the pursuit of bringing 'back to life' an historical figure, period, or item can occupy scholars for years. Others never caught up in such pursuits may, however, deserve some explanation of what the stories of Jane, her children, and their writing, reading, and playing with ephemera mean.

The British novelist, A S Byatt, explained the beginning of the prize-winning 1990 novel, *Possession*, in a way that sums up the intent of all historians and, most certainly, of those involved in bringing Jane's tale together. Byatt recounted the naming of her novel and its core purpose as follows:

The beginning of *Possession*, and the first choice, was most unusually for me, the title. I thought of it in the British Library, watching that great Coleridge scholar, Kathleen Cobun, circumambulating the catalogue. I thought: she has given all her life to his thoughts, and then I thought: she has mediated his thoughts to me. And then I thought 'Does he possess her, or does she possess him? There could be a novel called *Possession about the relations between living and dead minds*'. (emphasis not in the original; Byatt, 1990).

It is just this relationship - that of minds across the years engaged in similar activities with surprisingly common materials and mean - that explains 'possession' by an historical figure and his or her time. For in no search of an individual's history can a scholar avoid being drawn also into the social and cultural activities of the period.

In the case of all ephemera, and especially for children's toys, games, and literacy-related artefacts, it may seem strange to assert that their makers create them, and their users take them up 'to conceal a deeper game'. However, it is in the very nature of all play, and most markedly within literacy supports in play, that these ephemera are about much more than their surface appeal. No strategy of a children's book illustrator is without purpose, and authors of works for children know that their greatest strength is in the ambiguities of their language and pictures, allowing imagination to take their readers to a host of possible interpretations. Children outstrip most adults in their powers to fantasise, parody, and riddle in wild and unpredictable directions. It is precisely their engagement in play that fuels the imaginations of the young.

This idea and others that became prominent in child development, school reform, and literacy studies in the twentieth century appear evident throughout the nursery library of Jane. In many ways, Jane's nursery library reflects theories of learning that came to prominence only in the twentieth century. Yet the core of most of these ideas lies within the writings of John Locke and some of his contemporaries. For example, she demonstrates the cognitive underpinnings of 'the educated mind' proposed throughout the 1980s by Kieran Egan, Canadian scholar (see especially Egan, 1997). He asserts the importance of bodily understanding, the drawing in of information and skills to one's own person. He further argues the power of what he terms the 'mythic,' or that which includes opposites, parody, metaphor, and rhyme. And, like Jane, he pushes for the 'romantic,' that which links the exotic and heroic across contexts and persons. He also does not leave aside the philosophical or the principle-driven understandings of the tenets by which cause and effect, change, contradictions, and separations of facts and truth govern our world. Finally, he proposes for the 'educated mind' engagement with the 'ironic,' surely a quality embraced in Jane's work.

Certain 'truths,' 'discoveries,' or 'theories' (note that educators use all these terms and often to refer to the same concepts) seem to have to be discovered and rediscovered. Such truths have to be newly announced and claimed every few decades. Such is the case for much within the socio-historical work of Lev Vygotsky and his teachers as well as his followers. The case is the same for imagination, creativity, and experiential learning, as well as many other ideas in education that became 'current' in recent decades. John Dewey, Howard Gardner, David Perkins, and proponents of the Reggio Emilia approach would all understand that what appear to be redundancies across centuries are in fact good evidence of the sustained importance to human beings of the learning of the young and the role that adults can and must play in promoting this learning in the best possible ways. These scholars would also know that their urgings repeat time-worn arguments surrounding how 'best' to make the learning that occurs beyond school more pleasurable and intimate than that within school can generally be (cf. Boreman, 1736). All such arguments rest in large part on the obvious need to take into account motivation, and investment in role engagement for the young learner.

Less well-known and certainly less 'current' than those ideas about education noted above is one other that is evident within Jane's work and that of the most celebrated authors and illustrators of children's literature. That is the power of role and performance combined. And here it is necessary to make what may seem a divergence to note a particular contextual feature of the time in which Jane and her children, Robert and Barbara, were writing - the linkage of stage and page, of the visual and the verbal of public performance spaces. This contextual feature surely figured strongly in the background of the creative artistic work of Jane and in her uses of the materials with her children.

Throughout Jane's materials are both direct and indirect references to eighteenth-century 'readerly theatre' (Fishman, 2005). Moveable scenery entered the public stage only in the second half of the seventeenth century. From that point on, stage effects and complements to the mainpiece plays spread throughout the provinces from the British playhouses in London. For a five-act play, the occasions between scenes and even after the main play allowed for all sorts of new characters (see, for example, Bevis, 1970). These newcomers were just that - *characters* often in the sense of caricatures and not real persons playing the parts of real people whose speeches had been scripted. These entertainers were jugglers, pantomimists, dancers, singers, and harlequins, and contortionists. Plays became the vehicles of 'gallantry and trick' - both highly entertaining.

On stage, during the mainpiece plays, actors took on new forms of silent expression. All these innovations moved away from the auditory entertainment orientation of the early modern stage. Audiences were no longer mere listeners, but they were pulled toward the role of spectator-reader. The facial, gestural, emotive expressions, and person-centred role interpretations of characters had to be 'read' rather than heard.

Long scenes in which an actor said little or nothing often centred in that actor and depended on the fact that onlookers would 'read' his intentions, motives, and backgrounds of actions (for more on this phenomenon, particularly through pantomime, see Sawyer, 1990). Pantomime depended on visual elements that had to be 'read' in an actor's body for a performance to be interpreted in the context of the ongoing script realised only partly in the words of other actors. Moreover, with pantomime and greater focus on indications of motive and intention through gesture and facial expression, actors had to attend to one another on the stage, creating what came later to be called 'the fourth wall' between the stage and the audience/onlookers.[8]

Perhaps best known among actors who forced viewers to read this form of acting was David Garrick, known to Robert and Barbara Johnson, no doubt, not only through his prominence in the theatre, but also as a member of the Bath group of 'poets' (see chapter 6). Before Garrick was Charles Macklin, who made his debut in 1741 and, unlike Garrick, travelled widely to regional playhouses with troupes of travelling players before taking to London stages. It was as a pantomimist that Macklin began his career (Appleton, 1960). He and others who relied on mime enjoyed the support of scenery that attended provincial public stages, including makeshift performance spaces in country markets and on fairgrounds. All these together supported onlookers in being entertained as well as in gleaning the drama's narrative through what they could see rather than through the words they surely could not hear in such public spaces.

The 'so what?' of the stories of Jane and her family has then many answers. Foremost among these is the endurance of play and 'the play of it all' in certain basic human interactions that young and old alike enjoy. Jane's placement of her illustrations - character facing character, each precisely cut from two different sources so as to illustrate the narrative behind the card's intention - imitate what she saw on the public stage in actors' and entertainers' uses of their bodily postures, facial expressions, and backdrops to tell the stories. Moreover, many of Jane's illustrations are themselves of the strolling players and the assorted entertainers who accompanied them: acrobats, dancers, musicians, etc. In many of her cards, Jane takes her cue from the mix of the between-acts and after-play characters along with the core narrative of the mainpiece play. Entities within this mix need not be all of a central theme or even related in their purpose; each has its entertainment 'to delight' value. It is also telling that the rewards for virtue in the 'Castle of Pleasure and Delights' in Jane's *A Very Pretty Story*, include watching puppet-shows and plays.

In some ways, Jane also creates her children as part of a 'home stage' and the dramas of that place. They perform, play roles, and act against backdrops within her cards. No doubt, the games and play that went along with the uses of the cards called further on the performative abilities of the children.

Authenticity, reality, and rigor need their mediations, as does the learning of skills and subjects that have marked academic pursuits for centuries. Reading, writing, classifying, observing, and reflecting in pursuit of understanding mathematics, botany, zoology, philosophy, and theology: central to all of these is finding one's way into and through the 'lessons' of both play and school. Jane reminded her children thusly in the familiar verse:

> This is Jack Woodhouse
> a Riding to School,
> To Play with the
> Boys, and Learn
> Latin by Rule. (Set 17, item 37)

Jane links wonder and play with dogged persistence. Her writings echo the sentiment she enters in the couplet 'Reasons, whole pleasures, all the joys of sense, lie in 3 words - health, peace, competence'. Along with these, she adds imagination and empathy, qualities essential to sustaining a vitality in and for life that carries one from the private to the public, from childhood to adulthood, from child's play to the 'deeper game' of growing up.

Notes

1. This chapter was completed while the author was a Distinguished Fellow at the Institute for Advanced Study, LaTrobe University, Melbourne, Australia, August-October, 2005. The author acknowledges the Institute with gratitude for its commitment to scholarship and recognition of the need for seclusion to speed the conclusion of projects. Immeasurable appreciation goes also to Jen Fishman, Department of English, University of Tennessee, Knoxville, for her help in tracking down possible sources for

the entertainment references and illustrations used by Jane Johnson and in providing her expertise in seventeenth- and eighteenth-century drama in a substantial way throughout this chapter.

2.   Records of the activities of strolling players, including scenery that accompanied them, are extensive for some areas of the provinces. See chapter 3, footnote 21, of Fishman (2004) and Rosenfeld (1939).

3.   Points made throughout this chapter, and especially in the final section, illustrate Jane Johnson's awareness of the array of public entertainments increasingly popular throughout the eighteenth century. Many of these included the scatological. Some of these caricatures may have been based on actual figures, but their 'performers' and 'performances' endured. Jane's illustration of a monkey man defecating and her mention of this character provide an example of her inclusion of elements of such public characters in her nursery library. Both Francis Coventry and Oliver Goldsmith have characters called Monkeyman. In Coventry's *The History of Pompey the Little: or, The Life and Adventures of a Lap-Dog*, the Count explains, 'I am obliged to call on lord Monkeyman, who desires my opinion on some pictures he is going to buy' (1751: 194). In Goldsmith's *The Citizen of the World; or Letters from a Chinese Philosopher, Residing in London, to his Friends in the East* (London, 1762), a fictional Englishwoman writes to a fictional woman correspondent from the east, describing a colonel thus: 'As I live, my dear Charlotte, I believe the colonel will carry it at last; he is a most irresistible fellow, that's that. So well dress'd, so neat, so sprightly, and plays about one so agreeably, that I vow, he has as much spirits as the marquis of Monkeyman's Italian greyhound' (p165). The woman is describing a man, indicating that the 'marquis of Monkeyman' may have been a colloquial reference to men who exhibited certain kinds of behaviours. In Colley Cibber and Sir John Vanbrugh's *The Provoked Husband*, a character identified as 'Mask' names some of the men to be found at the masquerade, and his list includes 'Sir Powder Peacock,' 'Beau Frightful,' and 'the marquis of Monkey-man' (London, 1728: 92). There is also a reference to the 'monkey-man' in a book of entertainment entitled *The Juvenile Roscius: or, Spouter's Amusement. Being a Collection of Original Prologues, Epilogues, ... Imitations* (London, 1770). There, in a 'Prologue in the Character of a Reforming Constable,' the monkey-man appears 'bedaub'd with lace,' and he is possessed of 'mincing step' and 'round unmeaning face'. He appears to be a French fop, and the scatological overtone (*bedaub'd* recalls Swift and characters covered in sh-t). See also footnote 34 in Chapter 3.

4.   All references to lesson cards, sets and numbers are from the Manuscript Nursery Library, Lilly Library, Indiana University, Bloomington, Indiana.

5.   Oxford, Bodleian Library, MS. Don.c.190 fol 1.

6. See McCarthy (1999) on Anna Barbauld and conversation and the work of Michèle Cohen on the relationship between domestic education, conversation and the construction of the dramatic from the page.

7. See, for example, primers that contained rhymes such as 'C was a Captain all cover'd with Lace, D was a Drunkard, and had a red Face, J was a Joiner, and built up a House, K was a King and governed a Mouse…' quoted in Gumuchian (1941: 341).

8. Though the term 'the fourth wall' did not come into use until the beginning of the nineteenth century, its scenic elements as well as shifts from the auditory to the spectacular of the stage began at the end of the seventeenth century, see Hunt (1807). See especially Stephens (1998) and Fishman (2004) on the history of the competition of the visual and verbal, the image and the word.

Figure 27. Courtesy of the Lilly Library, University of Indiana, Bloomington, Indiana.

Appendix i

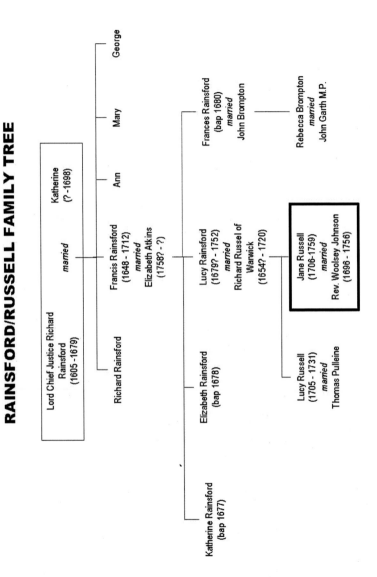

RAINSFORD/RUSSELL FAMILY TREE

Lord Chief Justice Richard Rainsford (1605-1679) *married* Katherine (? -1698)

Richard Rainsford

Francis Rainsford (1648 - 1712) *married* Elizabeth Atkins (1758? - ?)

Ann

Mary

George

Katherine Rainsford (bap 1677)

Elizabeth Rainsford (bap 1678)

Lucy Rainsford (1679? - 1752) *married* Richard Russel of Warwick (1654? - 1720)

Frances Rainsford (bap 1680) *married* John Brompton

Lucy Russell (1705 - 1731) *married* Thomas Pulleine

Jane Russell (1706-1759) *married* Rev. Woolsey Johnson (1696 - 1756)

Rebecca Brompton *married* John Garth M.P.

JOHNSON FAMILY TREE

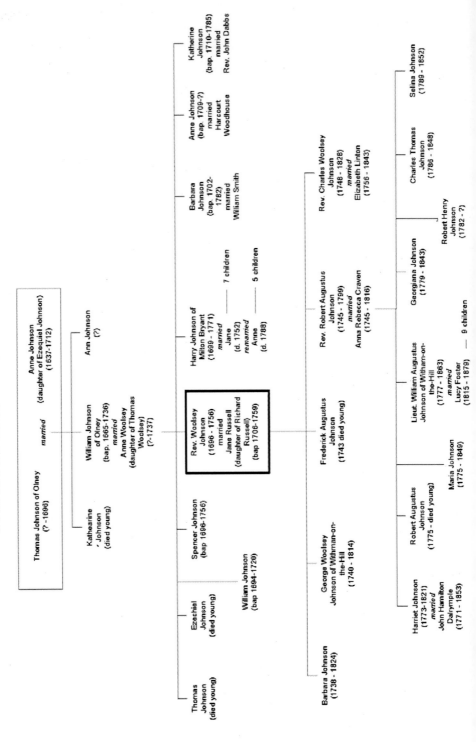

Appendix ii

Texts cited and referenced in Jane Johnson's commonplace book

We include a list of the texts cited in Jane's commonplace book as a matter of interest and as a starting point for anyone who may want to carry out further research - many of the quotes remain unidentified. We have transcribed the references she gives *verbatim*, but we have ordered them alphabetically and identified the probable sources in brackets.

'Advice to a Female Friend' [? quotation **not** found in Madam de Pompadour's, *Advice to a female friend*]

'Arabian Nights Entertainment'

'C.J.' [?]

'Cato'

'Cowley' [not Cowley but from Thomas Spateman's *A sermon preach'd before the Sons of the Clergy at their anniversary meeting in the Cathedral Church of St. Paul, February 25, 1730* (1731)]

'D. Jackson' [?]

'Epitaph on a Girl of Eight years old' [Owen Felltham, 'On the Lady E.M.', *Lusoria*, 1661]

'From a newspaper'

'Hales Tracts' [John Hales, from 'Of enquiry and private judgement in religion']

'Hamlet' [Shakespeare]

'Horace'

'Juvenal' [from John Dryden's translation of *The Satyrs of Decimus Junius Juvenalism* 1735]

'Labelle Letters' [?]

'Letters of the English Nation' [probably by John Shebbeare, 1756]

'Lord Bolingbroke' [Lord Henry St. John Viscount from a letter to Jonathan Swift 1723]

'Lord Lansdone' [George Granville Lansdowne, 'Letter to my Nephew Mr. Bevil Granville, upon his entering into Holy Orders' in *The Genuine Works in Verse and Prose*, 1736]

'Martial'

'Milton': *Il Penseroso* and *Paradise Lost*

'Moses Brown, Sunday thoughts' [*Sunday thoughts. Containing the publick, family, and solitary duties* 1750]

'The Mourning Bride' [William Congreve 1697]

'Mr H. Sermon (1756)' [probably Richard Hurd]

'Mr Locke' [John Locke, *An essay concerning human understanding*, 3.6.12, 1690]

'Nelsons Rights of the Clergy' [William Nelson, *The Rights of the Clergy of that part of Great-Britain called England*, 1715 (2nd ed)]

'Old Book of Emblems' [Geffrey Whitney, 'Sol non occidat super iracundiam vestram', *A Choice of emblems and other Devises*, 1586]

'Pericles' [Shakespeare?]

'Persian Letters' [George Lord Lyttleton, *Letters from A Persian in England to his Friend at Ispahan]*

'Persius, the fifth Satire' [Dryden]

'Plato'

'Plautus'

'Plutarch'

'Pompey the Little' [Frank Coventry, *The History of Pompey the Little: or, the Life and Adventures of a Lap-Dog*, 1751]

'Pope's Homer's *Iliad*' and '*Odyssey*'; 'An Essay on Criticism (1709)'; 'Of taste, an epistle to the Right Honourable Richard Earl of Burlington (1732); 'epitaphs' ['On Mrs Corbet, who died of a Cancer in her Breast' (1736) and 'On the Monument of the Honourable Robert Digby' (1727)]

'Resolves' [Owen Felltham, *Resolves, divine, moral, political*, 1677]

'Rollin' [Charles Rollin, from *The Method of Teaching and Studying the Belles Lettres or An Introduction to Language, poetry, Rhetoric, History, Moral Philosophy, Physicks, &. ?*]

'*Spectator*'

'Spencer Fairy Queen' [Edmund Spenser, *The Faery Queen*]

'Sr Philip Sydney' [from ?]

'St Austin' [quote from *The Turkish Spy*]

'Swift' [*Cadenus and Vanessa*, 1726]

'Tatler'

'Telemachus' [François de Salignac, Fénelon, *The Adventures of Telemachus*]

'The Life of Sir Francis Bacon' [from ?]

'The Rambler'

'Tompsons poems' [James Thomson, *Winter*, 1726]

'Turkey Spy' [Giovanni Marana, *The Eight Volumes of Letters Writ by a Turkish Spy Who Liv'd Five and Forty Years Undiscovered at Paris*, first published in French, 1684]

'Vissions' [Nathaniel Cotton, *Visions in Verse, for the Entertainment and Instruction of Younger Minds*, from *Vision V Happiness*, published anonymously in 1751]

'Young's Midnight thoughts' [Edward Young, *The Complaint: or, Night-thoughts on Life, Death and Immortality*, 1756]

[various Biblical verses]

Appendix iii

Texts cited and referenced in Robert Augustus Johnson's Journal (1771 - 1777)

N.B. This is an incomplete list as we have not worked so comprehensively on these references as on Jane's commonplace book (above). Some of Robert's reading has proved difficult to track down, but we have made a start and future researchers may complete the task.[1]

Abercromby, David (1688) *Versions of the Psalms of David*

Abercromby, David (1685) *Discourse of Wit*

Abercromby, David (1687) *Academy Scientarum*

Akinside, Mark (1744) *Pleasures of the Imagination: A Poem*

Barlow, Rev. Frederick (1775) *Complete English Peerage* [*The Complete English Peerage Or, a genealogical and historical account of the peers and peeresses of this realm to the year 1775 inclusive*]

Boswell, James (1785) *Journal of a Tour to the Hebrides with Samuel Johnson*

Chesterfield, Lord Philip (1776) *Dear Boy: Lord Chesterfield's letters to his son*

Chesterfield, Lord Philip (1778) *Letters to Alderman*

Ferguson, Adam (1767) *An Essay on the History of Civil Society,* (1966 edition)

Gibbon, Edward (1776-81) *The History of the Decline and Fall of the Roman Empire*

Gordon, Thomas (1719-1720) *The Independent Whig*

Hume, David (1740) *A Treatise concerning Human Nature*

Hume, David (1777) *Enquiries Concerning Human Understanding*

Hume, David (1779) *Dialogues Concerning Natural Religion*

Jenner, Charles (1771) *Letters from Altamont in the Capital to his Friends in the Country*

Littleton, Sir Thomas (1581) *Dialogue on Institutions of Laws of England*

Montesquieu, Charles Baron de (1751) *L'Esprit des Loix*

Mosheim, Johann (1765) *Ecclesiastical History: Ancient and modern*

Paine, Thomas (1791) *The Rights of Man: Being an answer to Mr Burke's attack on the American Revolution*

Paley, William (1785) *The Principles of Moral and Political Philosophy*

Price, Richard (1768) *Dissertations 1. Providence 11. Prayers* [Four dissertations: I. On providence. II. On prayer. III. On the reasons for expecting that virtuous men shall meet after death in a state of happiness. IV. On the importance of Christianity, the nature of historical evidence, and miracles]

Robertson, William (1769) *History of Charles V* [The History of the Reign of the Emperor Charles V]

Robertson, William (1759) *History of Scotland* [during the Reigns of Queen Mary and of King James VI]

Rousseau, Jean Jacques (1761) *La Nouvelle Heloise*

Rousseau, Jean Jacques (1758) *Lettre a d'Alembert* [sur les spectacles]

Rousseau, Jean Jacques (1763) *Emilius and Sophia: Or, a new system of education*

Shakespeare, William *Merchant of Venice*

Shenstone, William (1765/77) *Works in verse and prose of William Shenstone*

Smith, Adam (1759) *Theory of Moral Sentiments*

Wollaston, William (1726) *The Religion of Nature Delineated*

Note

1.   There are one or two occasions when the date of publication of texts comes slightly later than the date of Robert's journal entry. As we are usually talking about dates a year or so adrift, the only conclusions we can draw are that i] either the original date of publication is incorrect (and we know this sort of leeway still happens today between proposed and actual date of publication, as well as the latter and sales in bookshops) **or** ii] since Robert and George were such bibliophiles, they might have been able to get hold of some copies of books before general publication **or** iii] some publications may have appeared in serial form or in magazines in advance of publication. We have not had time to research the latter.

Select Bibliography

Main Manuscript Sources

Bodleian Library

Papers of Jane Johnson of Olney, Buckinghamshire and of her family, 17th-19th centuries: MSS. Don. b. 39-40, c. 190-6, d. 202, e. 193-200.

Centre for Buckinghamshire Studies
Correspondence, and other papers relating to the Johnson family of Olney: D/X 827

Leicestershire, Leicester and Rutland Record Office
Johnson Family collection: DE5122

Lincolnshire Record Office
Johnson I/2, Johnson I/3 and Johnson I/5.

Lilly Library
Manuscript Nursery Library: Johnson, J. mss.

Public Record Office
Johnson family wills

Websites

http://www.englishorigins.com
http://www.familysearch.org
http://www.documentsonline.pro.gov.uk
http://www.a2a.org.uk
http://www.british-history.ac.uk
http://www.londonancestor.com
http://www.theclergydatabase.org.uk

Primary Sources

Anon (1767) *A Little Pretty Pocket-book Intended for the Instruction and Amusement of Little Master Tommy and Pretty Miss Polly,* London: Printed for J Newbery, at the Bible and Sun in St. Paul's Churchyard

Anon (1749) *A New Play Book for Children, or, An easy and natural introduction to the art of reading.* London: Printed for Thomas Harris

Anon (1751) *A Pretty Book for Children, or, An easy guide to the English tongue Vol. I.* London: Printed for J Newbery, J Hodges and B Collins

Anon (1746) *Little Master's Miscellany, or, Divine and moral essays in prose and.* London: Printed and sold for Jacob Robinson at the Golden Lyon in Ludgate Street

Anon (1743) *The Child's New Play-thing: Being a Spelling-book, intended to make the learning to read, a diversion instead of a task.* London: Printed for M. Cooper at the Globe in Pater-noster-Row

Anon (circa 1760) *The Famous Tommy Thumb's Little Story-book: containing his life and surprising adventures.* London: Printed for S. Crowder and sold by B. Collins

Anon (between 1702 & 1714) *The First Book for Children, or, The compleat school-mistress.* London: Printed by and for C. Brown and T. Norris and sold by Charles Hartley at the Bible and Heart in Alderman-bury, near London Wall

Aulnoy, Madame d' (circa 1725) *The History of the Tales of the Fairies.* London: Printed and sold by E. Midwinter, at the Looking-Glass and Three Crowns in St Paul's Churchyard

Austen, J. (1971, first published 1815) *Emma,* Oxford: Oxford University Press

Bickham, J. (1737) *Fables, and Other Short Poems: collected from the most celebrated English authors. The whole curiously engrav'd, for the practice & amusement of young gentlemen & ladies, in the art of writing.* London: Printed and sold by William and Cluer Dicey

Boreman, T. (1736). *A Description of a Great Variety of Animals and Vegetables Extracted from the most considerable Writers of Natural History: and Adapted to the use of all capacities, especially for the entertainment of yough being a supplement to A Description of Three Hundred Animals.* London: Printed by J. T. for Thomas Boreman near Child's Coffee House in St. Paul's Church Yard

Boreman, T. (1741) *Curiosities in the Tower of London.* London: Printed for Thomas Boreman

Bunyan, J. (1686) *A Book for Boys and Girls.*

Bunyan, J. (1684) *The Pilgrim's Progress.*

Byatt, A. S. (1990) *Possession,* London: Vintage.

Coventry, F. (1751) *The History of Pompey the Little: or, the life and adventures of a lap-dog,* London: Printed for M. Cooper

Fénelon, F. (1713) *Instructions for the Education of a Daughter Done into English, and Revised by Dr. George Hickes.* London: Printed for Jonah Bowyer

Hoole, C. (1660) (Facsimile reprint 1969) 'A Petty Schoole' in *A New Discovery of the Old Art of Teaching Schoole,* Menston: The Scholar Press

Johnson, R. (1753) *The Statutes and Ordinances of me Robert Johnson Clerk, Archdeacon of Leicester, for and Concerning the Ordering, Governings, and Maintaining of my Schools and Hospitals of Christ in the County of Rutland, whereof I am Founder and Patron.* Stamford

Johnson, R. (1776) *Juvenile Sports and Pastimes. To which are prefixed, memoirs of the author: including a new mode of infant education.* London: printed for T. Carnan

Locke, J. (1693) 'Thoughts Concerning Education' in J A Axtell (ed.) (1968) *Educational Writings of John Locke,* Cambridge: Cambridge University Press

Locke, J. (1706) *Posthumous Works of Mr John Locke: His new method of a common-place-book.* London: printed by W.B. for A & J Churchill at The Black Swan in Pater-Noster-Row

Locke, J. (1750) *Elements of Natural Philosophy: by John Locke, Esquire. To which are added, some thoughts concerning reading and study for a gentleman*, London: printed for J. Thomson, S. Dampier and R. Bland

Marana, G. (1730) *The Eight Volumes of Letters Writ by a Turkish Spy: who liv'd five and forty years undiscover'd at Paris*. London: printed for G Strahan, W Mears, S Ballard, F Clay, J Hooke, B Motte, R Williamson, and the executors of H Rhodes

Miller, A. (1776) *Poetical Amusements at a Villa near Bath*, vols I and II. London. printed for Edward and Charles Dilly

Platt, H. (1594) *Jewell House of Art and Nature*. London: Theatrum Orbis Ferrarum, Amsterdam

Quarles, F. (1753) *Emblems and Hieroglyphicks on a Great Variety of Subjects, Moral and Divine*. London: Printed for M Cooper, W Reeve and C Sympson

Richardson, S. (1740) *Pamela* Vol I, M Kinkead-Weekes, (ed.) (1991) London: Everyman's Library

Richardson, S. (1740) *Pamela* Vol II, M Kinkead-Weekes (ed.) (1984) London: Everyman's Library

Richardson, S. (1753) *Æsop's Fables: with instructive morals and reflections*. London: Printed by S. Richardson for T and T Longman

Rollin, C. (1742) *The Method of Teaching and Studying the Belles Lettres or An Introduction to Language, Poetry, Rhetoric, History, Moral Philosophy, Physicks, &.* Dublin: printed by M Rhames

T. H. (1730) *A Guide for the Child and Youth*. London: Printed by J Roberts, for the Company of Stationers

Watts, I. (1715/1971) *Divine Songs*, Oxford: Oxford University Press

Watts, I. (1721) *The Art of Reading and Writing English*, (Facsimile reprint 1972). Menston: Scolar Press

Watts, I. (1859) *The Improvement of the Mind to which is Added a Discourse on the Education of Children and Youth*, Halifax: Milner & Sowerby

Secondary Sources

Books

Amussen, S. (1988) *An Ordered Society: Class and gender in early modern England*. Oxford: Basil Blackwell.

Appleton, W. (1960) *Charles Macklin, An Actor's Life*. Cambridge, MA: Harvard University Press.

Armstrong, N. (1987) *Desire and Domestic Fiction: A Political History of the Novel,* Oxford: Oxford University Press.

Ballaster, R. et al (1991) *Women's Worlds: Ideology, femininity and the women's magazine*. London: Macmillan.

Bartine, D. (1989) *Early English Reading Theory*. Colombia, S.C.: University of South Carolina Press.

Bayne-Powell, R. (1939) *The English Child in the Eighteenth Century*. London: Butler and Tanner.

Belton, J. J. (1951) *The Story of Packwood Warwickshire*. Private publication.

Bevis, R. W. (ed.) (1970) *Eighteenth-Century Drama: Afterpieces*. London: Oxford University Press.

Borsay, P. (1989) *The English Urban Renaissance: Culture and society in the provincial town 1660-1770*. Oxford: Oxford University Press.

Boyd, P. (comp.) (1939-55) *Boyd's Inhabitants of London*. Unpublished manuscript.

Bowers, T. (1996) *The Politics of Motherhood: British writing and culture, 1680-1760*. Cambridge: Cambridge University Press.

Brewer, J. (1997) *The Pleasures of the Imagination*. London: Harper Collins.

Brophy, E. B. (1991) *Women's Lives and the Eighteenth Century English Novel*. Tampa: University of South Florida Press.

Burman, J. (1934) *Old Warwickshire Families and Houses*. Birmingham: Cornish Brothers.

Carter, P. (2001) *Men and the Emergence of Polite Society: Britain 1660-1800*. Harlow: Longman.

Chartier, R. (1987) *The Cultural Uses of Print in Early Modern France*. Princeton, N.J.: Princeton University Press.

Clifford, J. (1987) *Hester Lynch Piozzi*. Oxford: Clarendon Press.

Cohen, M. (1996) *Fashioning Masculinity: National identity and language in the eighteenth century*. London: Routledge.

Conant, M. P. (1908) *The Oriental Tale in England in the Eighteenth Century*. New York: Norwood Press.

Darnton, R. (1984) *The Great Cat Massacre and other Episodes in French Cultural History*. Penguin.

Darnton, R. (1990) *The Kiss of Lamourette: Reflections in cultural history*. London: Faber.

Darton, H. F. J. *Children's Books in England*. (revised by Brian Alderson, 1982). Cambridge: Cambridge University Press.

Davies, R.T. (ed.) (1965) *Samuel Johnson: Selected writing*. London: Faber.

Davies, W. J. Frank (1973) *Teaching Reading in Early England*. London: Pitman Publishing.

Deacon, G. (2002) *John Clare and the Folk Tradition*. London: Francis Boutle.

de Bolla, P. (1989) *The Discourse of the Sublime: Readings in history, aesthetics and the subject*. Oxford: Basil Blackwell.

Dictionary of National Biography on CD-ROM (1995) Oxford: Oxford University Press.

Doubleday, H. A. (ed.) (1949) *A History of Buckinghamshire. The Victoria history of the counties of England*. London: University of London, Institute of Historical Research.

Dugdale, W. (1765) *The Antiquities of Warwickshire*. Coventry: John Jones.

Earle, P. (1989) *The Making of the English Middle Class*. London: Methuen.

Earle, P. (1994) *A City Full of People. Men and women of London 1650-1750*. London: Methuen.

Egan, K. (1997) *The Educated Mind*. Chicago: University of Chicago Press.

Fishman, Jen (2004) *Active Literacy: Performance and writing in Britain 1642-1790*. Unpublished Ph.D. dissertation, English Department, Stanford University.

Foster, J. (ed.) (1887) *London Marriage Licences 1521-1869*. London: Bernard Quaritch.

Gottlieb, G. (1975) *Early Children's Books and Their Illustration*. New York: Pierpont Morgan Library with Oxford University Press.

Goswami, U. and Bryant, P. (1990) *Phonological Skills and Learning to Read*, Hove: Lawrence Erlaum.

Great Britain War Office. (1760-1771) *List of the General and Field Officers as they Rank in the Army*. London: Printed for J Millan.

Heath, S. B. (1983) *Ways with Words*. Cambridge: Cambridge University Press.

Hilton, M., Styles, M. and Watson, V. (eds.) (1997) *Opening the Nursery Door: Reading, writing and childhood 1600-1900*. London: Routledge.

Hoggart, R. (1961) *The Uses of Literacy*. London: Chatto and Windus.

Houston, R.A. (1988) *Literacy in Early Modern Europe, Culture and Education 1500-1800*. London: Longman.

Hunt, L. (1807) *Critical Essays on the Performers of the London Theatres*. London, np.

Hunt, P. (ed.) (1995) *Children's Literature: an Illustrated History,* Oxford: Oxford University Press.

Hunter, J. P. (1990) *Before Novels: The cultural contexts of Eighteenth-Century English fiction*. London: W W Norton.

Jackson, M. V. (1989) *Engines of Instruction, Mischief and Magic: Children's literature in England from its beginnings to 1839*. Aldershot: Scolar Press.

Ketcham, M.G. (1985) *Transparent Designs: Reading, performance and form in the Spectator papers*. Athens, Georgia: The University of Georgia Press.

Klein, L. E. (1994) *Shaftesbury and the Culture of Politeness: Moral discourse and cultural politics in early eighteenth-century England*. Cambridge: Cambridge University Press.

Kymer, T. (1962) *Richardson's* Clarissa *and the Eighteenth Century Reader*. Cambridge: Cambridge University Press.

Laurence, A. (1994) *Women in England 1500-1760*. London: Weidenfeld and Nicolson.

Lechner, J. M. (1962) *Renaissance Concepts of the Commonplaces*. New York: Pageant Press.

Lewis, W. S. (ed.) (1973) *Selected Letters of Horace Walpole*. London: Yale University Press.

Lockridge, K. A. (1992) *On the Sources of Patriarchal Rage: The commonplace books of William Byrd and Thomas Jefferson and the gendering of power in the eighteenth century*. London: New York University Press.

Lonsdale, R. (1990) *Eighteenth Century Women Poets*. Oxford: Oxford University Press.

Lloyd, M. (1983) *Portrait of Lincolnshire*. London: Robert Hale.

Manguel, A. (1997) *A History of Reading*. London: Harper Collins.

Martin, Julia (2002) *Self and Subject in Eighteenth Century Diaries*, unpublished D Phil, University of New South Wales.

Mason, H.T. (ed.) (1998) *The Darnton Debate: Books and reading in the eighteenth century*. Oxford: Voltaire Foundation.

Matthews, B. (1994) *By God's Grace: A history of Uppingham School*. London: Whitehall Press.

Michael, I. (1987) *The Teaching of English*. Cambridge: Cambridge University Press.

Michael, I. (1993) *Early Textbooks of English*. Swansea: Colloqium on Textbooks, School and Society.

Muir, P. (1954) *English Children's Books 1600-1900*. London: Batsford.

Namier, L. and Brooke, J. (1964) *The History of Parliament. The House of Commons 1754-1790*, vol II. London: Her Majesty Stationery Office for the History of Parliament Trust.

Neuburg, V. E. (1971) *Popular Education in Eighteenth Century England*. London: The Woburn Press.

Nussbaum, F. A. (1989) *The Autobiographical Subject: Gender and ideology in eighteenth century England.* Baltimore: The Johns Hopkins University Press.

O'Connell, S. (1999) *The Popular Print in England.* London: British Museum Press.

O'Day, R. (1982) *Education and Society 1500-1800.* Harlow: Longman.

O'Malley, A. (2003) *The Making of the Modern Child: Children's literature and childhood in the late eighteenth century.* London: Routledge.

Pickering, J. S. (1981) *John Locke and Children's Books in Eighteenth Century England.* Knoxville: University of Tennessee Press.

Pickering, J. S. (1993) *Moral Instruction and Fiction for Children 1749-1820.* London: University of Georgia Press.

Pinchbeck, I. and Hewitt, M. (1969) *Children in English Society*, Vols I and II. London: Routledge and Kegan Paul.

Pollock, L. A. (1983) *Forgotten Children: Parent-child relations from 1500-1900.* Cambridge: Cambridge University Press.

Porter, R. (1990) *English Society in the Eighteenth Century.* London: Penguin.

Porter, R. (2000) *Enlightenment.* London: Penguin.

Privately printed (1875) *Johnson of Wytham-on-the-Hill. Co. Lincoln.* London: Mitchell and Hughes.

Raftery, D. (1997) *Women and Learning in English Writing 1600-1900.* Dublin: Four Courts Press.

Ratcliff, O. (1900) *History and Antiquities of the Newport Hundreds.* Olney: Cowper Press.

Ratcliff, O. (transc.) (1907-1910) *The Register of the Parish of Olney, co. Bucks. 1665-1812*. Olney: Bucks Parish Register Society.

Raven, J., Small, H. and Tadmor, N. (eds.) (1996) *The Practice and Representation of Reading in England*. Cambridge: Cambridge University Press.

Richardson, A. (1994) *Literature, Education and Romanticism: Reading as a social practice 1780-1832*. Cambridge: Cambridge University Press.

Roque, J. (1982) *The A to Z of Georgian London* (introductory notes by Ralph Hyde). Lympne Castle: Published for the London Topographical Society by Harry Margary in association with Guildhall Library, London.

Roscoe, S. (1973) *John Newbery and his Successors, 1740-1810*. Wormley: Five Owls Press.

Rosenfeld, S. (1939) *Strolling Players and Drama in the Provinces 1660-1765*. Cambridge: Cambridge University Press.

Rothstein, N. (ed.) (1987) *A Lady of Fashion: Barbara Johnson's Album of Styles and Fabrics*. London: Thames and Hudson.

Rouse, W. H. D. (1898) *A History of Rugby School*, London: Duckworth & Co.

Rowe Townsend, J. (1994) *Trade and Plumb-cake For Ever, Huzza! The life and work of John Newbery, 1713-67*. Cambridge: Colt Books.

Rugby School. (1933) *The Rugby Register,* vol. 1 (1675-1857) (revised and annotated by G A Solly). Rugby.

Schiller, J. G. (1997) *Digging for Treasure: An adventure in appraising rare and collectible children's books*. Bloomington, Friends of the Lilly Library, Indiana University.

Sharpe, K. (2000) *Reading Revolutions: The politics of reading in early modern England*. London: Yale University Press.

Shefrin, J. (2003) *Such Constant Affectionate Care: Lady Charlotte Finch - Royal Governess and the children of George III.* Los Angeles: The Cotsen Occasional Press.

Spence, C. (2000) *London in the 1690s: A Social atlas.* London: Centre for Metropolitan History.

Spufford, F. (2002) *The Child that Books Built.* London: Faber.

Spufford, M. (1981a) *Small Books and Pleasant Histories: Popular fiction and its readership in seventeenth-century England.* Cambridge: Cambridge University Press.

St Clair, W. (2004) *The Reading Nation in the Romantic Period.* Cambridge: Cambridge University Press.

Stephens, M. (1998) *The Rise of the Image, the Fall of the Word.* New York: Oxford University Press.

Stewart, S. (1993) *On Longing: Narratives of the miniature, the gigantic, the souvenir, the collection.* London: Duke University Press.

Stone, L. (1979) *The Family, Sex and Marriage in England 1500-1800.* London: Penguin Books.

Styles, M. (1998) *From the Garden to the Street: Three hundred years of poetry for children.* London: Cassell.

Summerfield, G. 1984 *Fantasy and Reason. Children's Literature in the Eighteenth Century.* London: Methuen & Co.

Society for Army Historical Research (1931), *The Army List of 1740.* Sheffield: W C Leng & Co.

The Lincoln Record Society (1936) *Lincolnshire Church notes made by William John Monson, 1828-1840,* vol. 31.

The Little London Directory of 1677: List of merchants and bankers of London. London: John Camden Hotten (1863).

Thwaite, M. F. (1963) *From Primer to Pleasure: An Introduction to the history of children's books in England, from the invention of printing to 1900*. London: The Library Association.

Trumbach, R. (1978) *The Rise of the Egalitarian Family: Aristocratic kinship and domestic relations in eighteenth century England*. London: Academic Press.

Vallone, L. 1995 *Disciplines of Virtue: Girl's culture in the eighteenth and nineteenth centuries*. New Haven: Yale University Press.

Venn, J. and Venn, J.A. (comp) (1922) *Alumni Cantabrigiensis*. Cambridge, Cambridge University Press.

Vickery, A. (1998) *The Gentleman's Daughter: Women's lives in Georgian England*. London: Yale University Press.

Vincent, D. (1989) *Literacy and Popular Culture in England 1750-1914*. Cambridge: Cambridge University Press.

Warner, M. (1994) *From the Beast to the Blonde: On fairytales and their tellers*. London: Chatto and Windus.

Watson, V. (ed) (2001) *The Cambridge Guide to Children's Books*. Cambridge: Cambridge University Press.

Weatherill, L. (1996) *Consumer Behaviour and Material Culture in Britain 1660-1760*. London: Routledge.

Witham-on-the-Hill Historical Society (2000) *A Piece of the Puzzle: The Journey of a village through history*. Stamford: BJs Print Design Ltd.

Whyman, S. (1999) *Sociability and Power in Late-Stuart England: The cultural worlds of the Verneys 1660-1720*. Oxford: Oxford University Press.

Articles

Alderson, B. (1999) 'New Playthings and Gigantick Histories'. *Princeton University Chronicle*. Vol. 60, no.2. (pp178-195)

Arizpe, E. & Styles, M. (2004) 'Love to Learn your Book': Children's Experiences of Text in the Eighteenth Century. *History of Education*. Vol. 33, no.3. (pp337-352)

Avery, G. (2001) 'Jane Johnson and her Children'. Introduction to *A Very Pretty Story by Jane Johnson*. Banbury: Bodleian Library, University of Oxford, (pp7-17)

Bator, R. J. (1971) 'Eighteenth Century England versus the Fairy Tale'. *Research Studies*. Vol. 39, no.1. (pp1-10)

Brewer, J. (1996) 'Reconstructing the Reader: Prescriptions, texts and strategies in Anna Larpent's reading'. In Raven, J, Small, H and Tadmor, N (eds.) *The Practice and Representation of Reading in England*. Cambridge: Cambridge University Press, (pp226-245)

Burke, V. (2001) 'Ann Bowyer's Commonplace Book (Bodleian Library Ashmole MS 51): Reading and writing among the middling sort'. *Early Modern Literary Studies*. Vol. 6, no. 3. (pp1-28)

Clanchy, M. T. (1984) 'Learning to read in the Middle Ages and the Role of Mothers'. In Brooks, G and Pugh, A K (eds.) *Studies in the History of Reading*, Reading: Centre for the Teaching of Reading, University of Reading School of Education and the United Kingdom Reading Association, (pp33-39)

Clancy, P. A. (1982) 'A French Writer and Educator in England: Mme Le Prince de Beaumont'. *Studies on Voltaire and the Eighteenth Century*. Vol. 201. (pp195-208)

Clapinson, M. (1997) 'Notable Accessions'. *The Bodleian Library Record*. Vol.16, no. 2. (pp165-170)

Clarke, N. (1997) "The Cursed Barbauld Crew': Women writers and writing for children in the late eighteenth century'. In Hilton, M,

Styles, M and Watson, V (eds.) *Opening the Nursery Door. Reading, Writing and Childhood 1600-1900*. London: Routledge, (pp91-103)

Cohen, M. (2005) "To Think, To Compare, To Combine, To Methodise': Notes towards rethinking girls' education in the eighteenth century'. In Knott, S. and Taylor, B. (eds.) *Women, Gender and Enlightenment*. New York: Palgrave Macmillan, (pp173-187)

Ezell, M. J. M. (1983) 'John Locke's Images of Childhood'. *Eighteenth Century Studies*. Vol.17, no. 2. (pp139-155)

Gumuchian, K. (1941) 'From Piety to Entertainment in Children's Books'. *The American Scholar*. Vol. 10, no. 3. (pp337-350)

Heath, S. Brice (1997) 'Childs Play or Finding the Ephemera of Home'. In Hilton, M, Styles, M and Watson, V (eds.) *Opening the Nursery Door. Reading, writing and childhood 1600-1900*. London: Routledge, (pp17-30)

Immel, A. (2002) 'A Very Pretty Story by Jane Johnson: A Facsimile of a Manuscript Held by the Bodleian Library'. *CBHS Newletter 73*. (pp28-30)

Ingram, M. (2005) 'Men and Women in Late Medieval and Early Modern Times'. *English Historical Review*. Vol. CXX, no. 487 (pp.732-758)

Jones, V. (2002) 'Introduction and Notes to *Evelina'*. In Burney, F. (1798) *Evelina,* (edited by Edward A. Bloom) Oxford: Oxford University Press.

Kinnell, M. (1996) 'Early Texts Used by Children'. In Hunt, P. (ed.) *International Companion Encyclopedia of Children's Literature*. London: Routledge, (pp141-151)

Lovell, T. (1995) 'Subjective Powers? Consumption, the reading public, and domestic woman in early eighteenth century England'. In Brewer, J. and Bermingham, A. (eds.) *The Consumption of Culture 1600-1800*. London: Routedge, (pp23-41)

Machor, J. L. (1993) 'Introduction: Readers/texts/contexts'. In Machor, J. L. (ed.) *Readers in History. Nineteenth-Century American Literature and the Contexts of Response.* London: The Johns Hopkins University Press, (ppvii-xxix)

Mandelbrote, S. (2001) 'The English Bible and its Readers in the Eighteenth Century'. In Rivers, I. (ed.) *Books and their Readers in Eighteenth Century England: New Essays.* London: Leicester University Press, (pp35-78)

McCarthy, W. (1999) 'Mother of All Discourses: Anna Barbauld's lessons for children'. *Princeton University Chronicle.* Vol. 60, no. 2. (pp196-219)

McDermid, J. (1989) 'Conservative Feminism and Female Education in the Eighteenth Century'. *History of Education.* Vol. 18, no. 4. (pp309-322)

McKay, B. (2001) 'John Atkinson's Lottery Book of 1809: John Locke's theory of education comes to Washington'. In Isaac, P. and McKay, B. (eds.) *The Moving Market: Continuity and change in the book trade.* Delaware: Oak Knoll Press, (pp127-144)

Michael, I. (1993) 'Seventeenth Century Teachers' Views on Reading and Spelling in Brooks', G., Pugh, A. K. and Hall, N. (eds.) *Further Studies in the History of Reading.* Wandsworth: United Kingdom Reading Association, (pp35-42)

Monaghan, E. J. (1991) 'Family Literacy in Early 18th Century Boston: Cotton Mather and his children'. *Reading Research Quarterly.* Vol. 26, p. 4. (pp342-371)

Myers, M. (1991) 'Romancing the Moral Tale: Maria Edgeworth and the problematics of pedagogy'. In McGavron, J. H., *Romanticism and Children's Literature in Nineteenth Century England,* London: University of Georgia Press, (pp96-128)

Myers, M. (1999) ''Anecdotes from the Nursery' in Maria Edgeworth's Practical Education (1798): Learning from children 'abroad and at home'', *Princeton University Chronicle.* Vol. 60, no. 2. (pp220-250)

Myers, M. (1986) 'Impeccable Governesses, Rational Dames, and Moral Mothers: Mary Wollstonecraft and the female tradition in Georgian children's books', *Children's Literature.* Vol. 14. (pp31-59)

Patterson, S. W. (1979) 'Eighteenth-Century Children's Literature in England: A Mirror of its culture'. *Journal of Popular Culture.* Vol. 13, no. 1. (pp38-43)

Pearson, J. (1996) 'Women Reading, Reading Women'. In Wilcox, H. (ed.) *Women and Literature in Britain, 1500-1700,* Cambridge: Cambridge University Press.

Plumb, J. H. (1975a) 'The New World of Children'. *Past & Present.* Vol. 67. (pp64-109)

Plumb, J. H. (1975b) 'The First Flourishing of Children's Books'. In Gottlieb, G., *Early Children's Books and their Illustration.* New York: Pierpont Morgan Library with Oxford University Press.

Plumb, J. H. (1983) 'Commercialization and Society'. In McKendrick, N., Brewer, J. and Plumb, J.H., *The Birth of a Consumer Society: The Commercialization of eighteenth-century England.* London: Hutchinson, (pp265-334)

Raven, J. (1996) 'From Promotion to Prescription: Arrangements for reading and eighteenth-century libraries'. In Raven, J., Small, H. and Tadmor, N. (eds.) *The Practice and Representation of Reading in England.* Cambridge: Cambridge University Press, (pp175-201)

Rowe, A. (2000) 'Learning the Letters'. In Bearne, E. and Watson, V. (eds.) *Where Texts and Children Meet.* London: Routledge, (pp146-158)

Sawyer, P. (1990) 'The Popularity of Pantomime on the London Stage, 1720-1760'. *Restoration and Eighteenth-Century Theatre Research.* Vol. 5, no.2. (pp1-16)

Shefrin, J. (1999) "Make it a Pleasure and Not a Task': Educational games for children in Georgian England'. *Princeton University Chronicle.* Vol. 60, n. 2. (pp251-275)

Shevelow, K. (1996) 'Fathers and Daughters: Women as readers of the *Tatler'.* In Flynn, E. A. and Schweickart, P. (eds.) *Gender and Reading: Essays on readers, texts, and contexts.* Johns Hopkins University Press, (pp107-123)

Spufford, M. (1981b) 'First Steps in Literacy: The Reading and writing experiences of the humblest seventeenth-century spiritual autobiographers'. In Graff, H. J. (ed) *Literacy and Social Development in the West: A Reader.* Cambridge: Cambridge University Press, (pp125-150)

Spufford, M. (1997) 'Women Teaching Reading to Poor Children in the Sixteenth and Seventeenth Centuries'. In Hilton, M., Styles, M. and Watson, V. (eds.) *Opening the Nursery Door: Reading, writing and childhood 1600-1900.* London: Routledge, (pp47-64)

Styles, M. and Arizpe, E. (2004) 'Reading Lessons from the Eighteenth Century'. In *Children's Literature in Education.* Vol. 35, n. 1 (pp53-68)

Tadmor, N. (1996) "In the Even my Wife Read to me': Women, reading and household life in the eighteenth century'. In Raven, J., Small, H. and Tadmor, N. (eds.) *The Practice and Representation of Reading in England,* Cambridge: Cambridge University Press, (pp162-174)

Thomas, K. (1986) 'The Meaning of Literacy in Early Modern England'. In Baumann, G. (ed.) *The Written Word. Literacy in Transition.* Oxford: Clarendon Press, (pp97-132)

Thomas, K. (1989) 'Children in Early Modern England'. In Avery, J. and Briggs, J. (eds.) *Children and their Books.* Oxford: Clarendon Press, (pp45-78)

Thwaite, M. F. (1966) 'John Newbery and his First Books for Children', introduction to John Newbery's, *A Little Pretty Pocket-book.* Oxford: Oxford University Press.

Tucker, N. (1997) 'Fairy tales and their Early Opponents: In Defense of Mrs Trimmer'. In Hilton, M., Styles, M. & Watson, V. (eds.) *Opening the Nursery Door: Reading, writing and childhood 1600-1900.* London: Routledge, (pp104-116)

Watson, V. (1997) 'Jane Johnson: A Very pretty story to tell". In Hilton, M., Styles, M. & Watson, V. (eds.) *Opening the Nursery Door. Reading, writing and childhood 1600-1900.* London: Routledge, (pp31-46)

Whitley, D. (1997) Samuel Richardson's *Aesop'.* In Hilton, M., Styles, M. & Watson, V. (eds.) *Opening the Nursery Door. Reading, writing and childhood 1600-1900.* London: Routledge, (pp65-79)

Young, B. (2001) 'Theological Books from The Naked Gospel to Nemesis of Faith'. In Rivers, I. (ed.) *Books and their Readers in Eighteenth Century England: New essays.* London: Leicester University Press, (pp79-104)

Index